How To Think Like a Collector

How To Think Like a Collector

Harry L. Rinker

Emmis Books
Cincinnati, Ohio

Dedication

To spouses whose marriages this book saves because they now better understand how their collector spouse thinks,

To family and friends who now understand that those who collect are really the normal and sane members of society,

And to Bruce Chaney of Roanoke, Indiana, who wrote the following in response to a column I wrote defining an antique as anything made before 1963:

> You are the reason that we go into so many "antique" shops and malls and see nothing but second-hand furniture and junk! So many of the younger generation have no idea what an antique truly is now.

> If you consider post-WWII items as antique, you should keep your opinions to yourself, for you certainly are not knowledgeable, but quite ignorant.

For further information, contact the publisher at

Emmis Books
1700 Madison Road
Cincinnati, OH 45206
www.emmisbooks.com

Library of Congress Cataloging-in-Publication Data

Rinker, Harry L., 1966-
    How to think like a collector / by Harry Rinker.
        p. cm.
    Includes index.
    ISBN-13: 978-1-57860-202-5
    ISBN-10: 1-57860-202-5
    1. Antiques as an investment. I. Title.
    NK1125.R564 2005
    332.63--dc22

                                        2005010158

Cover designed by Carie Reeves
Interior designed by Dana Morykan

Contents

Acknowledgments

I want to thank all the trade and daily papers who continue to run "Rinker on Collectibles" in spite of threats by advertisers to pull their advertisements and subscribers to cancel their subscriptions because my column appears. I also forgive those papers who gave in to these threats.

I thank my readers, especially those who wrote a letter to the editor and made their views known, even when they disagreed with mine. I decided from the start not to respond to these letters. I had my say. They had their say. It is time to move on.

I have been pleased over the years with a group of employees who have given unselfishly of their time and efforts to make Rinker Enterprises a nationally recognized antiques and collectibles educational and information resource center. Of these, Dana Morykan deserves special mention. She has proofed and criticized her fair share of "Rinker on Collectibles" columns. They are better because of this.

I am excited about my new publisher, Emmis Books. Special thanks to Jack Heffron and Andrea Kupper.

Finally, may Gary Thoe and Jon Quick sleep restlessly for the balance of their lives for failing to keep in mind the adage, "You never know what will come back and haunt you."

How To Tell Harry What You Think

This book is filled with my opinions. I would like to know what you think. Okay, so your e-mail or letter might wind up in one of my columns or the dedication of one of my future books. So what! I read all e-mails and letters whether complimentary or critical. They make me think, just as I hope what you are about to read will make you think.

Write to Harry Rinker, 5093 Vera Cruz Road, Emmaus, PA 18049 or e-mail harrylrinker@aol.com.

Preface

When someone asks me to describe Harry Jr., my son, I tell them: "He is arrogant, obnoxious, and opinionated, obviously traits he learned from his mother." Those who know me well start laughing immediately. Those traits describe me to a "T."

Do not forget to add curmudgeon. You will find it along with "national antiques and collectibles authority, editor, author, columnist, appraiser, consultant, lecturer, private collector, and dedicated accumulator" at the top of the biography sheet I provide my clients.

I admit it. I am extremely outspoken and blunt. I have lost track of the number of times during conversations and lectures when someone viciously asked, "Why don't you tell us exactly what you think?"

The inside of my poor mother's coffin is round from the number of times she has turned over in her grave based upon remarks I made in conversation or print. Josephine Prosser Rinker, my mother, was a kind and gentle person, a member of the "if you cannot say something nice, do not say anything at all" generation. My "tell it like I see it" style did not come from Paul Rinker, my father, either. I am not certain where and when it started. However, ask any of my relatives, and they will tell you I always was like this.

While attending one of my Class of 1963 Lehigh University reunions, I was joking around rather sarcastically. When I finished, one of my classmates turned to me and said, "Harry, you have not changed a bit since we went to school together." We laughed. I thought to myself, "Was I always this bad?" The grin on my face revealed that my self-reflection was far from pious.

Tact is not one of my attributes. I am frequently faced with the "What do you think of that?" question, especially when invited to someone's home for dinner. As my mother's son, I tried initially to hide behind safe phrases, such as (1) I do not know anyone who would enjoy the piece more than you, (2) The piece certainly has found a good home, (3) I cannot think of a more appropriate place for the piece, or (4) I can tell by the smile on your face how much you like it. You get the message.

I assumed so did the person with whom I was talking, until the following happened. I was attending another social event when one of the attendees came up to me and said, "I heard you were at so-and-so's house, saw his favorite piece, and really admired it."

"Are we talking about the same object?" I thought. We certainly were.

Now I take a much more direct approach when someone asks me "What do you think about this piece?" If I do not like it, I say, "It is a piece of crap." Since I began this practice, I find that no one misinterprets my remarks any longer.

I enjoy telling it like it is, at least from my point of view. As the old adage says, I have positively, absolutely no trouble "calling a spade a spade."

"Rinker on Collectibles," my weekly column, began in 1987. The column had a renegade, cutting edge style from its inception. Rather than focus on antiques, I decided to write about twentieth-century collectibles, the objects of my parents' and my generation and not those of grandparents' and other past generations. Collectibles were just emerging as one of the viable segments of the antiques marketplace. It has been my pleasure to watch collectibles reach a point where they are now the dominant segment of the antiques marketplace. I am proud to take credit for being one of the individuals who made this happen. I like antiques, but I love collectibles.

Prior to "Rinker on Collectibles," antiques columns utilized a question-and-answer format. I wanted to be different. As a result, I decided to alternate weekly between a question-and-answer column and a text column. Eventually the text columns became a vehicle to poke, probe, and analyze developments within the antiques and collectible industry.

I had no qualms revealing trade secrets, questioning existing practices, and touting changes that attacked the antiques community's traditionalism. Needless to say, not everyone agreed with what I wrote. My name has appeared more often in the "Letters to the Editor" sections of the trade papers that carried or carry "Rinker on Collectibles" than it did on the masthead of my column. *Antiques & Auction News*, the trade paper that launched my column, threw it out for being too controversial. I take great pride in this fact.

I am often asked: "What is your goal in writing 'Rinker on Collectibles'?" My stock answer is: "I want to piss off everyone in the trade at least once a year!" I could have used "anger," but the true Harry Rinker never equivocates.

I found that getting people angry makes them think. This is the goal of "Rinker on Collectibles." I want to make people think.

Let me make one thing perfectly clear. It is not my goal to convince everyone to agree with me. Heaven forbid! One Harry Rinker in this business is enough. The wonderful thing about the antiques and collectibles field is that there is not one right answer to trade issues or questions. There are many correct answers. Discussion of what these answers are and how they apply is critical to making the trade better.

"Rinker on Collectibles" is now in its eighteenth year. Hopefully, it still retains the cutting edge it had when it began. You can judge for yourself. *How To Think Like a Collector* is a compilation of "Rinker on Collectibles" columns. Once again, there is that word "think." This is not the first compilation of my column. In 1989, Wallace-Homestead published *Rinker on Collectibles,* a book featuring the first two and one-half years of my text columns. A great many text columns, more than 375, have followed since. Deciding what columns to include in *How To Think Like a Collector* was a difficult task. For those who have followed "Rinker on Collectibles" over the years, I trust you approve of my choice.

I love the antiques and collectibles business. Connie Moore, my second wife, used to call it the mistress with which she could not compete. Fortunately, Linda Houck, my present wife, recognizes that the business is only inanimate and that the animate thing I love more than anything else is her.

When asked why I have devoted my professional life to the antiques and collectibles business, I tell people the answer rests with a principle I learned while a member of the Boy Scouts of America—leave the campsite a better place than you found it. The antiques and collectibles business is my campsite. Hopefully, time will judge that Harry Rinker did indeed leave it a better place than he found it.

Introduction

I know something you do not know. *There is a collecting gene in our DNA.* Before you shake your head no, think about it. Collecting is more fully developed in some people than others. The necessity to collect sometimes passes from parents to their children. Other times, it skips a generation. Yet, every family has one or more collectors in it.

If the above is true, and I certainly believe it is, then the following is equally true. People who collect are normal, and people who do not collect are sick. Because of this, I have answered the call to go out into the world and cure as many sick people as I can by teaching them how to collect. I want them to experience all the fun and joy that is inherent in collecting, such as the exhilaration one experiences when finding a special treasure.

I need your help. This is not a one-man job. We need to teach the world to collect. They can sing or drink a Coca-Cola as part of the collecting process.

Réne Descartes's "I think therefore I am" did not go far enough. If he really understood life, he would have said, as I have on many an occasion, "I collect therefore I am." Collecting is natural, as instinctual and necessary as breathing. A person who does not collect is not whole.

I live in America, a nation of collectors. eBay and others have commissioned surveys to determine what percentage of the American adult population collects. The survey results range in the 30 and 40 percentile. Their pollsters need to go back to the drawing board. They did not ask the right questions. I know the answer is in the 70-plus percentile. My best guess is that three out of four Americans collect. I want to raise the percentage to ten out of ten.

When I meet someone who tells me he does not collect, I begin asking a few simple questions: (1) Do you own things that belonged to your parents, grandparents, or great grandparents? (2) Did you save objects from your childhood? (3) Do you have ten similar items that are fifteen years old or older? In almost every single instance, the person answers yes to one or all three of these questions.

You do not have to be aware that you collect in order to be a collector. Collecting just happens. As I already have shown, deep down inside everyone is a collector. Awareness heightens the pleasures associated with collecting. It is fun to add items to existing collections. It is even more fun to start a new collection.

I try to buy an antique or collectible every day. It is not an apple a day that keeps the doctor away, it is a collectible. If I buy more than one object in a day, I do not count the extras against the days ahead. If I did, I would not have to buy anything until 2020. There is no fun in this. Today's purchases are today's purchases. The slate is wiped clean at the end of each day.

I also start a new collection each month. The result is that I have more than 250 collections housed in the former Vera Cruz Elementary School, home and office to Linda and me. When you tell someone you live in a schoolhouse, they think "little one-room schoolhouse on the top of a hill." No, no, no! The Vera Cruz Elementary School had six classrooms, an all-purpose room with a stage, a large kitchen, two offices, and three storage areas, a total of fourteen thousand square feet. It is not full, but I am working on it.

When I tell people the above, they look at me and ask, "Why?" My response is simple. I tell them they are asking the wrong question. The correct question is, "Why not?" For far more of my life than I would like to admit, I led a "why" life. Ten years ago, I switched to a "why not" life. What a difference it has made.

The antiques and collectibles field is in the midst of the greatest change in over a century. More change occurred in the 1990s than in the previous nine decades of the twentieth century. The first signs of change appeared in the mid-1970s. It continues today. I consider myself privileged to be one of the writers who has and continues to document and comment on that change.

Change began with the collecting revolution of the mid-1970s and early 1980s. In fact, I am proud to admit that I was one of the revolutionaries.

"What revolution?" you ask. The revolution that overturned the traditionalists' control of collecting by dictating what should and should not be collected. Only their precious antiques were worth collecting. Everything else was junk. The revolutionaries pooh-poohed that attitude. They took the position that everything is collectible. It is the act of collecting that is important, not what is collected.

The revolutionaries removed hundreds of collecting categories from the closet and brought them out in the open. Collecting gained a freedom it had never before experienced.

America became collecting-conscious in the 1970s and 1980s. The world quickly followed. Collecting stories became standard fare in newspapers and on radio and television. The old-timers were shocked when stories focused on Elvis memorabilia and lunch boxes and not their precious antiques. Why not? Young collectors identify with Elvis and lunch boxes. In fact, today's young collectors much prefer to collect post-1960 objects. It is hard to adjust to the fact that the objects with which I grew up in the late 1940s and 1950s are now far less desirable than the objects with which Harry Junior and Paulanne, my children, grew up. Time marches on and waits for no man.

[**Author's Note**—If you haven't figured it out already, I love clichés. In fact, my writing is full of them.]

I have been around long enough to remember life before the antiques mall. In 1982, I flew to Fresno, California, to visit a store that had been converted to house forty antiques dealers. Within ten years, the antiques mall became a major selling venue in the antiques and collectibles trade.

A second collecting revolution is currently taking place thanks to the personal computer and the Internet. It is hard to believe that 2005 marks the tenth anniversary of eBay. Most individuals would tell you it has been around much longer than this.

[**Author's Note**—The same applies to me. Most individuals think I have been analyzing and talking and writing about the collectibles trade for three or four decades. Actually, I began editing *Warman's Antiques and Their Prices* in 1981 and launched "Rinker on Collectibles," my weekly column, in 1987. I have yet to celebrate my twenty-fifth anniversary. Yet, I am an institution of sorts, realizing fully that my detractors would much rather see me institutionalized.]

This second revolution is a fascinating one. While the Internet is much bigger than eBay, it is eBay that is the leader of the antiques and collectibles revolution. I have watched eBay evolve and grow. I remain convinced its impact on the trade is still in its infancy.

eBay has increased the size of the collecting pie tenfold or more and created a global marketplace. It has redefined scarcity in many collecting categories and, as a result, redefined value as well. eBay has taught collectors to comparison shop.

When people ask me where all the young collectors and dealers are, I tell them to look on eBay. Can the traditional marketplace attract these new collectors and dealers? This is the greatest challenge the trade faces today. If the answer proves "no," the impact of this second revolution will be greater than anyone imagined.

Will there be a next revolution? You bet there will. The Internet and eBay are not the final answers. I cannot wait. I am an advocate of change. I just hope I have the strength and energy to participate in it.

CAST OF CHARACTERS:

I write from a personal perspective. I have no trouble laughing at myself and sharing my embarrassments. No one collects in isolation. My family and friends appear in this book. You should be aware of at least some of the cast of characters:

Antonio: Frederick Vogt's (Connie's son) son

Connie: Connie Moore, my second wife

Dana Morykan: Co-worker and friend. I do not like titles and never use them unless absolutely necessary. Dana's name often appears in my columns accompanied by the title Associate Editor or Senior Researcher. She is much more than this, much more.

Harry Jr.: Harry L. Rinker Jr., my son

Krystalee: Frederick Vogt's daughter

Linda: Linda Houck, my third and present wife. God willing, she will be my last one as well.

The Prossers: My mother's extended family. I think they all go to church on Sunday and say a silent prayer that my last name is Rinker.

CHAPTER 1

What Is It—Antique, Collectible, or What?

"What is an antique?" is one of the most frequently asked questions that I encounter. In 1963 when I was a graduate student at the University of Delaware, I had the opportunity to study with the Winterthur Fellows. I was told an antique was something made before 1830, a date marking the beginning of the industrial age in America. This is the purist definition.

Traditionalists define an antique as anything that is one hundred years old or older. While this definition works for the United States Customs Service (i.e., no duty is charged on goods more than one hundred years old exported to the United States), it does not work in the field. I am in my sixties, and I am an antique.

The definition of what is and is not an antique constantly evolves. This is demonstrated by the columns I've collected in this chapter. They illustrate the evolution of my own definition of antiques. Some accept the change willingly. Others fight it tooth and nail.

I am one of the evolutionists. If you are a traditionalist, I strongly suggest you skip Chapter 1 and begin this book with Chapter 2.

Antiques, Collectibles, Desirables, Country, Reusables, and Junk

The problem with the word "antiques" is that it is used both in a general and a narrow sense. In its broad sense, antiques is a generic term that describes a secondary marketplace for resold or recycled goods. In its narrow sense, it describes one specific portion of that broader secondary marketplace.

Antiques collectors attend antiques shows and malls where they buy antiques from antiques dealers. These antiques can be Early American period furniture or 1920s-30s Colonial Revival furniture. A large number of younger collectors think things from the 1950s are antiques.

The relatively simplistic antiques market of the 1950s and earlier decades is gone, never to return again. The 1995 antiques market is a complex entity. It is no longer comprised of a single unit (antiques), but six units—antiques, collectibles, desirables, Country, reusables, and junk.

An antique is anything made before 1945, a definition I began touting in the late 1980s. Acceptance continues to grow. 1945 was sixty years ago. While I personally object to the concept that something sixty years old is old, I confess that a critical evaluation of myself in the mirror each morning lends credence to this argument.

A collectible is an object made between 1945 and the mid-1970s. In addition to the date of manufacture, there are two other keys that are critical to classifying an object as a collectible. The first is the recognition that it is part of an established collecting category, i.e., a category that appears regularly in general price guides. The second is the establishment of a viable and trustworthy secondary resale market. Like antiques, collectibles have stood the test of time. Enough have been destroyed so that a point is reached where supply and demand are about equal.

A desirable is a newer object, in some cases days or weeks old. The key difference between a desirable and a collectible is that a desirable's secondary resale market is highly speculative. Individuals collect desirables. It is the act of collecting that makes them part of the antiques market. Desirables have not stood the test of time. They might be desirable today, but totally unwanted in the future.

Country is unique. It stands apart from the main components of the antiques market—antiques, collectibles, and desirables. This is a difficult concept to grasp. Are not the objects involved in Country either antiques, collectibles, or desirables? Yes, they are. Despite this, Country collectors and dealers do not view them in those terms. They are Country—pure and simple. When an object is labeled Country, it is removed from the mainstream and becomes an entity unto itself. Country is a look, a feeling, a mood. If you are into Country, you understand. If you are not, you do not. There is no sense belaboring the point.

During the last twenty-five years, we have lost sight of the role reusables or recyclables play in the antiques market. We have become so engrossed with the concept of collecting that we have forgotten there are individuals who buy older objects to reuse them, i.e., continuing their utilitarian function. Prior to the 1960s it was easy to argue that it paid to buy antiques because they usually cost less than a similar new object. My belief in this concept helped me furnish my first apartment.

I have been concerned for some time that the antiques purists have forgotten that the members of the garage sale and swap meet communities are a vital part of their world. It is time to correct this mistake. Every fine antique that sits in a china cabinet or on a shelf as an object of worship was once new and lived through a time when its principal role was one of reuse. Value rests with the object's utility, not its collectibility.

What is an antiques dealer, really? History tells us that the first antiques dealers were trash or junk dealers who worked the rural market fairs. We separated from our unsavory origins in the late nineteenth century. Antiques shop owners quickly learned to look down their noses at trash/junk dealers and still continue the practice today.

Modern collecting trends and methodology have changed the traditional transformation process whereby an object becomes an antique. The old pattern was new, recyclable, collectible, and antique. Today's objects are saved as soon as they are produced. Once an object is played with or used, its long-term collectible value is tainted. Fortunately, foresight is not sufficient to predict everything that will eventually become a collectible and antique. There remains, and always will remain, a role for the reuse/recyclable portion of the antiques market.

Why include junk as an antiques market category? Have you recently attended Brimfield, Renningers, or any of the thousands of flea markets and antiques malls across this great country of ours? If you have, you know why junk has its own category. I have never seen so many objects that anyone with a grain of common sense would recognize as belonging in a landfill being offered for sale as something worth collecting. It is as though Americans have taken the concept of taste and flushed it down the toilet.

We appear to have adopted the concept that something is worth saving simply because it has survived. We have fallen victim to an Emperor's-new-clothes problem. We look at the stuff and know it's junk, but we hesitate to identify it for what it is. What is wrong? If it is brown, sausage-shaped, gooey, and smelly, it does not take a genius to figure out what the product is.

It is time for some of the more outspoken members of our fraternity to do a little finger pointing and start calling a spade a spade. When you see junk, tell the seller you are not a dummy. You know what he is selling and that it belongs in the landfill, not his booth or shop. If the effort proves successful, I eventually will be able to drop junk as one of the components of the antiques marketplace. Here's hoping!

I introduced the concept of desirables primarily because of limited editions. The mere fact that something is collected does not make it a collectible. As used by the trade, a collectible is clearly defined as an object made between 1945 and the mid-1970s with a viable secondary sales market.

Manufacturers of limited edition material are extremely sensitive. They are acutely aware that if some of us had our way their products would be part of the junk, not the desirable category. But the issue is one of collectibility, not value judgments. People collect limited edition material, and it is part of the antiques marketplace.

I chose the term desirable because I felt it accurately describes the motivation behind the purchase of most limited edition objects. People buy them because they desire them. True, the desire may result from clever sales manipulation by a manufacturer. However, once again, this is irrelevant. The fact remains that people collect these objects.

Most manufacturers of limited edition objects have dropped all suggestions from their sales literature that their products are good, long-term, financial investments. History has shown just the opposite is true. They encourage individuals to buy the objects because they like them and will derive pleasure from owning them. I support this approach. It places the emphasis where it belongs.

A desirable as defined has two principal characteristics—it is of recent origin and it has no reliable secondary market. This is only a temporary state. Eventually, the object will survive long enough and be traded frequently enough that a reliable secondary market will be established. I believe this process takes approximately thirty years. Hence, Rinker's Thirty Year Rule: "For the first thirty years of anything's life, all its value is speculative."

Although I developed the concept of desirables to apply primarily to limited edition objects, in truth, it applies to anything new—from comic trading card sets to Mighty Morphin Power Rangers. We are collectible conscious. Stashing—or, perhaps more correctly, hoarding— new objects against the possibility that they will become the valuable collectibles of the future is a common practice. It is a trend more likely to accelerate than decline. The field needs a term that describes this phenomenon. Further, the term must be neutral, avoiding making a value judgment as to whether or not the practice or the object is good or bad. The term of choice is "desirable." Let's learn to use it.

Why Does the General Public Have So Much Trouble Accepting the Concept That Post-1945 Objects Are Valuable?

I participate in dozens of verbal appraisal clinics each year. No matter where I do them, from the East Coast to the West Coast, the vast majority of items brought by individuals for appraisal are manufactured prior to 1940. In fact, more than half are made before 1920. Even when I personally promote an appraisal clinic in the local media and plea for individuals to bring post-1945 items, pre-1940 objects dominate.

The general public is under the false assumption that an object has to be old to be valuable. Many antiques and collectibles television shows lend credence to this notion. *Antiques Roadshow* is an excellent example. It focuses on high-ticket, pre-1920 objects. An appraisal of thousands of dollars is seen as having much more entertainment value than one hundreds of dollars.

While the concept that age created value enjoyed considerable validity throughout much of the twentieth century, it lost its credibility in the 1970s. Today age is either a minor value consideration or can be negated completely. Today's market is trendy. As such, desirability has become the dominant value consideration.

Why does the general public have so much trouble accepting the concept that post-1945 collectibles are valuable? 1945 was sixty years ago. Objects made in the 1940s, 1950s, and 1960s are old. Ask anyone in his twenties or thirties. They do not identity with black-and-white television and 1958 Chevrolets. Most have only heard about Elvis from their parents.

It should come as no surprise that the answer to the question that I posed does involve age. The general public tends to become involved with antiques and collectibles late in life. It is critical at this juncture to understand that I am discussing individuals who are not serious collectors. Collectors are an entirely different matter.

Most individuals buy household furnishings and objects needed for daily living based upon their utility. They live with them, often for decades. Value is determined by how long the objects remain useful. No thought is given to long-term secondary market collectible value.

Further, the longer an individual lives with an object, the less likely he will remember what he paid for it new. The object loses its cost base. In the owner's mind the cost base is zero.

Test yourself. Look around the house and locate several objects you purchased twenty, thirty, or forty years ago. Ask yourself two questions—what did you pay for them and what are they worth today?

You should ask yourself if there are collectors for these objects. If so, what are they willing to pay? If you do your homework, you will find that there are collectors and other groups of buyers for a surprising number of these "recent" objects—and that they are willing to pay far more than you ever imagined the objects would be worth.

The best time to maximize the secondary market return on objects from your childhood and young adulthood is when you are in your late forties or early fifties. This is the period when your contemporaries are paying a premium price to recapture their past.

Unfortunately, most individuals do not sell during this period. They wait until they reach their late sixties or early seventies. Interest in the secondary market value of objects is generally triggered by one of three events an individual has to deal with: (1) handling the estate of a deceased relative, (2) estate planning for himself, or (3) downsizing to move into a smaller home. Obviously, individuals involved in the second and third circumstances are generally at least over fifty and usually well into their sixties. The average age of individuals handling the estate of a deceased relative is increasing, thanks in large part to increased life expectancy.

Individuals do not like to admit that the things with which they grew up and played are old. If they do, they have to accept the fact that they are old also. Today older individuals take better care of themselves. They do not think of themselves as old when they reach their sixties. They retain this thinking throughout their seventies and well into their eighties.

There are two simple truths to which the general public still remains unaware. First, the value of many post-1945 objects far exceeds the value of many objects that are a hundred years old and more. Second, it is easier to sell post-1945 collectibles than it is to sell antiques. In today's trendy market, the vast majority of buyers want post-1945 items.

Thanks to television, especially cable channels such as the History Channel, people's perception of what constitutes the "past" is changing. The "past" is the mid-twentieth century. The eighteenth century, nineteenth century, and first third of the twentieth century are largely ignored. For those under fifty, the 1950s and 1960s are old.

Today's young collectors have cast aside the traditionalist "antique" mindset. While they willingly accept the antiques they inherit, their principal buying focus is on post-1945 collectibles. One needs no further proof than the continuing aging of the collector base in dozens of traditional "antique" collecting categories.

While serious collectors have "seen the light" and joined the twenty-first century, the general public is still stuck in the past. Although I find this resistance to change hard to understand, my verbal appraisal clinic work has demonstrated how deeply the old values continue to hold sway.

I once believed that what I saw happening inside the collectibles community applied to the wider community as well. It does not. The battle to educate the general public to the importance and value of post-1945 collectibles remains a challenge.

What's an Antique?

How do you define an antique? This is a question I have been asked hundreds of times. Sometimes the simplest question is the hardest one to answer.

When I reach the question-and-answer portion of a lecture or seminar, I tell the audience members three rules apply if they want to ask me a question. First, do not ask the question if they do not want me to answer it. Second, there is nothing in the trade about which I do not have an opinion. Third, if they expect me to tell them what they want to hear, it probably is better that they do not ask their question.

The only difference between the questions "How do you define an antique?" and "What is an antique?" is the first question recognizes that the definition is very much a matter of opinion. Many questions in the antiques and collectibles field have multiple correct answers. Experienced scholars in the trade know it is better to put forward a broad "an" answer than a definitive "the" answer.

The antiques and collectibles field is in a constant state of flux. It has redefined itself multiple times during the past two decades. The definitions that apply in 2005 will be out of date by 2020. While I find this stimulating and challenging, there are others who find it frightening. The latter prefer a stable, predictable, traditional marketplace similar to the one that occurred for the first eight decades of the twentieth century. Alas, the past is past. We live in the here and now.

The purpose of this column is to explore some of the standard responses to the "How do you define an antique?" question.

An antique is something that is old. Old is a relative term. What is old to a person in her twenties is vastly different than what is old to a person in her sixties.

When I lecture or teach about antiques and collectibles, I tell my audience not to use "old"—to strike the term from their vocabulary. I cite the following example: "When I was twenty, forty-year-old women were old. When I was batching it in my early sixties, forty-year-old women were just right." Actually, I found fifty-year-old women just right, but fifty just does not work as well as forty in the story.

Old is a state of mind. I am sixty-three. I do not consider myself old, albeit society has a far different impression. I strongly suspect I am not going to consider myself old when I am in my seventies. I am at the front edge of a new generation of individuals whose life expectancy runs into their nineties. Okay, maybe I will be old in my eighties.

My parents, my father born in 1905 and my mother in 1907, were of a different mindset. They considered themselves old when they were in their fifties. They dressed and acted old. My mother felt life was not worth living past seventy. When she reached seventy, she died.

During the Hippie and Beatnik era, "do not trust anyone over thirty" was a famous phrase, a phrase that has come back to haunt these individuals now that they have raised a generation of children, many of whom are in their thirties.

The Yuppies, Dinks, and Me generations consider themselves failures if they are not at the peak of their business career by their mid-forties. Try to get a new job today if you are in your fifties. While the potential employer will find other justifiable reasons not to hire you, the simple truth is that most applicants are victims of age discrimination.

There is a real conflict here. Those in their twenties, thirties, and forties consider anything over fifty old. Those in their sixties and seventies believe they are still young. When I attend a fundraising meeting at Lehigh University, my alma mater, and they ask the members of the younger classes to stand up, I always jump out of my seat and stand. I will be damned if I am going to let any member of a younger generation define whether I am old or not.

An antique is something that belonged to my grandparents. On the surface, I happen to like this definition. The only problem is that I am a grandparent. I have a twenty-year-old granddaughter, a nine-year-old grandson, and more grandchildren on the way. If they apply this definition, this means that the things that I have saved from my late 1940s and 1950s childhood and 1960s early adulthood need to be considered antiques.

Face facts: The grandparents of today grew up in the 1940s and 1950s and were young adults in the 1960s and 1970s. While it is true that the spread between generations is increasing, the previous statement was based on three (not four) generations per decade.

If you were ten when John F. Kennedy was shot, you are now fifty-two. If you were ten when man landed on the moon in 1969, you are now forty-six. Look in the mirror. You have reached middle age. Senior Citizendom looms around the corner. Chances are your children have graduated from high school. If you are not grandparents already, you most likely will be within the next decade.

In 2005, it is far more likely that Grandma and Grandpa's house will be furnished with 1950s or 1960s furniture and decorative accessories than objects from the 1920s and 1930s. Like it or not, many items the twenty-, thirty-, and forty-something generations of collectors consider antiques were manufactured after 1945.

An antique is something that is one hundred years old. One has to have his head buried in sand to believe this definition. This definition lost its meaning by the early 1980s. A hundred years is not old. It is ancient.

Car collectors have the right idea. They define a classic car as a car that is between twenty-five and forty-nine years old. An antique car is a car over fifty years old. According to their definition, a car made in 1955 or earlier is an antique. I like this approach. First, it floats. Each year the definition of what constitutes an antique car moves forward. The critical question is whether or not twenty-five and fifty years are the correct break points. While convenient, do they reflect significant time differences in technology and design? They do not.

An antique is something found in antiques malls, shops, and shows. If this definition was used and antiques malls were the principal defining source, one could easily be led to believe that an antique was any object made before 1990. We all know this is not correct.

While the vast majority of merchandise offered at antiques shops and shows dates prior to 1940, 1950s through 1970s items are becoming more and more common. Clearly antiques shop and show dealers offer objects from the 1920s, 1930s, and 1940s without hesitation. These decades clearly are antique.

The antiques show community has avoided the inclusion of large quantities of mid-twentieth century material by creating Modernist shows, shows focusing on objects from the 1930s through the 1980s. Modernist shows are the hottest game in town. However, most buyers are buying the objects as antiques rather than collectibles.

Retro, a period term in jewelry that defines examples from the early 1940s, has been broadened in the collecting community to describe all objects made between the late 1930s and the late 1960s. No matter the term used, it is impossible to disguise the fact that buyers view these objects as antiques rather than collectibles.

When asked "How do you define an antique?" my stock answer for years has been any object made before 1945. When I first put forth and defended this point of view ten-plus years ago, a hue and cry was raised by those who felt I was demeaning the trade. Over the years, more and more individuals accepted my definition. There are still traditionalist detractors who argue in favor of the hundred-year rule, 1915, or 1940. However, I believe the supporters of the 1945 date are in the majority.

As you may have guessed, I am beginning to question the 1945 date. Recently, when asked, "How do you define an antique?" I find myself increasingly answering, "Any object made before 1963." Why? I will provide my reasoning in my next "Rinker on Collectibles" column.

An Antique Is Anything Made Before 1963

An antique is anything made before 1963. I have been hinting at this for the past three years. It is time to come right out and state it.

This proposition is not going to be popular, even among some of the more progressive thinkers in the antiques and collectibles trade. Too bad! It has never been my goal to win a "Mr. Popularity" contest. My goal has been to analyze trends and developments in the antiques and collectibles trade and report my conclusions.

It has been over a decade since I put forth the proposition that an antique was anything made before 1945. Viewed as "head of the curve" at that time, this definition has gained widespread acceptance. 1945 was sixty years ago. The vast majority of auctioneers, collectors, dealers, and others associated with the antiques and collectibles trade accept that as a long time ago.

1945 was a convenient break point. It marked the end of World War II, the growth of suburbia, the arrival of women in the workforce,

America's emergence as a true world power, and, most important, the beginning of the television era. Life in America in 1948 was very different than life in America in 1938. Americans thought, acted, and lived differently.

Americans tend to think in decades, e.g., the Fabulous Fifties, the Psychedelic Sixties, etc. Rarely does a shift from one decade to another represent a significant change in lifestyle. Those who experienced the change from the twentieth to the twenty-first century know nothing changed radically between 1999 and 2001. Although the temptation to use an even decade year, e.g., 1950, 1960, 1970, etc., to define shifts in lifestyle or in this case collecting trends is great, it does not make sense. One needs to look for an event or series of events that trigger such a shift, and then ask: In what year did they occur?

When asked when the twenty-first century began in America, future historians will cite September 11, 2001. The 9/11 tragedy changed America's mindset. America's role abroad in 2005 is very different than its role in 1995. America is far more polarized—economically, politically, socially, religiously, etc. In 2026, the question that will define the twenty-something and thirty-something generations will be: "Where were you when you heard that the planes hit the twin towers?"

Generations are separated by the questions they can answer. Where were you when you heard Pearl Harbor was bombed? Where were you when you heard President Kennedy was shot? Where were you when you heard man landed on the moon? Where were you when you heard the *Challenger* exploded? Where were you when you heard the *Columbia* exploded?

The impact of many of these events was felt worldwide. The Kennedy assassination is an example. Some questions are national in scope. The *Challenger* explosion is an example. If you live in Europe, a critical question that will separate generations is: "Where were you when you heard the Berlin wall fell?"

I know where I was when Pearl Harbor was bombed. I was three months old and living in a crib in Dundalk, Maryland. My father was employed by Bethlehem Steel and was working at the time in the Sparrows' Point ship building yards. Obviously, I have no personal memories of the event. In fact, I have no personal memories of World War II, not even V-E or V-J day.

Most long-term personal memories begin at age six or seven. I am sixty-three. Putting these two pieces of information together, the simple truth is that you have to be almost seventy years old or older to have any personal memories about where you were when you heard Pearl Harbor was bombed. Pearl Harbor has been relegated to the history books and the History Channel.

Where were you when you heard President Kennedy was shot? I was in the basement of the library at Washington University in St. Louis where I was attending graduate school. President Kennedy was assassinated on November 22, 1963. Forty-one plus years have passed since that tragedy took place. If long-term memory begins at age six or seven, this means that you are highly likely to be fifty or older if you can tell personal stories of where you were when you heard President Kennedy was shot. The result is all the twenty-somethings, thirty-somethings, and the vast majority of forty-something collectors have only read about the Kennedy assassination in history books. The 1950s and even the 1960s are a long time ago to the generation who grew up following the Kennedy assassination.

America in 1960 was a very different country than America in 1965. America in the 1960s was still experiencing the return to prosperity and world power status introduced during the Eisenhower era. The country was optimistic and content.

The mid-1960s were a period of great change. It was an era when social causes, ranging from banning the bomb to saving the whales, became a central focus. Civil rights questions tore the nation apart. Opposition to the Vietnam War polarized the country. Beatniks and Hippies were harbingers of the Age of Aquarius. The Beatles came to America. Polyester arrived on the scene. Colors became bright and bold. Abstract design reigned. Peter Max and popular Pop artists such as Andy Warhol were cult heroes. America became home to the drug culture.

If you were a 1950s conservative, the mid-1960s were a cultural shock. America and the world had turned upside down. Adapt and change or be left behind. "Do not trust anyone over thirty" had a far broader meaning—reject any established tradition and lifestyle.

I like to tell people I survived the 1960s and 1970s. Having grown up in the 1950s, I see a distinct parallel between the Eisenhower and Reagan elections and their impact on the American lifestyle.

Car collectors define a vintage car as a car that is between twenty-five and forty-nine years old. An antique car is fifty years old or older. A 1955 car is now an antique. I like the way car collectors define their category because the date constantly moves forward.

Until this column, the car collectors were ten years ahead of my 1945 date in defining what is antique. Now I am eight years ahead of them. By the time the antiques and collectibles trade stops debating the issue and accepts 1963 as the new key date dividing antiques and collectibles, chances are the trade and car definitions will coincide.

If an antique is anything made before 1963, how do I define collectibles and desirables, the other two units that comprise the complete "antiques" collecting market? For the moment, I am defining a collectible as anything made between 1963 and 1980. Although it's an even decade, I like 1980 as a dividing point primarily because of the lifestyle shift immediately following the first Reagan election. Antiques and collectibles are joined together by a trustworthy and stable secondary resale market—albeit with the market currently as trendy as it is, one has to question what "stable" really means. A desirable is an object made after 1980. Desirables have a speculative secondary market.

I confess that I am looking long and hard at 1980 as the end date for collectibles. My head tells me to change the date to somewhere in the mid- to late 1980s. The problem is that I have no firm lifestyle shift to which to attribute it.

Further, such a change seriously challenges a rule I have touted for years, Rinker's Thirty Year Rule, which states "for the first thirty years of something's life, all its value is speculative." Has the time come to put this rule under the microscope and see if it still applies? Rinker's Thirty Year Rule was created before the arrival of the Internet. Clearly, the Internet has and remains in the process of redefining how the antiques and collectibles field operates.

I am not ready to take off my thinking cap quite yet.

CHAPTER 2

Inside the Mind of the Collector

Is there a portion of the brain that governs one's desire to collect? I think there is. It is located between the portions of the brain that focus on memory retention and pleasure sensation. The amount may vary from individual to individual, but it is present in everyone.

WARNING! Collecting is addictive. It is worse than alcoholism, gambling, or smoking. Once you have experienced the joys of collecting, you are hooked. No matter how hard you try, you never will be able to shake the addiction.

Besides, why would you want to? Collecting adds passion, excitement, and purpose to life. Collecting is an adventure. Many simply love the hunt. The hunt holds only minor fascination for me. I love the goodies.

I am a member of the "he who dies with the biggest pile wins" club. My pile is big now, but nowhere near as big as it is going to be when I die.

Having fun is essential to the collecting process. Sharing the fun adds to the pleasure. Read on as I share some of my fun experiences with you.

Memories

Memory plays a major role in what is and is not collected. A recent e-mail, press release, and radio quiz raised some serious concerns about memory's impact on collecting, especially the issue of what constitutes the past.

The Internet is an information pipeline. It has replaced the photocopy and fax machines as the means of passing along office jokes ranging from acceptable to politically and socially incorrect, food for thought, and other useful information. Much of the information is transmitted in a pass-it-down-the-alley style.

I recently received such an e-mail. It began: "Just in case you weren't feeling too old today, this will certainly change things. Each year the staff at Beloit College in Wisconsin puts together a list (of events) to try to give the faculty a sense of the mindset of this year's incoming freshman…. The people who are starting college this fall (2002) across the nation were born in 1984."

The list was lengthy. I have selected ten: (1) they are too young to remember the space shuttle blowing up; (2) the CD was introduced the year before they were born; (3) they have always had an answering machine; (4) they have always had cable; (5) Jay Leno has always been on *The Tonight Show*; (6) they do not know who Mork was or where he was from; (7) they never heard "Where's the Beef?" or "de plane Boss, de plane"; (8) they do not care who shot J.R. and have no idea who J.R. even is; (9) they do not have a clue how to use a typewriter; and (10) bottle caps have always been screw off and plastic.

The Class of 2006 represents the next generation of twenty-some-thing collectors. For them, the 1970s is old. Forget about the 1950s or 1960s. By the time they graduate, even the early 1980s is going to seem old. Their parents were born in the late 1950s or early 1960s and did not become young adults until the 1970s. If born in the late 1950s, the parents are part of the social cause generation, i.e., civil rights, make love not war, etc. If born in the early 1960s, the parents are part of the Yuppie generation.

The next generation of twenty-something collectors comes from smaller, more mobile families. They have very limited roots in the past. They are a technology-driven generation and more interested in look-ing ahead than behind. Their exposure to the past is derived from cable television and periodicals.

Through the 1980s, the antiques and collectibles field was influ-ential in guiding new collectors toward what to collect. This influence lessened in the 1990s. By 2006, the field's ability to direct collectors will be marginal. Collecting trends will be established by outside sources. Further, collecting trends will be measured in months, not years. Serving the collecting needs of the Class of 2006 will require major changes in how the antiques and collectibles field operates.

Reuters released a story on November 9, 2002, by Angela Moore titled "Retro Reflex: Toy Makers Bank on Nostalgia." The story begins:

> With consumers facing a dizzying selection of modern toys for the winter holiday season—from motorized cats to muscled action figures and video games—some toy makers want to cash in on the nostalgia factor.
>
> Mattel, Inc. and Toys R Us are among the companies that have revived old favorites such as Cabbage Patch Kids and He-man in the hope of catching the eyes and hearts of "Generation X" or "Baby Boomer" parents.
>
> Among the toys back on the front shelf are Care Bears, Magic 8 Balls, Hasbro's updated version of the Trivial Pursuit board game. Next year also sees the revival of Teenage Mutant Ninja Turtles and the Strawberry Shortcake doll collection.
>
> "The advantage is that you don't need to spend a ton of money to gain brand recognition," said John Taylor, a toy analyst with Arcadia Investment Corp. "If you put something on ice for a decade, kids grow up and have kids of their own."
>
> Bringing back old brands can spark interest in a product that's been forgotten by mainstream buyers, or freshen up an old name by adding a new spin to it.

Excuse me?! How old do you have to be to have played with Cabbage Patch dolls, Care Bears, Teenage Mutant Ninja Turtles, and Strawberry Shortcake? Heaven help us. Next thing you know they will be reissuing My Little Pony toys. There are some aspects of the 1980s that time simply should forget.

These are toys from the 1980s. I have more than a dozen period Teenage Mutant Ninja Turtles objects put aside in the closet that houses the purchases from my annual "$250 and a Closet" column. The 1980s is yesterday. It is too recent to evoke long-term memories.

In the process of proofing this column, Dana Morykan, my senior researcher, mentioned that her eighteen-year-old son, Zack, recently rediscovered the Turtles. Maybe the toy industry *is* on to something.

Note that the toy industry is banking on the late Baby Boomer and Generation X parents to look no further back than their own children's childhood for the memories they want to pass along to their grandchildren. I have argued for some time that the newest generations of collectors looks back no further than their parents and their own experiences for their collecting memories. Forget the things that belonged to their grandparents, great-grandparents, etc. Collecting is "me" focused.

The toy industry is making no effort to reissue the television-related toys of the 1950s through the 1970s. It is fun to watch the old shows on Nick at Night. It is even safe to say a new generation of youngsters is being exposed to these shows. However, this has had no impact on the value of period collectibles licensed by these shows and has not resulted in any desire on the part of toy companies to reissue old products or create new ones. The 1950s, 1960s, and 1970s are not historic to the toy industry, they are ancient.

A quiz was a regular feature of *Whatcha Got*, a weekly antiques and collectibles call-in show I did previously on KLTF in Little Falls, Minnesota. The death of Margaret "Peg" Phillips, who played the tart-tongued shopkeeper Ruth Anne Mille in the television series *Northern Exposure,* prompted this question: "What year did 'Northern Exposure' go off the air?"

Take a minute and write your answer on a sheet of paper before reading further.

The first caller guessed 1989. Before the correct answer of 1995 was given callers offered 1987, 1990, 1991, 1992, 1994, 1997, and 1999. The show first aired in 1990.

How accurate is intermediate- and short-term memory? Over the years I have noticed a tendency on my part to date things up to a decade earlier than they actually occurred. Recently, I was asked to provide a list of three television shows from the 1960s that generated a large group of collectibles. I am embarrassed to report that two of the shows on the list I gave a reporter were from the 1970s.

I have come to the conclusion that the time period that individuals remember most accurately is the one they experienced from early grade school (age seven) through young adulthood (age thirty). By this time, an individual's tastes are firmly established. Everything that happens later is either ignored or relegated to a position of lesser importance.

My goal is to keep abreast of shifting collecting trends. Yet, I find myself constantly having to relearn events that occurred during my lifetime. While I can define the 1940s, 1950s, and 1960s with a reasonable degree of accuracy, I am having difficulty defining the 1970s and 1980s. Admittedly, understanding the 1970s is becoming easier.

Historians, writers, and the media define a generation. They decide what memories are required to trigger the requisite feeling of nostalgia. We are told what to remember.

The 1970s and the early 1980s will be defined in this first decade of the twenty-first century. I am anxious to see what objects make the list. Why? Because these are the items the next generation of collectors will collect. Keep your eyes open.

How Many Are Too Many?

How many examples are required to have a bona fide collection? Normally, when someone asks me this question, I quickly reply "ten or more." My answer is derived from an early (late 1980s) "Rinker on Collectibles" column titled "Rinker's Rule of Ten."

I wrote: "Rinker's Rule of Ten is quite simple. When somebody asks me whether something is collectible, I ask myself one simple question: Would I own ten of them? Think about this for a minute. A real collection requires at least ten items."

I chose ten for several reasons. Convinced that almost every American collects something, a proposition that I still strongly believe, I wanted a count that was easily achievable if someone simply looked around and did an honest count. Equally important was a number that could quickly be surpassed by someone starting a new collection.

Every collection begins with the second example. However, two or three or four examples do not make a collection. A sense of having a collection is the key to defining a collection. This sense is number-driven.

As collecting enters the twenty-first century, I am concerned that ten is far too small a number to define a collection. Today's collections usually number in the hundreds and even thousands. Serious collectors dismiss individuals who only own ten, twenty, or even fifty of something. Even if one owned the top ten examples in a specific collecting category, the majority of the collectors in that category and certainly the general public would consider the collection as inconsequential. Collecting is no longer about quality, it is about quantity.

The big number game arrived on the scene in the 1980s and became dominant in the 1990s. The boom times of the 1990s led to a conspicuous consumption mentality on the part of collectors. Large collections were the order of the day. Gaudy displays followed as collections that initially consumed a few shelves or at most a wall expanded to include an entire room, rooms, or a special addition to the home to house the collection. The collector's goal is to overwhelm any general visitor and cause a deep case of envy when showing off his collection to a rival.

The media is one of the driving forces behind the emphasis on quantity collections. Newspapers, magazines, radio, and television often features stories about individuals who collect. In almost every case, these individuals have "one of the biggest collections of (blank)." It is a collection's size that attracts attention.

In 2002 Home & Garden Television launched two new antiques and collectibles shows, *Collector Inspector* and *Ultimate Collector*. Where *Collector Inspector*, the show that I host, downplays the role of collectors, *Ultimate Collector* takes just the opposite approach. *Ultimate Collector* seeks out collectors with the biggest pile in a specific collecting category. It fuels the myth that he who dies with the biggest pile wins.

Even when a collection's focus falls outside the traditional collecting categories, the mere fact that the approach is unusual is not enough unless the number of items is large. A collector of hotel soap with a mere five hundred examples would attract no media attention. In fact, I doubt if five thousand examples would be enough. How many examples would it take? Ten thousand might do it, but my bet is on twenty thousand plus. Not possible? My suspicion is that there are probably five or more individuals who would qualify.

Is quantity a bad thing? As a dedicated accumulator and a major quantity collector, I am hardly in a position to "call the kettle black." I have more than my fair share of collections that number in the hundreds and one major collection, jigsaw puzzles, that numbers in the thousands. I accept quantity collecting as a necessity.

In today's checklist-driven collecting community, the desire to own one of all known examples is a prime collecting motivator. It is why collectors often focus on one or two subcategories within a major collecting category. The goal is to assemble a "complete" collection. It is impossible in most cases. Yet, it more than any other goal is responsible for keeping the collector focused and dedicated to the hunt.

The true collector never has enough. The "How many are too many?" question is fallacious. One never has enough. Having enough implies a high degree of satisfaction. Continual dissatisfaction is a hallmark of the serious collector.

Collectors are haunted by the "how many" accumulating questions asked by spouses, children, and friends. Examples include: (1) Why do you need another one when you already have one just like this? (2) Isn't that just like the one you bought last week? (3) Don't you have enough? and, (4) There is no room left; where are you going to put that? Nothing puts a collector on the defensive more than having to justify what he bought. In an ideal world no justification either to himself or an outside entity is required from the collector. The mere fact that he wants to own it, can afford to own it, and has purchased it is sufficient.

There is no valid answer to the "How many is too many?" question until a collector runs out of space. No collector worth her salt will ever run out of space. Collectors are inbred with the ability to find space when they need space. They are among the best when it comes to packing, piling, and stacking. If they do not have sufficient space, they will create the space they need or acquire new space. I speak from experience.

Usable space is everywhere. Attics, closets, basements, and garages are just the most obvious. Under the bed is one of the spaces collectors most frequently overlook. Under the bed is ideal because temperature and humidity are most regulated in the bedroom. It is also free from continued attack by ardent cleaners, one of the reasons parents frequently hide Christmas gifts there.

Floor space is rapidly becoming a premium at Rinker Enterprises. I tend to pile and stack. You would be amazed at how many cardboard file boxes I can stack on top of one another without crushing the bottom boxes. Alas, in many cases, my piling and stacking is simply objects on top of one another.

I use shelves, but find myself constantly torn by the desire to buy another object for one of my collections rather than invest in storage shelving. I am fully aware that in my school, which features rooms with high ceilings, the most underutilized space resides upwards. I have resolved to do better in the future.

Collecting became increasingly more sophisticated during the final two decades of the twentieth century. As a result, it is difficult to identify general collecting rules that apply universally. "Rinker's Rule of Ten" has fallen victim to this development.

Today it is necessary to divide collecting into categories in order to understand it. "Rinker's Rule of Ten" still applies to the general public. Ten objects do constitute a collection when the desire is to create a collection with the sole purpose of fun and enjoyment. In order to be considered an average collector, the number jumps to a minimum of one hundred. Those wishing to be considered serious collectors need a minimum of five hundred examples. Major collectors assemble collections numbering in the thousands.

These numbers are based on an average unit cost of less than fifty dollars per object in the collection. When the average unit cost per object is between fifty and one hundred dollars, reduce the numbers by one-quarter. When the average unit cost per object is above two hundred dollars, half the number is required for the serious and major collector and one-third for the average collector.

In the final analysis, it is a numbers game after all.

My Most Favorite Piece

While I was appearing on a radio show recently, the interviewer asked what seemed to be a rather simple question. "What's your most favorite piece in your collection?"

Normally, I always have a ready reply to any question I am asked. But this question made me pause.

My first reaction was to answer, "I do not have a single favorite piece." This response ducked the question and provided an easy way out. I should have taken it.

Instead, I thought back to my home and office where stacks of boxes and drawers are filled with the diversity of my collecting manias ... Hopalong Cassidy, charge tokens and credit cards, comic books, political buttons, games, quilts, Pennsylvania Dutch material, postcards, shopping bags, etc. The list is endless. In truth, I am the true eclectic eccentric collector.

If disaster struck and I could save only one object from the totality of my collections, which one would I save? The very thought surpasses the horror of Frankenstein or the fear of Hell. That interviewer's question gave me nightmares.

The dedicated collector doesn't have a favorite item. He has favorites, plural! Worse yet, he loves them all.

The more I think about it, the more convinced I become that single objects merge into a unified whole and lose their identity in the mind of the dedicated collector.

The collection is the all-controlling force that dominates his life. Everything is related to everything else. Objects are viewed only in their relationship to other objects.

I sat back and thought about the great collectors that I know. One individual came immediately to mind.

He was afflicted with a love affair with cars, acquired during his boyhood. His first acquisition was an old Chevy. As he prospered, he branched out into vintage cars.

When space and storage became a major consideration, he switched to scale models and miniatures as well as assembling a toy collection of tin, lead, cast iron, and plastic automobiles, trucks, fire engines, and even trains.

The next collecting phase saw him branch out into automobile memorabilia ranging from giveaway premiums from manufacturers and dealers to match safes embossed with an automobile. If it had to do with automobiles or had a picture of an automobile on it, he wanted it.

By now his collecting obsession was the major focus of his life. His days, nights, and weekends revolved around buying. His collection expanded to include automobile art, lithographs, oil paintings, posters, porcelains, and sculptures.

He ran out of space again. He built more rooms, creating his own personal museum where he could browse among the sum total of his collectibles. When he ran out of this new space, he added another room and more display cases.

At this point, something happened. The mania was still there. But the original sex appeal and chemistry began to lag. It was getting harder and harder and more and more expensive to find exciting new material.

While still faithful to his original mistress, he now is embarking on a new romance: a collection of baseball memorabilia. This is dedication. This is craziness.

But could he name his favorite automobile piece? No way! Absolutely not! Everything in the collection is precious to him.

I was back to square one. How to answer the darn question?

I have met people who are in love with one specific antique or collectible. Almost without fail, they are a casual dilettante collector, not a dedicated collector. Like the Sunday painter, the dilettante collects on a whim, buys on impulse (a few dollars here, a few dollars there), and shies away from making a commitment to assembling a meaningful collection. They are trendy and willing to shift allegiance to a collecting category the minute their current interest becomes unfashionable.

What they want more than anything from the antiques and collectibles they own is bragging rights. We need these persons in the market, but we don't have to like them. So much for this approach.

Then, I had an inspiration and the answer became crystal clear. "What's my favorite piece?

"Why, the next one, of course."

Passion

A life without passion is no life at all. Assuming this is true, I can think of dozens of collecting categories, especially in the antiques sector, that are in deep despair. They have become so staid and conservative they are slowly bleeding to death. I cannot think of anything more deadly than being stuck for hours in a room filled with collectors of Queen Anne period furniture.

SALOPIAN COLLECTORS OF THE WORLD UNITE. Just kidding! Do you even know what Salopian ware is? Do not worry. You are in the majority. Salopian ware collectors are as extinct as the dinosaurs. The last one died over two decades ago when the passion vanished from the collecting category.

While there is a hundred times more passion found in collectors of collectibles than in collectors of antiques, it is not enough. Collecting is the most fun when it takes place in a fever-pitched atmosphere, a setting charged with passion.

Many of the collectibles categories that originated in the 1970s and 1980s are becoming complacent as they mature. The collectibles market as a whole does not seem anywhere near as exciting as it did twelve years ago when I launched my "Rinker on Collectibles" column. It has not retained the high level of excitement that fueled its initial appearance.

I have thought about this carefully. I wanted to make certain that my conclusion was not driven by my own aging process. It is not. This is an analytical statement of fact.

My first thought was to explain this growing lack of passion and excitement by introducing a new analytical concept—collecting category burnout. The key questions are: (1) Can any collecting category maintain a high level of passion indefinitely? (2) If the answer is no, what is the average length of time that passion runs high? and (3) What are the factors in the growth of a collecting category that diminish the passion? I am working on a series of timelines that will allow me to predict the potential level of passion within a collecting category at any given moment of time. Nothing concrete yet, but I am making progress.

The same set of questions applies to collectors. Can a collector maintain a high level of passion for a lifetime? The answer is yes. The proof is empirical. I know of many such collectors. Dave Bausch, Betty Newbound, and Allan Petretti are good examples. Alas, far more collectors lose their passion than retain it. Again, it is worth asking why.

One can achieve no greater high than one resulting from collecting. Collecting often produces an adrenaline rush. I do not understand why people need mind-altering drugs when antiques and collectibles are available. My collectibles highs last far longer and have no side effects (except maybe a financial one now and then).

I am still as excited about collectibles as I always have been. No one will ever accuse me of lack of passion, especially when the subject is collectibles. I love this business and its objects. Love and passion are intertwined. You cannot have one without the other. I learned long ago that I was not put on the face of the earth to be a wimp.

The collectors, dealers, and other individuals in the collectibles field that I like the most are those who get excited about what they buy and sell. When they talk about their things, the pitch of their voice rises slightly, they speaker faster, their eyes sparkle, and they become animated. It does not take a genius to figure out that they are trying to transfer to the listener the excitement and passion they feel for their objects. Their zealousness rivals that of the most ardent religious missionary.

An inanimate object is no fun. It is just a thing. Collectibles are neutral only if someone allows them to be. Passion breathes life into an object. Giving life to objects is one of the many joys of collecting.

When a collector says, "That object sings to me," I immediately ask why. The answer is always insightful. There is a collecting psyche. Sharing it is a mind-expanding experience.

I like the concept that objects sing because it suggests that objects really do have inner souls. They are deeply hidden, but they are there. It is shared only with those who have the passion to seek them out.

On more than one occasion, I have been at a flea market, antiques mall, shop, or show and have heard a voice calling: "Over here. I am over here. Come buy me. I am meant for you. We belong together." I have learned to listen to this bewitching song. I give no credence to

those individuals who contend these songs are from seductive collectibles sirens. Trust me, they are the voices of collectibles angels.

John Gallow, president of Butterfield and Butterfield, once told
me, "No one loves a child like its own mother." John was referring to
foreign collectors buying back objects in the American market that
were made in their homeland. I interpret the comment differently.

Never criticize a child to its mother. Perhaps I should use parent
instead of mother, but experience has shown that mothers are far more
possessive and defensive of their children than fathers are. Having married a woman with children from a previous marriage, I know well of
what I speak.

The truth is the antiques and collectibles business is my child. I
adopted it and made it mine. Mess with it and you mess with me.
Attack it and you attack me. I will go to war to defend my child, something I have done on more than one occasion.

But the child does not escape without discipline. I am a harsh
father. I expect a lot from my child. I set a higher standard for my child
than I do for anyone else's. When my child does not meet that standard,
I have no trouble pointing out his errors and suggesting a better path.

I have no trouble getting up on a soapbox when I have something to
say. Nor do I allow the bounds of modesty and, in some cases, common
decency to prevent me from saying what I think needs to be said. I try not
to demand that the listeners agree with me, just that they hear me out.

Often what I have to say pushes some buttons. People get angry.
They violently disagree. This does not bother me, rather it pleases me.
Passion is as much about love as it is about anger. Either way, neutral-
ity is cast aside.

I recently spoke to the graduate students in the University of
Delaware's Winterthur fellowship program. Winterthur sent the students to me because they requested information on twentieth-century
collectibles, a chronological time period not included in the Winterthur
mission statement. The students were totally unprepared for what they
encountered.

Instead of just talking about twentieth-century collectibles, I
decided to attack some of the basic tenets of the modern museum system, especially those of museums whose focus is the eighteenth and
nineteenth centuries. I called these future leaders in the museum field

everything from "upper-class, white elitist snobs" to "preservers of an obsolete, out of touch with reality, history."

Suffice it to say I got their blood boiling. The good news is they attacked right back. They rose to the defense. The discussion was heated and passionate.

The day ended with neither side conceding the field. However, no one who was involved in the battle will ever be able to look at the issue in the same complacent way they did before, not even me.

Is there a place for passion in the antiques and collectibles field? You bet there is! And there always will be, as long as I draw a breath.

P.S.: Thomas Turner made ceramic Salopian ware at Caughley, located near Broseley, Shropshire, England, in the eighteenth century. The ware has a polychrome transfer. Initially collected as "Polychrome Transfer Ware," it was collected as "Salopian Ware" in the 1950s. '60s, and '70s because it was marked with an "S" or "Salopian" impressed or painted under the glaze. The term also developed a generic meaning—applying to all early polychrome decorated wares.

Is the Hunt Enough?

The hunt is an integral part of collecting. For some collectors, it is the heart and soul of collecting. When the thrill of the hunt is missing from the buying process, it seems tainted. Few like easy prey. But is the hunt enough?

The hunt is an involved process. First, the collector identifies a specific object or objects she wishes to acquire. This allows the collector to select the best hunting grounds to bag her trophy. Each jungle—in this instance a generalization for antiques malls, antiques shops, antiques shows, auctions, flea markets, or the Internet—offers different game.

Few collectors go shopping for the sheer fun of shopping. Collectors go hunting expecting to buy. If they do not return home with something, they feel unfulfilled. Hunting is not about the experience. It is about the buy.

Second, anticipation is a key element in the hunt. The decision to go hunting is rarely instantaneous. Once a decision to go hunting is made, a great deal of planning is necessary. Questions, such as where should I hunt, how much time should I allow, what should I take with me, and what are my chances of finding what I am seeking, have to be answered. These decisions are not easily made. They need to be stewed over, churned, and stirred. So much depends on making the correct decisions.

Thinking about the hunt over several days or weeks tends to heighten the experience. In fact, a true hunter dreams about the hunt for days before participating in it. Dreams are always about what will be found, never about what has been bought. I have spoken to dozens of collectors who have told me they experienced a strange sense of déjà vu when finding a treasure. "It is as though I bought it before" is their comment. Of course, they have—in their dreams.

Third, victory, i.e., one or more successful purchases, is assumed. Collectors sense victory long before it is achieved. Failure is not an option.

Fourth, while a buy is essential to a successful hunt, it alone is not enough. For a hunt to be truly successful, to create a sense of elation, the buy has to be a bargain—A STEAL! When this happens, the collector achieves a collecting high, a feeling at least equal to and normally far in excess of any high achievable by other means.

Look into the eyes of a collector when he talks about the hunt. They shine. His face glows. His voice's pitch changes. The conversation becomes animated. The collector relives the hunt in its telling. The process is mystical.

As I write this column, I am celebrating my sixty-second birthday. [**Author's Note:** I was born October 1, 1941.] Earlier today, I received a birthday card from Dana Morykan and Virginia Reinbold, my staff at Rinker Enterprises. It read "Aging Is Inevitable. Maturing Is Optional." I constantly tell people one of my main goals in life is never to grow up. I am not a victim of the Peter Pan syndrome. I merely want the enjoyment of youth to always be a part of my adult life.

As I look in the mirror and notice the continuing graying of my locks, I have to accept the fact that I am aging. Note I said aging and not maturing. Yet, I do find that the aging process has changed some of my attitudes.

Heresy that it is, I no longer find the thrill of the hunt as exciting as I once did. While I am not ready to attribute my change in attitude to age, it plays a factor. Far more critical is a busy personal schedule that no longer allows time for the hunt. I consider myself lucky when I find an hour to go hunting. A day to hunt is a luxury I no longer have.

Yet, I continue to adhere to my philosophy that "buying an antique or collectible a day keeps the doctor away." Forget about apples. This is about mental not physical health. A day that passes without my buying something or a package arriving at the office with something I bought previously is a day that is incomplete. Thank goodness for eBay. I cannot even imagine how I survived before it arrived on the scene.

Feeling as I do now about the hunt, I find myself continually asking, "Is the hunt enough?" For the aging (alright, mature) collector the answer is no. The hunt is only one part of a far larger total experience.

In the ideal world where I would be able to spend a day or more actually hunting, I would do so only if the experience was total. A total experience consists of four ingredients: (1) a great place to hunt, (2) a hunting companion, (3) a fabulous dinner, and (4) superior accommodations. I am a Hilton camper, i.e., I prefer sleeping in a hotel or motel bed over spreading my sleeping bag on the rock-hard ground.

I define a great place to hunt as a location where there are multiple buying sources within a ten-mile radius—a combination of antiques malls, flea markets, antiques shows, or antiques shops. If an auction is nearby, life is complete. Such places do exist. The Adamstown (Pennsylvania) antiquing strip along Route 272 is one example. There are Interstate exits that provide access to three or more malls and flea markets. America is blessed with dozens of "antiquing towns," i.e., towns that have downtown areas filled with malls and shops.

I no longer like shopping alone. The hunting experience is enhanced by sharing it with friends. I am blessed. I get to see collecting through the eyes of others. Each individual brings a different perspective to the collecting experience. The learning process is continuous.

I do not go antiquing with a collecting rival. I am not stupid. When rivals go hunting together, friendship stops at the entrance to the jungle. Not everyone has the ability to understand and respect this. Therefore, save yourself grief and preserve friendship with your rivals by not going shopping with them. By shopping with someone who collects in a totally different collecting category, you double the eyes looking for things. Jealousy and rivalry are eliminated. Both share in the joy of each others' purchases.

Celebrating the hunt with a fabulous dinner is something I learned from Stanley Greene, the first owner of Warman Publishing following the demise of E. G. Warman. Stanley told me as I left on one of my first field research trips, "If you have a good day, take the time to celebrate with a good meal." He was absolutely right. I took his advice then and have ever since. I have a list of favorite restaurants near every hunting ground I have visited. Many are not found in local guide books. I have long considered sharing these favorites with my readers but could not justify doing so because they were not "antique" related. Now, I believe they are. As a result, expect to find restaurant recommendations in future "Rinker on Collectibles" columns.

A great place to hunt, a terrific hunting companion, and a gourmet meal need to be capped by a fabulous place to spend the evening if the hunting experience is to be considered truly complete. I spend a great deal of time in motels. There are excellent chains. However, nothing beats a great bed and breakfast or a renovated old downtown hotel. When faced with the choice of one or the other, I always opt for the downtown hotel. You have not lived until you have spent a night in the Omni, formerly The Netherlands, in downtown Cincinnati.

Do not confuse the hunt with a buying fix. A buying fix is when you decide you want something and you want it immediately. Alas, this is the attitude the majority of young collectors bring to the buying experience.

When I want a fix, I shop on eBay. eBay provides instant gratification. Well, maybe not instant. Sometimes I have to wait several days for the auction to close. This anticipation is not good for my soul. I like knowing if I have won or lost immediately. However, when you cannot experience the hunt, eBay is a viable alternative.

I buy antiques. I breathe. The two are inevitably linked. It is a great life. I hope it is for you as well.

Are Collectibles Your Mistress?

I am a closet country music fan. Rollin' down the highway to a speaking commitment or travelin' the back roads of Upper Milford Township on the way to my office, my car radio blasts with the Nashville sound. Before my more upscale readers tune me out, I also confess to listening to National Public Radio's *All Things Considered* on the way home from work. I do not have a one-track mind. I'm really a wild and crazy guy at heart.

Recently, I was struck by the similarity in theme between Highway 101's hit "Whiskey, If You Were a Woman" and some of my observations in the collectibles field. The song's premise is simple. The singers lament an individual's addiction to whiskey with which the spouse cannot compete. If only the addiction was another person, then the spouse would have a chance.

I wonder how many collectors' spouses wish that their husband or wife had a two-legged mistress or lover instead of a collectibles mistress. My own guess is that the two-legged variety requires far less time and costs far less to keep. I would not know. I have had a collectibles mistress as long as I can remember.

[**Author's Note:** There are both collectibles mistresses and collectables lovers. Since I am male and write primarily in the first and third person singular, you will read about the collectibles mistress in what follows. Be assured there are just as many collectibles lovers out there. The victimized spouse is male just as often as female.]

Most individuals who have two-legged mistresses are reasonably discreet about their activities. Individuals with collectibles mistresses are not. Evidence of their indiscretion is everywhere. They make no attempt to hide it. In fact, they display it openly—the more visible, the better. Nary a day passes without a collector's spouse being visually reminded of her proper place in the order of things.

Watch a collectibles collector handle his collection. You are witness to an act of love. The eyes take on a distant, reverential appearance. There is a brief interlude of silence as a bond is established between collector and object. A gentle whisper of love is occasionally uttered. Each piece is stroked, fondled, and caressed. When was the last time that you looked at your spouse this way? Think about it.

The collectibles mistress in dominant. I am amazed at how many collectors think they control their collecting habit. Forget it. Collectibles are the controller; the collector is the controllee. Once hooked, you are in for the long term. There is no "quickie" in the collectibles field. Ask any individual who has stood in line for over an hour waiting for a collectibles show to open.

Collectors plan their lives around their mistress more than they do their spouse. They mark their next year's calendar with major show dates before their spouse's birthday or their anniversary. Getaway vacations are more likely to happen if there is a show or collector in the area.

Collectors think nothing about interrupting established routines or plans to spend time with their mistress. I no longer do jigsaw puzzles at home. Once I start a puzzle, I feel compelled to finish it. I often would work into the wee hours of the morning. Jigsaw puzzles can have a decidedly negative effect on one's sex life. I speak from experience.

Consider the following scenario between a collector and his spouse:

"We have a few minutes. Do you mind if I stop at this antiques mall?"

"Of course not. I'll wait in the car."

"Are you certain? Don't you want to come in?"

"No. I brought along a book to read."

"Great. I won't be long."

Collectors find it impossible to be fully open with their spouses about their collectibles mistress. There are some things they simply prefer not to discuss, e.g., how much they just spent on their latest "prize" piece and why the car or home repairs are not going to get done this month because of it. The first few times this happens relationships are seriously tested. Eventually, the spouse becomes worn down by these experiences and grudgingly accepts the inevitable.

Spouses are not always passive. One afternoon shortly after we had moved to our home in Zionsville, Connie answered a knock at the door. A husband and wife dealer team was delivering a tall case clock that I had purchased and about which I had forgotten to tell Connie.

When asked by the dealers where she wanted the clock, her reply was a classic: "Put it on the bed. He is sleeping with it tonight."

What can a spouse do? Most spouses find it impossible to share the same collectibles mistress. I know a number who have tried. They failed miserably. Collectors are simply too possessive.

One solution is for the spouse to take a collectibles lover in another category. This approach is doomed from the start. A competition for space begins immediately. Sources of supply only occasionally overlap. Each spouse is pulled in a different direction. A collectibles collector is not the type of person to suffer in silence when forced to act civilized among a group of people whose interests in no way reflect his own.

Some individuals actually try to be supportive of their spouse's collectibles mistress based upon the belief that anything is better than the two-legged variety. Wrong, wrong, wrong! When they give birthday, anniversary, and holiday gifts that enhance the collectibles mistress's charm, all they do is frustrate. They set the collector's mind racing—how did she find this instead of me? Is she turning my sources against me? How much did she pay? I am certain I could have gotten a better deal. She has obviously had this for some time; why did she have to wait so long to give it to me? Doesn't she know that I already have two of these in my collection? These are not the kind of responses that build loving relationships.

Collectibles collectors' spouses have little choice but to suffer and endure. In this era of social relevance, one wonders why having a collectibles mistress has not been classified as a form of spousal abuse. In my opinion, being married or involved with a collector for longer than ten years is more than enough to earn a place in heaven.

Further, I have not yet heard of a court case where a collectibles mistress has been cited as the ground for divorce. The concept is not abstract. The woman does exist. This is fertile ground for an imaginative and enterprising divorce attorney.

CHAPTER 3

Understanding How the Market Works

I believe it is possible to quantify and predict the antiques and collectibles market. I have devoted a good portion of my professional career to proving this. Rinker Enterprises Inc., my antiques and collectibles educational and research center, contains the reference resources to track more than 1,500 antiques and collectibles categories, many over a fifty-plus-year period.

Assigning a dollar value to an object is providing only a partial answer to what it is worth. There are three additional key questions critical to determining an object's value: (1) What are the factors that make an object worth something at a specific moment in time? (2) How has the object's price reached this point? and (3) What are the factors that are likely to change the object's value in the future? These are the questions I thrive upon.

An educated collector is a smart collector. Alas, no college or university offers a degree in antiques and collectibles. Most collectors learn "by the seat of their pants." "Rinker on Collectibles," my weekly column, is my contribution to shortening the learning curve. Read on and learn.

When Did Americans Become Collectibles Conscious?

The following excerpt is from Jason Vest's article, "Lawyers Hold All the Cards / Baseball Cards: An Innocent Hobby or a Gambling Mojo for Kids?" that appeared in the December 2, 1996, issue of *U.S. News & World Report*: "The value of baseball cards from the '50s and '60s exploded in the late '80s because of a shortage of supply. 'It's the story almost every man who came of age at a certain time tells—as soon as he went off to college or got married, his mother threw out the baseball cards and comic books,' says David Leibowitz, an analyst with Burnham Securities.

"But boomer mothers have thrown the industry a curve ball. 'They're of the generation that used to collect cards themselves,' Liebowitz says, 'and they know darn well not to dispose of them.' With more people holding on to cards and companies churning out tons more, the result has been a glut—and little appreciation in price."

Scarcity is one of the Big Three value components for any collectible. Condition and desirability are the other two. Just as every collectible has a value at which it will not sell, every collecting category has a fixed, limited number of potential buyers, be they collectors, dealers, decorators, investors, or speculators. The number of potential buyers for most collectibles categories—those consisting primarily of objects made between 1945 and the early 1970s—ranges between one thousand and five thousand individuals. The number of potential buyers in some narrow collectibles categories is less than two hundred.

There are some desirables categories—those consisting primarily of objects made within the last thirty years—where the number of buyers exceeds ten thousand individuals. Three examples are contemporary Precious Moment figurines, sports trading card collectors, and Holiday Barbies. Individuals who buy desirables are primarily trend-driven, short-term oriented, and financially focused. I question if they are true collectors. They are better described as speculators, hoarders, foolish, naïve, or some combination of these terms.

An object becomes a collectible when it achieves a stable secondary resale market value. This value is achieved when an object has been bought and sold enough times on the secondary market so that collectors trust the object's value. This process takes time, between twenty-five and thirty years for most objects. In the interim, any secondary resale market value is speculative.

Collectibles must stand the test of time. During the interval from manufacture (the beginning of the desirables period) to collectibles status, collectors shape the market by (1) deciding which objects are worth collecting and (2) the level of importance assigned to specific objects within a collecting category. Which objects are ultimate units, upper echelon, above average, common (or core), or junk? Objects move about in levels during the desirables period as collecting trends shift, causing collectors to change their minds about an object's importance. Once an object is classified as a collectible, it tends to remain at that level of collecting importance.

Not all objects pass the test of time. Survival alone is not enough to create value. Age is now far down the list of factors that determine an object's value. There are dozens of late-nineteenth-century pattern glass goblets and wines worth $40 or less; there are hundreds of comic books from the 1950s and '60s with values exceeding $50.

The law of supply and demand applies to collectibles. When a collectible is in short supply and collector demand is high, an object's value is high. Competition among collectors drives values upward. When a collectible's supply is large and collector demand low or fulfilled, an object's value is low. If the supply is extremely large, an object can lose its appeal altogether. There is little fun in owning what everyone else has.

More and more collectors of post-1970s objects are now asking a very basic question—how many examples have survived? In most cases, this question is very difficult to answer. Obviously, collectors and dealers want the number to be small. It is to their advantage. More often than not, the number exceeds their highest guesstimates. The safest course is to assume a high number. Unfortunately, most collectors and dealers are not prepared to make this mental leap to reality.

Americans became collectibles conscious sometime in the mid-1970s. Collectibles consciousness is defined as understanding that an object has the potential to appreciate in value above its initial cost. Further, it is highly likely that this may occur within the lifetime of the collector.

Prior to the creation of a level of collectibles consciousness, objects followed this life path: (a) purchased and used, (b) recycled or discarded, both limiting the supply, (c) surviving objects stored for twenty to thirty-plus years, and (d) survivors discovered, identified, and collected. Instant collectibility was not a concept. The number of collecting categories was narrow.

The development of a collectibles consciousness changed everything. Objects survived in numbers far exceeding the ability of the collectibles market to absorb. Instant collectibility and speculation became viable market concepts. Hoarded objects went from store shelf to storage area, raising condition demands for post-1970s objects from very good to excellent and placing an importance on packaging almost equal to the object found within it.

Individuals collecting objects made after 1970 apply a totally different set of collecting criteria to their items than do those individuals who collect objects made before 1970. Unity within the collecting community has been replaced by diversity.

What made America collectibles conscious? Because this development occurred in the mid-1970s, some suggest that events associated with the celebration of the Bicentennial is the answer. This is wrong. The celebration of our nation's two hundredth anniversary had nothing to do with it.

The media's discovery that America's fascination with antiques and collectibles, particularly their value, was a viable news story created this consciousness. Antiques and collectibles became news. Auction house hype accelerated the trend. Before long, reports of record prices at auctions and the development of new collecting trends was front page news. The arrival of national and regional trade papers, specific collecting and/or price guides on almost every conceivable subject, and the explosion of flea markets and antiques malls and shows fueled the growth of a national collectibles consciousness.

Everyone wanted to get into the act. Before long, collectors no longer played a major role in the marketplace, supplanted by decorators, impulse buyers, and individuals looking for pieces of their lost youth.

In the early 1990s a continuing stream of holiday toy shortages that mated with a "must have" buying mentality among the general public provided proof of a collectibles consciousness that now alternates between sanity and madness. The dictionary definition of a collector as "one that makes a collection" is meaningless. Today the motivation behind the act of collecting defines a true collector, and the act of collecting itself does not. An individual with a five-year hoard of Holiday Barbies is not a collector, at least not in my mind.

There are positives associated with the growth of a national collectibles consciousness. Collecting is more egalitarian. Collecting elitism, most commonly associated with antiques collectors and a long way from dying, is under attack. The number of acceptable collecting categories has doubled. Everything is collectible became a concept worth discussing, not dismissing. The post-1945 collectible not only achieved acceptability but became dominant in the marketplace.

Some view the changing collecting parameters of the 1990s as offering new opportunities to expand the collecting field. Traditionalists see them as major threats in a world in which they have achieved a high comfort level. Too bad for them. Nothing is going to stop the changes that are underway. America's collectibles consciousness is changing the way American's collect.

The Test of Time

This column marks the twelfth anniversary (1999) of "Rinker on Collectibles." I do not remember the exact moment when I realized that an anniversary or birthday celebration denotes the conclusion of a year rather than the beginning of a new one. I know it occurred when I was an adult, not a juvenile.

Mentally reminiscing about past columns, I wondered if "Rinker on Collectibles" had reached the point where it had stood the test of time. Everyone secretly wishes for immortality in one form or another. My mind easily leaps from specific to general principles. I realized that my own concern was really an abbreviation of a much larger question: What exactly does it take to stand the test of time in the antiques and collectibles field?

My assumption has always been a minimum of thirty years. This was a prime consideration when I postulated Rinker's Thirty Year Rule: For the first thirty years of anything's life, all its value is speculative. Maturity does not occur in twenty-one years. It takes thirty years or longer. Accepting this premise, "Rinker on Collectibles" has a long way to go before I can feel assured it has stood the test of time. I plan to revisit this theme again when I write my thirtieth anniversary column in 2016.

In an era where "old" is no longer a major collectibles value factor, age alone is an insufficient measure of a collecting category's or object's ability to stand the test of time. Making a successful transfer from one generation to the next, demonstrating an ability to recycle, and remaining useful and/or appealing are far more important considerations.

The ability of a collecting category to attract a second or, even better, a third generation of new collectors is a major indicator of whether or not a collecting category, personality or character, sales venue, or trade periodical has stood the test of time. This is especially applicable today when generations are measured in thirty-year intervals rather than twenty-year intervals as they were in the past.

The passing of the collecting category's mantle from one generation to the next is critical. The 1980s introduced the concept of one-generation collectibles: collecting categories in which the objects that comprise the category decline significantly in value when the generation that grew up, played, and lived with them dies.

Although not readily recognized as such, memory is a critical value component of any collectible. The general public and collectors buy what they know. What they know is what they remember. Remaining a viable and recognizable image in the mind of the current generation is the biggest hurdle any collecting category or object faces. Ask anyone under thirty-five to identify English salt-glazed ware, a Leeds platter, Findley glass, Eddie Cantor, Ed Wynn, or a Shmoo. Chances are they cannot.

I recently acquired a 1932-33 RCA Radiotrons advertising jigsaw puzzle featuring Jessica Dragonette and Jack Pearl. Jessica and Jack who? As soon as I returned to my office, I consulted a radio show reference guide to find out who they were. Jessica Dragonette was a featured singer on NBC's *Cities Service Concerts* radio program from 1929 to 1956. Jack Pearl was the host and star of NBC's *Jack Pearl Show* that aired from 1932 to 1937. Although I now know who they are, they still mean little to me. Although they were two of the queens and kings of 1930s radio, they fall into a growing category of "who cares" collectibles. They failed to stand the test of time.

Most personalities fail to stand the test of time. It is human nature. When researching a question about a child's baseball glove bearing the signature of Lloyd "Sprout" Waner submitted by a KFGO *Whatcha Got* listener, I was surprised to find that he was a member of the Baseball Hall of Fame. As a test, I reviewed the names of all the members in the Hall of Fame whose careers ended prior to 1950. I recognized less than a quarter of them. I suspect my batting average is higher than most.

As the twenty-first century dawns, there is less and less tendency to look to the past, let alone revere it. Because of national media coverage, most individuals know that Gene Autry and Roy Rogers, the last members of the 1950s western cowboy television triumvirate (Bill Boyd's Hopalong Cassidy was the third), died in 1998. Shortly after Gene's death, another famous B-movie cowboy died. Can you name him? I am willing to bet you cannot. Bob Allen, a western "bad guy," is the answer. Much more important, do you even remember him? Chances are that 90 percent plus of the population does not.

The failure to transfer the love and joys inherent in a collecting category from one generation to another is a primary reason why many antiques collecting categories are decreasing rather than increasing in value. This transfer does not occur by osmosis. It is now understood that objects do not have an inherent quality that makes each succeeding generation love them. Each generation must teach the next generation how to love.

Collectors throughout much of the twentieth century assumed collecting categories automatically recycled. Categories fell out of favor only temporarily. This is no longer true. There were signs that this was true prior to the mid-1980s. Copper luster ware is a prime example. Antiques collectors viewed these as exceptions, not the rule. As the 1990s come to a close, the list of categories that may never recycle grows larger and larger. The future is not promising for a wide range of late-nineteenth- and early-twentieth-century objects ranging from Model T Fords to pattern glass. Some market analysts are even raising questions about some post-1945 collectibles. It saddens me to state that Hopalong Cassidy collectibles are among them.

Some collecting categories, such as dinnerware, flatware, furniture, and stemware, will survive based on the simple premise that they have reuse value. A major plus of today's younger collectors is their desire to use the things they collect in their daily lives. I am very encouraged by this development.

However, use alone is not enough. The object also has to appeal and relate. It is surprising how many historic forms, shapes, and patterns complement modern decorating themes. It is equally surprising how many do not. A failure to survive long-term threatens those that do not.

In this eclectic age when virtually anything goes, why is there a problem? If an object survives, has it not stood the test of time? The answer is no. Applicability/usability is a key 1990s value factor. Today's collectors shy away from things they cannot use, that do not display well, or that fail to function as good conversation pieces.

Individuals born during the period when "too good to throw out" was a national mindset have dozens of boxes in their attics, basements, storage sheds, or garages filled with objects they have not used or seen in decades. Although they have no use for them, they keep thinking someone else will. They need to face reality. The landfill may be the most appropriate home for this material.

I favor time in combination with applicability, relevancy, and use as the measure to determine if an object or thing has stood the test of time. These are the criteria that I continually apply to "Rinker on Collectibles." Will my column stand the test of time? I plan to do my best to see that it does.

Bueschel's Three Rules of Collecting

Talking with appraisers, auctioneers, authors, collectors, dealers, and other individuals involved with antiques and collectibles is one of my greatest pleasures. I am continually impressed by people's willingness to share. I learn something new from every conversation.

Most conversations involve factual information—the history of an object or object group, identification tips, pricing information, state of the market, etc. An occasional conversation deals with market theory. Something is said, a sentence or a phrase, that starts me thinking. I am constantly searching for new insights into how the antiques and collectibles trade functions. I write these ideas down the minute I hear them so that I do not forget them. My computer monitor is ringed by clip notes containing the best of these ideas. The vast majority eventually evolve into "Rinker on Collectibles" columns.

I like the whys of the antiques and collectibles business as much as I do the whats. Whys involve insight and analysis, understanding why something is happening and seeing if it confirms or refutes previously identified patterns. The process is subjective, no matter how objective it looks on the surface. I put my conclusions into print so they can be commented upon and challenged.

There are not a lot of why thinkers in the antiques and collectibles trade. I think I know why: Most simply do not care. Fortunately, a few do, among them Jane Sarasohn-Kahn, Gary Kirsner, Ann and John Koenig, Connie Swaim, and Gary Thoe. Do not talk to them unless you want to be mentally stimulated.

I purposely left one name off the list: Richard "Dick" Bueschel. Of all the people with whom I talk, he, more than anyone else, says things that start me thinking. I almost hate calling Dick. A simple query quickly develops into a theoretical discussion, often on topics far afield from my initial request. I called Dick recently to ask his help. As always, the conversation moved to other areas within minutes. So that no misunderstanding arises, Dick always answers my specific question first. In most cases, several pages of supporting documentation arrive via fax a few hours later.

Most individuals in the antiques and collectibles trade know Dick Bueschel through his articles and books about coin-operated machines and military aircraft. I am fortunate to know Dick as a fellow collector (although like me, he really is an accumulator) and market theorist. I remember with great fondness a series of correspondence and conversations we had about his can opener collection.

During a recent conversation, Dick mentioned that he had three basic rules of collecting. There was absolutely no way I was not going to take advantage of that opening.

"What are they?" I asked. He told me. "Do you mind if I share them with my readers and comment on them?"

"Absolutely not," Dick responded.

I have spent the last two months thinking about the implications and meaning in Dick's three rules. Time to put my thoughts into print.

RULE #1: If you look, you will find. If you don't, you won't.

This is very similar to a concept that I advocate: You do not see something until you start collecting it. Collectibles hunters are focused.

If you collect lithograph tin toys, you ignore everything else— Depression glass or art pottery, for instance. Collectors see only the things about which they care.

Whenever anyone shows me an object and says, "I have never seen one before," my immediate response is, "Where did you look?" The hunting range is vast; the survival rate higher than most people realize. The secondary market availability of collectibles is measured in hundreds, thousands, and, in some cases, tens of thousands. Rare has no meaning in respect to collectibles. Scarce is even a questionable term.

This is why the hunt is so much fun. Dick's rule is loaded with optimism. If you look, you will bag the game you seek.

Shortly after I started collecting jigsaw puzzles, I approached Sandy Marrone, a leading collector/dealer of sheet music, to enlist her aid in finding songs about jigsaw puzzles or sheet music with jigsaw theme covers. Sandy said that she had never seen any. I asked her to look. Over the years, Sandy has found more than a dozen different pieces of sheet music with a jigsaw puzzle connection. We are convinced this is only the tip of the iceberg.

I spent the past five years searching for a salt and pepper shaker in the shape of puzzle pieces or with jigsaw puzzle decoration. Thus far, my efforts have been in vain. Every salt and pepper collector and dealer with whom I have spoken has never seen one. Does this mean such a set does not exist? Not for one minute. I just have not found it. I have faith that I eventually will.

Making a continuing commitment to the hunt is a key to ensuring the validity of Dick's rule. The search never ends. There is always something new to be found. One cannot sit back and wait for things to come to her. Success requires hunting in the field.

RULE #2: If I had to do it all over again, I would do it all over again.

Dick has placed the emphasis clearly where it belongs: on the joys of collecting and not on what is collected. This rule affirms that collecting is a lifelong experience, not something to be enjoyed for a brief period of time. Collecting is a natural act. To collect is to be. Limiting collections to a specific time period is going against the natural order of things.

Why do it all over again? While no justification is needed other than because this is what I want to do, the best reason to collect is that it is fun. A pox on those individuals who take it too seriously. My favorite collectors are those individuals who tell funny stories about themselves, laughing wholeheartedly in the process.

This rule also demonstrates what I call a "no regrets" approach. Collecting should always be about looking forward, never looking back. Many spouses see collecting in terms of gifts never received, vacations never taken, home improvements never completed, and time spent in truly forgettable places. Too bad. Divorce is a viable option. It is imperative never to stifle the collector within.

RULE #3: The more you know, the less you will have to pay.

The more you know, the better able you are to walk away from a bad buy. A bad buy is one where the object is overpriced, in less than satisfactory condition, or both. Knowing whether an object is commonly found or scarce and in what price range it normally sells is a major advantage when deciding whether or not to buy.

There are several keys to implementing this rule: (1) learning where to buy, (2) comparison shopping, and (3) patience. Too many collectors buy the first example they find. They do not take the time to decide if they are buying in the most advantageous venue. There is a big difference between what is paid for the same item at a country auction versus a big city auction. The same applies to antiques shows, malls, and other sale environments. Today the market for antiques and collectibles is the world, thanks in large part to the Internet.

Comparison shopping is a good indicator of the number of examples of an item that have survived. It forces the buyer to focus on obtaining an object that meets two key criteria—condition and value. It also reveals when price fixing is in play. When three different antiques mall or show dealers feature the same object priced within 10 percent of each other, assume there has been an agreement to fix the price. Walk away. Do not buy the cheapest of the three. You will eventually find the object in the same or better condition at a different location for a much lower price.

If collecting is a lifetime experience, being patient is not a problem. The survival rate of any object made after 1880 is relatively high. Every time I bought an advertising jigsaw puzzle thinking that I would never see another one like it in my lifetime, I found that Don Friedman, my biggest rival, has owned an example for at least two years. There is no doubt in my mind that eventually I will find and own an example of every puzzle in Don's collection that I currently do not have—provided I am patient.

Celebrity Bounce

Only a small number of individuals, a distinct minority, are unaware that Mark McGwire of the St. Louis Cardinals broke Roger Maris' single season baseball home run record by hitting his sixty-second home run on September 8, 1998, off Chicago Cub starting pitcher Steve Trachsel. The percentage of those who care is far less than those compelled to read and hear about it.

Allentown, Pennsylvania, is hardly St. Louis. Yet, McGwire's achievement made the front page of the *Morning Call* two days running. This happened across much of America. Considering all the negative news from inside the Washington, D.C., beltway, anything positive is a welcome relief.

While traveling to a personal appearance at the Riverfront Antique Mall in New Philadelphia, Ohio, shortly before McGwire's achievement, I made a telephone call to check in with my office. A Connecticut newspaper reporter called to ask my opinion about an outstanding offer of one million dollars for the baseball hit by McGwire for his sixty-second home run. I quoted the old English proverb, "A fool and his money are soon parted."

Concerned that multiple home run balls would materialize following the record-breaking hit, the National League marked all the balls used in the games leading up to McGwire's accomplishment with a substance that was visible only under infrared light. There was an implied assumption that the person who caught the ball would return it. With an outstanding offer of one million dollars, one has to wonder.

While there have always been celebrity collectors, this collecting category moved from the minor to the major leagues during the last two decades. Initially celebrity collectors concentrated primarily on autographs and other two-dimensional objects. Now they want clothing, jewelry, and a variety of other professional and personal memorabilia.

During the last five years there have been several occurrences when a monumental event, not always positive, caused a significant jump in the value of items associated with a particular celebrity. Some of the most obvious examples are Princess Di, Pee-wee Herman, Jackie Onassis, and O. J. Simpson. It is a sad state of affairs when personal tragedy rather than accomplishment is the major trigger causing this value spike.

Perhaps this is why the Mark McGwire bounce is so refreshing. It is a positive-, not negative-driven event—assuming that you can put aside the controversy over McGwire's consumption of performance-enhancing substances.

It is easier to understand something if it has a name. "Celebrity Bounce" explains the price rise, stabilization, and fall associated with collectibles from celebrities whose "fifteen minutes of fame" stretches over a six-month to three-year period.

The celebrity bounce is temporary. The value of Mark McGwire's rookie baseball trading card has risen over the last several months from $200 to $2,000. Will it still be at $2,000 three years from now? Absolutely NOT! Will it increase in value? Highly unlikely. Will it decrease in value? Bet on it. In fact, it will probably be close to its mid-1998 value.

There is a definite cycle attached to the celebrity bounce. An event associated with the celebrity serves as the market trigger. Values rise rapidly, doubling and tripling in the space of a few weeks or months.

Values hold only as long as the celebrity remains front page news. As the public loses interest and the story moves to the middle of the paper or last ten minutes on the national news, value declines. When the story disappears, the market collapse is usually in full swing.

The celebrity bounce is selective. Entire categories of individuals, e.g., politicians, are immune. Do not look for a rapid rise in President Clinton collectibles as the result of the publication of Kenneth Starr's report.

Poor Monica, no publisher wants to meet her terms for a book deal. There is little left to tell. If Monica is looking for money, she should consider auctioning the famous semen-stained dress. There is little question its final value would far exceed any of Princess Di's gowns. There is not a lot of presidential DNA available within the collecting community.

Celebrities have to stand the test of time. There is no question that O. J. Simpson will be forgotten in 2098, hopefully before then. Will the same be true of Princess Di? Most people find the concept inconceivable. On the other hand, I see no long-term collectible future for Princess Di memorabilia. Name any of the daughters of Queen Victoria. She had more than one. Most individuals cannot. Yet, these princesses lived less than a hundred years ago.

Few individuals stand the test of time. Many American presidents rate only a few paragraphs in our history books. Name any Senator from your state who served during the nineteenth century. How about the name of a major silent movie cowboy star. It requires little effort to prove that memories fade. When memories fade, so does the value of the collectibles associated with that individual. Want to buy an Al Jolson record?

When I wear my reporter's hat, I am expected to provide fact and analysis, not opinion. Personally, I find the celebrity bounce phenomenon distasteful. If buyers and sellers ignored it, it would not happen.

Reality presents a far different picture. When a celebrity bounce occurs, there are those who simply cannot resist the temptation to try to capitalize on it. Those following this course are advised to consider the following points.

When a celebrity bounce occurs, it is time to sell, not buy. If you plan to jump on the capitalization bandwagon, you need to do it within the first three weeks when the material is still relatively cheap. Profit margin decreases as the purchase price moves further and further away from its pre-celebrity bounce starting point.

The market is decidedly short term. Get in and get out as quickly as possible. Sell the moment you achieve a sufficient profit margin, i.e., double or triple your initial purchase price. Do not think twice about someone making a few additional dollars on an object after you. They still have to sell what they bought to get their cash. You have cash in hand.

It is a mistake to hold out for absolute top dollar. The peak of the market lasts only a matter of days. Once the market starts to fall, potential buyers quickly disappear. The winner in the end is the person with the cash, not the person who owns the object.

Celebrity bounces are fun to track because they are so volatile. They are not for the weak of heart. If you have problems handling excitement, pressure, and stress, stick with the more traditional collecting categories. If you do not mind strapping on the six guns and venturing out at high noon, then participating in a celebrity bounce is just the thing to keep your adrenaline flowing.

Having begun this column by commenting on the accomplishments of Mark McGwire, it is only fair to end it by talking about Sammy Sosa. I was rooting for him to win the home run derby. Alas, he did not. This says it all.

Losers are only a footnote in history. Unless you lived through the famed Mantle-Maris 1961 home run race, you are not likely to remember who had the second-best home run record that season. I cannot tell you who was behind the Babe the year he hit sixty home runs.

McGwire celebrity bounce is probably going to last several years. Sosa's bounce will be measured in months. Unless, of course, he hits seventy-one home runs next year to lead the league. Go for it, Sammy. I am pulling for you.

Male Chauvinist Pigs—Or, Why I Really Love This Business

The collectibles business is loaded with male chauvinist pigs. I should know. I am regularly accused of belonging to that extremely large, oft maligned, male fraternity. If truth be known, my membership card in my wallet contains a very low number.

The issue of male chauvinism as a problem within the collectibles community moved to front burner status in my mind when Sharon Iranpour of Rochester, New York, wrote describing the geezerly and braggart nature of many of the male dealers she encounters. Sharon complained of constantly being ignored by such individuals when her only desire was to conduct business with them.

A few weeks ago, I enjoyed a pizza dinner with a couple who earn their livelihood from the trade. They own an antiques shop, work the show circuit, and refinish furniture. They have an active retail and wholesale business. The husband does the refinishing. The wife does the buying and selling. While in the field, the husband was approached by a dealer who had several pieces of furniture to sell.

"Come over and look at them," he said.

The husband went home and told his wife about the pieces. She called and made an appointment. This is an abbreviated version of the conversation upon her arrival.

"Where's the boss?"

She (being polite), "He's at home refinishing some pieces."

"I was expecting him."

"I do the buying for our business."

"Well, I do not sell to women."

"Thank you very much, I'll be leaving now." [I have too much respect for this lady to report what she actually said to the seller. Better her reputation remain intact than having herself viewed as "one of the boys."]

Two women who refinish and sell generic furniture from the early twentieth century are students at the Institute for the Study of Antiques and Collectibles. They cart and haul their furniture to indoor and outdoor shows in Pennsylvania and Ohio. They sell well. However, their business improves considerably when a male, usually one of their husbands, is in the booth.

Seeing two women and one male, prospective customers, both male and female, inevitably approach the male to ask questions and/or begin the bargaining process. The male directs the potential customer to one of the women. In most cases, the business discussion continues.

RENT A MALE—a creative antiques and collectibles business opportunity for some enterprising individual. The wonderful news is that the male does not necessarily have to be the stud and/or Robert Redford type. Based on my observations, any male will do, provided he has recently bathed and is clean-shaven. I know what is preferred, but fact is fact.

Do you see the same possibilities that I do? Life as a rent-a-male ... an attractive career alternative for the burnt-out executive ... all you do is stand around and refer potential customers to your female employer ... no pressures ... no hype. If you have to kiss ass to keep your job, it certainly has more pleasant possibilities than when you worked in corporate America.

I think of myself as an old-fashioned (no, not old fart) chauvinist. I was raised in the "respect the woman" camp. Even in my fifties, I still do my fair share of "Yes, ma'am," "Can I carry that for you, ma'am," "Take my seat, ma'am," "How can I help you, ma'am," etc.—you get the picture. I never thought I was demeaning any women or myself by opening a door for them.

Times change. People do not always change with them. I cannot help wondering if the actions of the offending male chauvinist geezers and braggarts in the collectibles field are governed by the notion that if you ignore a problem, it will simply go away. They did not play with girls growing up. Why should they play with women now that they have?

Males dominate far more collectibles categories than do women. In record collecting, they account for more than 95 percent of the collectors. One does not have to be a genius to identify those collecting categories where the percentage of males to females exceeds 80 percent. Toy soldiers, toy trains, farm toys, toys in general, art pottery, and large segments within the paper market, e.g., advertising trade cards, trading cards, and postcards, are just a few that come immediately to mind.

There is a major "good old boy" network in place in the collectibles field. Males constantly help and counsel other males. Few males serve as mentors for women. Women have to work twice—no, three or four times—as hard to survive in the trade.

Males buy primarily from other males. Once again, it is a relationship that they find extremely comfortable. If they are going to buy from a woman, the price has to be significantly below retail or they negotiate far longer and tougher than they would from a fellow male. If a male buys on a "winner takes all" basis, it is critical that he always gets the better of the deal when dealing with a female.

The name of the game is, and always will be, percentages. What percentage of book authors is male? What percentage of dealers at a flea market, mall, shop, or show are male? What is the ratio of male to female collectors within a collecting category? What percentage of the owners and editors of trade papers and periodicals are male?

Are you so naive as to believe that there are no glass ceilings in the collectibles business? There are plenty—and they are made of thick glass. It is highly likely that they will take much longer to crash than many of those in the corporate world.

What is a woman to do? I am not certain that I am the right person to answer this question. Honestly, I am rather comfortable with the way things stand at the moment. I do not want my tombstone to read: "Ended male dominance in his trade." I have other possible inscriptions in mind.

Those who are avid readers of this column know that I am not going to end it here, although God and I both know that I should. What follows is not about equality. It is about fairness and preserving the differences between the sexes. It focuses on power, not justice. As much as I want to be an idealist, deep inside I am a realist.

First, the worst thing that any woman can do is become one of the boys. Why would you want to be something you despise? Show these arrogant sons of guns that it is possible to do business in the trade with your head held high.

Second, vote with your wallet and speak with your middle finger. Money talks, especially when it walks. Ladies, more and more money, especially discretionary income, rests in your hands. Use it to force the equality you seek.

Third, more change occurs via inside control than through outside struggle. Move in, take control, and make changes. This is not something that is done overnight. It is a long-term process. This is one of the best-kept male secrets that I know.

Fourth, the key is to network. Help each other. Support each other. Do not rely on finding that one male mentor in a thousand who is open-minded enough to assist you.

Fifth, do not hesitate to muscle in on male turf. Actually, once you have overcome the initial resistance, you may be surprised how easy you find the going. Male chauvinists are far more poorly organized than you think.

Finally, when you are offended, confront the offender. Do not walk away on the premise of "why bother." If you love the collectibles field as much as I do, you cannot.

I have not run from this topic. Believe me when I tell you that I expect a fair amount of flack for what I have written. Too bad. The sex of those with whom I do business has never been the issue with me, only a person's competence, care, and curiosity to learn.

Time Is the Enemy

During a personal appearance at a West Palm Beach, Florida, antiques and collectibles show, I lectured on the topic, "What's Hot and What's Not in Antiques and Collectibles." During the question-and-answer session that followed my formal presentation, a member of the audience asked my opinion of the current market for Buffalo Pottery's Deldare.

My audience numbered slightly over seventy-five individuals, a great many of whom were sixty and older. As an experiment, I asked everyone who would recognize a piece of Buffalo Pottery's Deldare to raise his hand. I expected to see at least ten to fifteen hands. Instead, all I saw was the hand of one other person in addition to my own. I looked at the woman who asked the question and said, "Do you need further proof that the category is in trouble?"

For readers unfamiliar with Buffalo Pottery's Deldare, Buffalo Pottery produced this line between 1908 and 1909 and again between 1921 and 1923. Examples made during the first period feature hand-decorated scenes based upon the English artist Cecil Aldin's Fallowfield Hunt or generic English village scenes. The base color is an olive green. Only generic English village scenes were used during the second production period. Most pieces are artist signed.

In 1911, Buffalo Pottery introduced Emerald Deldare. These pieces had an Art Nouveau style border and a central image from Goldsmith's *The Three Tours of Dr. Syntax*. A few pieces with an Art Nouveau center motif also were produced.

In 1981 when I assumed the editorship of *Warman's Antiques and Their Prices,* Buffalo Pottery's Deldare and Emerald Deldare was considered high-end among American-produced ceramics. Prices ranged from the low hundreds for commonly found pieces to the low thousands for scarcer pieces. Several prominent dealers, especially Seymour and Violet Altman, kept market interest high.

It is now twenty years later. In fairness, interest in Deldare and Emerald Deldare remained strong throughout most of the 1980s. Collector interest waned in the early 1990s and has been declining steadily ever since on the national level. Modest collector interest remains in New England, the Mid-Atlantic states, and the eastern portions of the Midwest, Buffalo Pottery's home region. However, here as elsewhere, the average age of collectors continues to increase.

Will a time arise when collector interest in Buffalo Pottery's Deldare and Emerald Deldare disappears completely? The answer is yes. While it may not happen in my lifetime, I firmly believe it will happen one day.

Most collectors believe that designation as an established collecting category is enough to guarantee the collecting future of the category. This is not the case. Collecting categories disappear over time. Far more will fall by the wayside than survive.

Those opposed to this notion argue that there will always be a few collectors, at least a dozen or more, for every collecting category, no matter how obscure it becomes. They are correct. Few categories completely disappear. The objects have to go somewhere, if not to museums then to heirs or scholars.

In my capacity as a collection management consultant, I frequently am involved in the dispersal of collections assembled during the early and mid-twentieth century. In one instance, I was asked to recommend a method of sale for an individual who collected watermarked paper. Collecting early watermarked paper, especially American in origin, was very popular in the first half of the twentieth century. Today it is the provenance of a small group of specialists. Most paper dealers do not even check early paper for watermarks any longer. Their principal concern is the content on the paper.

Do the following quiz. It is relatively simple. All I want you to do is describe one piece from the following five categories:

Camphor Glass	Findley Onyx	Stevensgraphs
Castleford	Lowestoft	

Be honest. How did you do? I am willing to bet you had to consult an antiques and collectibles price guide or dictionary for three or more of them. If you answered all five correctly, chances are you have been in the business for more than twenty-five years and are well over sixty.

Perhaps it is not fair picking on antiques collecting categories. However, every antique was once one day old and was once a collectible. Many of yesterday's collectibles, especially those from the 1930s through the end of the 1950s, are now part of the antiques section of the market.

Time is the enemy. Collectors focus on the present. They have only a vague knowledge of how collecting interest developed in their favorite collecting categories, and they have little concern about their future. In the case of collecting, one is far better off not having a long-term perspective.

My questioning how long a collecting category lasts was triggered by a market report I wrote about Roseville Pottery. In researching the historical background for the report, I noted that the last piece of Roseville was manufactured in 1952.

"That is over fifty years ago," I thought, "I wonder how much longer Roseville has as a viable collecting category?" Will Roseville exhibit the same collecting interest in 2052 that it did in 2002?

Life without Roseville is a concept today's Roseville collectors do not want to imagine, let alone admit. Yet, it will eventually happen. Nothing is collected forever.

Collecting as a concept became popular in the last two decades of the nineteenth century. Initially it was the provenance of people of means and education. In the 1920s the concept expanded as everyone was encouraged to have a "hobby." Collecting as we define it today is the result of the collecting revolution of the 1970s. As a result, long-term tracking data is limited. Many collecting categories are relatively new.

Trade theorists are by necessity empirical. They conjecture. As data becomes available, their conclusions will be proven or disproved.

Based upon my observations, the disappearance of most collecting categories will occur within three or four generations. There will be fewer generations needed in the twenty-first century than there were in the twentieth century. Given this, the time span is between 100 and 150 years.

When does the time count start? The last day of manufacture is the most obvious starting point. However, I opt for the period when the average age of the generation that used the objects reaches sixty.

How do you know when a collecting category is a prospect for disappearance? Here are six potential indicators:

1. When the average age of collectors exceeds fifty-five.
2. When prices within the collecting category have been stable for ten or more years.
3. When the amount of coverage in a general antiques and collectibles price guide drops by half or the category has been placed in a general category rather than being given a category of its own.
4. When the collectors' club disbands and has not been heard from in ten years.
5. When pieces no longer regularly appear for auction or in the booths of dealers at antiques shows.
6. When the only place you see examples from the collecting category is a museum.

What is the point of all of this? It is nothing more than a reality check. For those who violently disagree with what I have written, remember that in time even I will be forgotten. Time is the enemy of us all.

CHAPTER 4

An Inside Look at How Prices Are Determined

While I wish more individuals were interested in the history of objects rather than value, I am wise enough to accept the simple truth that the most often asked question in the antiques and collectibles trade is: "What is my object worth?"

There is no simple answer to this question. Value is time sensitive. There are no fixed values in the antiques and collectibles trade. The age of the blue chip antique or collectible is a thing of the past.

Further, there are many different values, wholesale and retail being only two of them, in the antiques and collectibles field. When I am in the process of purchasing an antique or collectible, the only value about which I care is: "What am I willing to pay?" I have made value personal, something I strongly believe every collector should do.

In the final analysis, all antiques and collectibles are worthless. Their value is transitory. It is real only for the few moments during the sale when someone actually pays for the object.

Confused now? Do not be surprised if you are even more confused when you read what follows.

Book Value

I received the following letter from Claudine Fuhrman of Bethlehem, Pennsylvania: "During the time I have been reading your column, I have never seen you address the question I am about to ask…

"When you quote a reference, how much of the quoted value can someone realistically expect to get if he or she sells that item? For instance, if the price guide states a certain figurine is worth $100, what percentage of that amount would be a fair price to expect upon sale if it were in very good condition? I realize many factors enter in. I was just wondering about a ballpark figure. Judging from what I have read in your column, I have the idea that a stated value and real sale value are not the same."

I received this letter in mid-December 2000, which marked the beginning of my fifteenth year of writing "Rinker on Collectibles." In my column I make it a point not to revisit issues I have written about previously. However, I do recognize that many "Rinker on Collectibles" readers have not been reading my column since its inception and, hence, may not be familiar with some of my past columns.

Ms. Fuhrman's question is one I am asked repeatedly. Given the Internet's impact on antiques and collectibles pricing, it is a question worth revisiting.

My first recommendation is to take a very skeptical approach to the prices found in all antiques and collectibles price guides, my own included. Price guides are just what their name implies—price guides. They are not price absolutes. You cannot call up a price guide author and say: "I would like to buy one or more items at the prices you have listed. Send them to me." Antiques and collectibles prices are subjective. Value is very much dependent on time and place. Thanks to the Internet, the safe assumption to make these days is that they fluctuate wildly across the board.

You need to ask two key questions before you worry about what percentage of a price guide's value you can reasonably expect to obtain if you sell an object: (1) What are the qualifications of the author(s) of the price guide? and (2) What is the accuracy of the prices? Many price guide authors have a vested interest in seeing that the values in their price guide are high. Dealers often author price guides to validate the prices they charge their buyers. Collectors usually price objects based on what they would like to receive if they sell their collection, not what they paid for the objects nor what the objects currently realize on the open market.

Prices need to be field tested. Until recently, antiques malls and shows were the test ground. Unbiased price guide authors adhered to the assumption that prices should closely reflect the asking price found at antiques malls and shows. Since most antiques and collectibles are sold at a discount, ranging from 10 to 20 percent off the sticker price, a price guide value based on the asking price of an object is not a fully accurate reflection of an object's true market value. If anything, it is high.

Most price guides still use prices for goods found at the antiques malls and shows as the standard for their pricing. Prices realized on the Internet raise serious questions about the validity of this traditional standard. A price guide that does not take Internet pricing into consideration is worthless.

In the past, the assumption was that auction values often were low, largely because dealers buy the vast majority of items sold at auction. When placed for sale at antiques malls and shows, the final price is much higher. Again, the Internet has caused a major re-evaluation of this approach. While it is true that dealers use the Internet to acquire merchandise, a far higher percentage of the buyers are collectors and other end-users. As a result, Internet pricing, assuming it stabilizes, has the potential to become the most accurate reflection of what an object's "retail" value actually is.

Antiques and collectibles price guides must continue to use retail prices, i.e., what you would expect to pay if you were buying the object, as their standard if they wish to remain valid tools. The dealer is the key. Whether on the Internet or in an antiques mall or show, it is the dealer's selling price that is the key barometer.

Although antiques and collectibles are "old" objects, one needs to view them as "new" objects when buying them for one's collection or display. Somewhere between 60 and 70 percent of an object's fair market or book value is profit to sellers along the way. When considering what an object will bring when resold, especially within a year or two following its purchase, a return of thirty to forty cents on the purchase cost is doing exceptionally well.

Collectibles are not easily liquidated. They are not like stocks and bonds where one can call a broker, place an order to sell, and receive a return within a few percentage points of the current board listing. The closer one wishes to obtain book value, assuming it is correct, the more time, effort, and cost one is going to expend. When time, effort, and costs are deducted from the amount received, the end result is highly likely to be substantially less than half of book value.

Perceived value plays a major role in determining how close one can come to book value. The higher the value, the easier it is to obtain book value. If a collectible books at $10 or less, chances of finding a buyer for it at any price are slim. When the value is under $50, think fifteen to thirty cents on the dollar. The ability to obtain book value increases exponentially as the perceived value of the object increases. If an object books at $10,000, a seller can reasonably expect to sell at fifty to sixty cents on the dollar. Simply stated—the higher the book value, the more likely a seller is to achieve it.

The entire issue of book value is further complicated by the fact that today's market is extremely trendy. The above applies only to categories that are hot or in play. If a category is in decline, all bets are off. Buyers expect deep, deep value discounts when a collecting category has lost favor. Collecting trends can shift in a matter of months. Price guide values have lag times ranging from six to twelve months.

In light of the above, why use price guides at all? In areas with which you are familiar, you should rely primarily on your personal observation and field experience. Use a price guide only when venturing into a new collecting category.

The collectibles field enjoys an abundance, perhaps far too many, of antiques malls, shops, shows, and Internet sale sites. The same applies to price guides. One can easily find a second, third, and even fourth opinion for the value of almost every collectible. Given the subjective nature of pricing, one might expect these prices to vary considerably. More than likely, one will find they usually agree with each other. The polite assumption is that this results from due diligence in field research by the authors. Heaven help us all if the reason is copying or price fixing.

A good price guide gets you into the ballpark and up to the plate. It provides a sampling of prices that allows an overview of values within the collecting category. Whether you strike out or hit a home run using that information is your responsibility, not that of the price guide author. A price guide value should only be one factor among many in determining what to pay or ask for an object.

Tracking trends within a collecting category is one of the best uses one can make of a price guide. When you have identified a price guide that works well for you, buy it edition after edition. Do not throw out older editions. Keep them shelved as a unit. When you want to know if prices are rising, falling, or holding steady, examine the values for the past five years. You will be amazed how easy it is to spot trends if the price guide author has done the work properly.

This paragraph from the "A Buyer's Guide, Not A Seller's Guide" portion of the introductory section of my new *The Official Rinker Price Guide To Collectibles: Post-1920s Memorabilia, Fourth Edition* (House of Collectibles, 2000; $19.95) summarizes my views: "This book is not a seller's guide. Do not be mistaken and assume that it is. If you have an object listed in this book and wish to sell it, expect to receive 30 percent to 40 percent of the price listed if the object is commonly found and 50 percent to 60 percent if the object is harder to find. Do not assume that a collector will pay more. In the twenty-first-century antiques and collectibles market, collectors expect to pay what a dealer would pay for merchandise when buying privately."

What can someone realistically expect to get for an item? The correct answer is the amount of money placed on the table by a buyer. The difficulty with this answer is that it is valid only at that moment in time when it occurs. It is why I enjoy being part of the collecting game. Not everyone feels the same.

What Is the Right Price?

Recently I purchased a group of television show theme records. David Hofstede's "Singing TV Stars" article in *Baby Boomer Collectibles* magazine triggered my collecting urge. The fact that I watched many of these programs when they first aired made my decision to collect easier.

My initial purchases included: MGM, E-4088's "Richard Chamberlain sings" for $4; MCA-6150's *Miami Vice*: Music from the Television Series for $4; Atlantic SD-7210's *All in the Family* for $6; Peter Pan 822's "Kaptain Kool and the Kongs" for $7; and, Promenade 2089's "Bilko Marches" for $8. As you see I am taking a much broader approach to the subject than discussed in the Hofstede article. Hofstede focused solely on records by television series stars who actually performed the songs and/or music on the record. I plan to collect any television series record, with special emphasis on those with strong album cover images.

Shortly after making my purchases Scott Curtis' 52 Girls Collectibles Summer Catalog (P.O. Box 36, Morral, OH 43337) arrived in the mail. I quickly checked out Scott's offerings and was pleasantly surprised to find a number of television show theme records among them. I was even more delighted when I found the Richard Chamberlain (Dr. Kildare) record for which I had paid $4 listed at $19 and my $8 "Bilko Marches" record at $16.

Two questions arise: (1) Which of the two prices is the right price? and (2) How much did it actually cost me to but the four records? Years of collecting experience has taught me that the questions "What did I pay for something?" and "What did something cost?" are not synonymous. The cost of an object is the sum of the purchase price plus the acquisition expense costs.

When I returned from the buying spree that included the four records, I sat down and noted my purchase costs. I added up my out-of-pocket expenses and calculated the value of my time by taking the number of hours I spent in the field times what I normally charge a client per hour. I added these figures together and divided by the number of purchases that I made. Finally, I added this amount to each purchase. Now I knew how much each object cost to acquire. After doing this, Scott's prices proved very reasonable, so reasonable in fact that I purchased several of the television theme records from Scott's catalog.

The Rinker Enterprises, Inc., staff and I in our role as reporters and price guide editors face the "right price" issue every day. Locating prices is easy. Determining if the price is the right price is the challenge. The issue is easy to ignore. We cannot.

There is not one price in the collectibles field. There are many. Here are a few examples:

1. Advertised, sticker, or asking price: The price for which an object is offered for sale by a seller. This price rarely reflects the actual selling price. Negotiation frequently results in a final sale between 10 and 50 percent below this price.

Further, it is not safe to assume that the sticker is even close to the right price. I realize that raising this issue borders on heresy and is more likely to increase my enemies list than my list of friends. It is naïve on the part of the general public and field to assume that every seller has done the proper grading and research relative to price an object properly. In truth, most have not. Far more pricing in the trade is based on guesses and guts than any of us would like to admit.

2. Auction price: The price at which an object sells at auction. In the 1940s and '50s auction prices were assumed to be the true test of an object's worth. Today we realize that objects sell at auctions at a multiplicity of pricing levels. Dealers buy for resale. Obviously, they will ask more than they paid when they sell. It is about profit. Private collectors, often competing with the very sources from whom they buy at shops and shows, bid in an attempt to cut the profit margin of the middleman. Speculators buy, frequently in excess of current market value, in hopes that an object's upward pricing spiral will continue. Add to the mix individuals with a bad case of auction fever, feuding family members, and participants in the dealers' pool. What is the result? Price chaos. Each price paid has to be interpreted in the context of who bought it and their motivation.

3. Dealer's price: Price at which an object is sold when it passes from one dealer to another. Dealers normally trade with each other at discounts ranging from 10 to 30 percent of an object's sticker price. The buying dealer generally plans to price the object significantly higher than the initial sticker price. He has to do this to ensure his profit margin.

4. Book price: The price found in price guides. As I have stated in the past, price guides are a curse. They are used more often as price absolutes than as guides. They make sellers greedy. Sellers, especially novices, feel they are entitled to book price.

Once again, it is necessary to raise the question: What makes you think the prices in a price guide are right? Price guides, especially single subject guides, have been used to shape and manipulate dozens of markets within the collectibles field. Few price guide authors are independent. Hidden agendas from promoting a collection prior to sale to justifying prices charged customers abound. Users beware.

5. Private sale price: A price of approximately twenty to fifty cents on the retail dollar at which objects are purchased by pickers, dealers, and private collectors directly from the home of someone unfamiliar with the business. This is a sale venue where negotiation is intense and a "take it or leave it" attitude prevails. It is generally assumed that the "coming out" price is the lowest price for which an object will sell.

6. Garage sale or "I stole it" price: A price considerably below an object's potential worth. In spite of the tremendous wealth of pricing literature and media publicity about collectibles, the general public is largely unsophisticated when it comes to the actual worth of most collectibles. While one will not find a hundred dollar item for a dime or quarter at every garage sale, such finds occur thousands of times each weekend across America.

There are a number of price guides I would love to author, but doubt that I could find a publisher if I did. My favorite concept is the "What I Really Think It Should Be Worth Price Guide." A "What I Really Bought It for Price Guide" concept is a close second. I already have a database started for this guide.

Back to the question that began this column: What is the right price? The correct answer is: THERE IS NO RIGHT PRICE. This hour's right price can be next hour's wrong price. Value has reality only when an object is sold and then only at that specific moment and circumstance in time. All the rest of the prices are based on a best guess scenario.

The fact that there is no right price is what I love most about the collectibles business. Everyone, buyer and seller alike, is on his own. Each individual's skills determine how he does. Some turn the process into a contest—elated when they feel they have won and devastated when they feel they have lost. The smart ones make the process fun—make a purchase, put it behind immediately, and move on to the next. Laugh a little along the way.

Do not cloud your judgment by focusing or worrying about the right price issue. It is totally subjective. Bury it. The one and only price that counts is what you are willing to pay. Let this principle guide your collecting. You will be surprised how much more fun and pleasure you will have. Kudos to buyers who pay only what they want and have the sense to walk away when this is not the case. They have the proper perspective. I admire them. So should you.

Where Do Prices Come From?

How do dealers determine the price they ask for a collectible? Given the implied trust within the antiques and collectibles business that the price marked on a piece is a fair price, this is a question worth examining.

A fixed markup formula against price paid and researching price guide, auction, and field pricing for an object and determining a selling price based upon this research are the two methods buyers assume dealers use. Most dealers consider themselves lucky if they double their initial purchase cost for a collectible. Because most dealers sell on a part-time basis and are happy if they recover their costs, i.e., expenses and inventory replacement, plus buy a few objects for their personal collections, they are willing to work on short profit margins. Based upon informal surveys I have done over the last five years, less than 5 percent of the dealers in the trade pay themselves a salary. I wish I were in a position to work for nothing. Alas, I am not.

When lecturing at The Institute for the Study of Antiques and Collectibles, I urge dealers to set a goal of trying to sell at prices whereby they average three times inventory cost. Their immediate reaction when I first propose this is utter disbelief. "It cannot be done" is the normal response from seminar participants. It can be done. I have interviewed dozens of dealers, full- and part-time, who average three or more times inventory cost. The key is to buy right so one can sell right. Buying inventory properly, which appears so easy on the surface, is really the toughest part of the selling equation.

If a dealer used a standard two, two and one-half, or three times inventory cost to arrive at an asking price, few prices within his inventory would be the same. Yet, when one examines the prices on merchandise within a dealer's booth at a flea market, mall, shop, or show, one traditionally finds twelve to eighteen price points used by the dealer to cover every item in his inventory. The most common price points are eight, twelve, eighteen, twenty, twenty-five, forty-five, sixty-five, eighty-five, and one hundred or a multiple of them. If the dealer or selling environment has a fixed discount policy, add 10 to 20 percent to these prices.

Only a very small percentage of dealers use a fixed markup approach for pricing purposes. Assuming this is true, do most dealers research price guides, auction records, and field prices before establishing a final asking price? The answer is an emphatic no. While more dealers utilize the research route than the fixed markup approach, their number also is small.

Research takes time, and time is money. It is hard to justify an hour of research time when the end result is to raise the asking price of an object from $15 to $25. Research also requires commitment to building and maintaining or having access to a major research library. If the dealer specializes in five to ten collecting categories, a research approach to pricing is more likely than if the dealer is a generalist, i.e., sells objects from dozens of different collecting categories.

The research approach to pricing contains a number of flaws. First, experienced dealers know to be highly suspicious of some price guides' prices, especially those in single topic guides. Many authors and editors have private pricing agendas. Several antiques and collectibles price guide publishers are notorious for not reviewing and crosschecking the prices supplied by their authors and editors. The field, especially the collectibles sector, is filled with guides written by wunderkind experts whose longevity in the field is measured in single- and not double-digit years.

Second, auction prices need to be carefully interpreted. Dealers are the principal buyers at auction, even at major auction houses such as Bonham's & Butterfields, Christie's, Skinner's, and Sotheby's. Obviously, dealers do not buy objects with the intent of selling them at cost. Unfortunately, no auction house indicates on its prices realized if a lot was purchased by a dealer or private individual.

Third, while field prices are a far more accurate resource for the value of objects than price guides or auction prices, field prices also must be questioned. Although no charge of price fixing has ever been proven against any group of antiques and collectibles dealers, the truth is that price fixing is an unspoken about and common practice in the trade. My evidence is simple. Have you ever noticed at a flea market, mall, shop, or show that the price asked for the same object in several different dealers' booths rarely varies by more than ten percent? Many a helpful dealer has suggested to another dealer, "You have that object priced too low," or "You can get far more than you are asking for that object." If I were the seller in question, my response would be, "I would be happy to sell it to you and let you make the additional profit."

Further, price discounting is a standard selling practice in the collectibles field. As a result, the price marked on an object is rarely the price at which it is sold. The level of discount varies from dealer to dealer and depends upon the circumstances of the moment. Few dealers will reveal to anyone, reporter or rival, the price at which they actually sold an object. Buyers also jealously guard this number.

Given the above, what is the principal source that a dealer uses to determine his prices? I believe I know. The answer is the dealer's gut.

After buying an object and mulling over its market potential, the dealer reaches down into his gut and pulls out a price that he feels is right. Is there any rhyme or reason to the price? Experience, greed, and a desire to realize the top price possible—i.e., go for the jugular and achieve a braggable selling price—play a far greater role in gut pricing than any reasoned approach. Since selling is more a hobby than business for most dealers, they have no trouble carrying unsold merchandise, largely overpriced, in inventory for years.

There are two principal reasons gut pricing plays such an important role in determining the final selling price of an object. First, every collectible has a multiplicity of prices in today's market. A single object can appeal to collectors in a half-dozen or more collecting categories. In many cases, it is hard to determine the primary collecting category to which an object should be assigned. Each potential primary and crossover collector views the value of a collectible differently. As a result, there is no right price, but a number of right prices. The real right price is the one at which the dealer sells the object and that price is subject to a number of variables, e.g., time, place, circumstances of buyer and seller, etc.

The situation becomes even more complicated when the decorative, nostalgic, and impulse values of an object enter the pricing equation. There are no available statistics that compare the number of collectors who buy objects versus those individuals who buy them for decorative or nostalgic purposes or simply on impulse. Based solely upon my gut reaction, I think the latter group far outnumbers collectors in today's market.

A dealer shared a recent buy-sell experience that started me thinking about the role played by gut pricing. She acquired five of the Haviland/Parlon Tapestry I series limited edition collector plates at a garage sale for $10 each. These plates feature reproductions of medieval tapestries from the collection at The Cloisters in New York City. A unicorn is the central theme of each plate.

If the dealer used a fixed markup to triple her money, she would have asked $150 for the set. If she had researched the plates in a limited edition plate price guide, e.g., *The Official Price Guide to Collector Plates, 6th Edition* (House of Collectibles, 1996, $17), she would have found a current market value of $430, assuming she had the first five of the six plates in the series. Instead, she reached into her gut and marked the plates at $125 each, relying on the decorative value of the theme and the Haviland/Parlon name to carry the day. Right from the start, she saw no future in selling the plates to the collector segment of the collectibles market.

The dealer sold the five plates to the same buyer for $500, not a bad return on a $50 inventory cost and ample proof that averaging times three is not as impossible a task as many dealers claim.

When I became editor of *Warman's Antiques and Their Prices* in 1981, I called Don Mast, the individual behind Warman's pricing, to ask if he would share with me how he determined the prices that appeared in the book. "When you have been in the business as long as I have, you know what the right price should be," he replied. As a person with strong academic training, I was in a state of shock.

A decade and a half later, I understand what Don Mast meant. The most valuable tool anyone in the trade has is his gut. I now accept this concept. Finally, life would really be copasetic if it were not for the fact that some dealers appear to have a constant problem with indigestion.

Mommy, Why Are All the Prices the Same?

I am a comparison shopper. I do not buy the first example I see. The old argument of "buy it now, you may never see another" has no meaning. The reason is simple. Almost everything I buy was mass-produced.

As a result, condition and price are critical components when making my decision whether or not to buy an object. I only buy objects that are in fine or better condition. I do not adhere to the "buy a lesser quality object and trade up" philosophy. The few times I attempted to follow this philosophy, I inevitably found myself putting the lesser quality object into storage rather than disposing of it or trading up.

I am a bargain hunter. I admit it. I do not make a purchase until I find an example at a price that I am willing to pay. I have learned to walk away when the price does not please me. Eventually, and it always happens, I make my desired purchase. I may wait years, but I buy with a strong sense of satisfaction that the hunt was worth it.

As a price guide author, I track prices. I am especially fortunate because my travels take me to a wide variety of antiques and collectibles sale venues across the country. I like to think of my market perspective as national. Thanks to the Internet and my increasing travel overseas, I am expanding it to global.

Shopping antiques malls and shows recently, I noticed a disturbing trend. Prices asked for a specific object fell within a relatively narrow price range. For example, most 1940s/50s tin cake carriers ranged in value between $22 and $28. 1950s commonly-found glass cocktail shakers are priced between $18 and $30. The list goes on and on.

It is highly unlikely that each seller paid approximately the same price for these objects and used the identical markup percentage to determine their selling price. Some sellers had to acquire the examples at a much lower cost that in theory should enable them to set a lower selling price.

Price competition is a marketing tool. I encounter it every day—when I visit the grocery store, buy gas, go to a shopping mall, or comparison shop on the Internet. Yet price competition is surprisingly lacking in the collectibles field. The asking price for an object is far more likely to be similar than dissimilar.

Why are all the prices the same? At first glance, the culprit appears to be price guides. Sellers buy an object, research it in a price guide, fall victim to the myth that price guide prices are always accurate, and price their goods accordingly. Price guide prices are not always accurate. More and more often, especially in single subject price guides, the prices are market manipulative.

It is not fair to place the blame for uniform prices on price guides alone. The real culprit is market pressure by dealers, usually older established dealers, who think other dealers, especially new dealers, should sell at the same or higher prices than found on their own merchandise. There is enormous pressure to price conform.

New dealers traditionally undervalue their initial offerings. They know what each object costs, the profit level they want to achieve, and set their asking price accordingly. Sales are brisk.

Established dealers noticing their success are quick to offer the helpful suggestions: "Your prices are too low," and "You could easily have gotten more for that." They encourage the new dealer to raise his prices.

These established dealers have planted a seed that eventually haunts every new dealer. No matter what price he receives, the fact that he sold it is enough to indicate that he charged too little. "It sold too fast; I should have charged more" is a common dealer lament.

When I train new dealers, I encourage them to react to suggestions that they should charge more by saying to the dealer making this suggestion: "I am delighted with the price I have on the object. If you think it will bring more, I will be happy to sell it to you at my price and let you make the increased profit." When asked to back up their suggestion with money, most dealers will run for the hills.

Pressure to conform to established pricing norms is prevalent in the antiques and collectibles trade. Not wishing to offend, most new dealers quickly knuckle under to the pressure. Everyone wants to be part of the fraternity.

In truth, dealers are in direct competition with each other. In a competitive business environment, the advantage goes to the seller with the lowest prices. Instead of price similarities in the antiques and collectibles trade, one should see noticeable differences, differences that normally should range in the hundreds of percent.

No profit is made when an object sits unsold on a shelf or in a booth. Yet, the objective seems to be to fill antiques malls and shows with similar objects priced at a level that makes their probable sale iffy at best. A standard price, one seen on the same object mall after mall or show after show, is not an incentive to buy. It encourages buyers to take an "I will buy this when I am damned good and ready" approach. If a dealer wants to achieve a quick sale, the price needs to be attractive, i.e., a bargain.

Have I placed too much blame on dealer pressure as the principal reason for price conformity? Perhaps! There is another possible explanation.

When a dealer acquires an object and questions what to charge for it, he frequently will walk around an antiques mall or show to see what other dealers are asking for it. Using this information, he places basically the same price on his object.

Do you recognize the false reasoning? The reason the dealer found comparable objects is that they did not sell. The logical conclusion is that these objects are overpriced. If he wants to sell his object, he should place a lower, perhaps significantly lower, selling price on it.

Recently, I was asked to evaluate several booths at an antiques mall. Lack of sales is the prime reason I am asked to consult. During one of the evaluations, I continually asked the husband and wife dealer team what they initially paid for their merchandise. I was not surprised to learn that objects they acquired for a few dollars had price tags ranging from $15 to $50, almost all of them at or near price guide prices.

It does not require a college education to see why their sales were slow. They bought right. Greed and pressure to conform had caused them to set prices that challenged even the casual buyer.

My recommendation was to abandon price guide and comparison price research. Use a times three to times five profit margin and price the objects to sell quickly. Do not be upset if another dealer buys an item and sells it at a higher price. Make a quick profit and use the profit to buy more. Volume selling is profitable selling.

Do not draw the wrong conclusions. There are enough price differences within the antiques and collectibles trade that a price fixing accusation is unwarranted.

The correct conclusions are: (1) there is not as much price competition as there should be and (2) current trade practices and norms restrict rather than encourage such competition.

Will this change? I doubt it. However, change is not possible without a dialogue. Hopefully, this article will start one.

How Common Is It?

Overestimating the scarcity of an object is one of the most common mistakes made by buyers and sellers of antiques. Everyone wants their favorite object to be scarce, i.e., one that is difficult to locate—the greater the difficulty, the higher the level of scarcity.

As my readers know, I do not use "rare" to describe the availability of objects, even those made in the nineteenth century. In the twenty-first century, the vast majority of collectors, my guesstimate is ninety plus percent, collect objects made in the twentieth century. Almost all these objects were mass produced. Production is measured in tens or hundreds of thousands and, in some cases, millions.

This results in a high survival rate of objects in very good or better condition. Very good is the minimum condition grade at which objects should be collected. Today's collectors do not want objects that are damaged or incomplete. They want objects that are ready to be displayed or used, i.e., object that can go right from the seller into their home.

I use a five-level scale to determine the scarcity of an object—(1) extremely common, (2) common, (3) difficult to find, (4) extremely difficult to find, and (5) almost impossible to find. The criteria for each level is as follows:

Extremely common: Objects available daily. I see one or more in every antiques flea market, mall, or shop that I visit. One or more examples appear for sale on eBay several times within a week.

Common: Objects that I find within a day or two of wanting to locate them. In many cases, all it takes is a phone call. Even I am astonished at how common some objects are. I recently was asked to find in a span of four days or less a fifty-five-inch wide, "S" roll, refinished roll-top desk featuring an interior of thirty plus drawers and slots and a base with four drawers on the left, four drawers (or two drawers and a file drawer) on the right, and a center drawer. When the client called, I expressed concern that the task was virtually impossible on such short notice. I did promise to make a few phone calls. I called a friend. He made a few other calls and within two hours he located a dealer who had a desk matching the description. I looked at the desk later the same afternoon. In less than twenty-four hours, I had fulfilled my client's wishes. I accomplished this because, much to my surprise, roll-top desks turned out to be far more common than I thought. Had my phone efforts failed, I already had suggested to my client that she place a classified seeker advertisement in several of the trade papers. I was certain she would have her desk in a day or two after the advertisement appeared. The point is simple. Even objects from the late nineteenth and early twentieth century are common.

Difficult to find: Objects that take a week to several weeks to locate. Remember, we are talking about the survival rate of objects worth collecting or using. If the criteria was locating the object regardless of condition, the objects in this category would be classified as extremely common or common. Objects in this group appear for sale on eBay one to four times a month.

Extremely difficult to find: Objects that take several months to locate. This is a case where persistence pays. A prospective buyer has to put the word out and be patient. Sometimes he may have to renew his request. Most dealers forget client wants after a month has passed.

Almost impossible to find: Objects that take years to locate. Most are in the hands of collectors or private individuals who usually do not understand the scarcity level of what they own. The object appears for sale on eBay once or twice a year.

I am concerned that some may incorrectly interpret the above definitions based upon "the length of time it takes to find an object" criteria. My assumption is that the person seeking the object is familiar with the trade and can conduct the same level of search that I can. I know this is not case. This is why it is critical that experts familiar with the field and especially the collecting category assess and assign scarcity levels to objects.

I face the "How common is it?" issue every day. "How common is it?" is usually the first question I ask myself when evaluating an object. Scarcity is one of the Big Three criteria for valuing an object. Desirability and condition are the other two. Scarcity ranks third on the list behind desirability and condition. Yet, no object can be valued without taking scarcity into consideration.

During the taping of *Collector Inspector*, my antiques and collectibles show on Home & Garden Television, I see a great many items that have been passed down through the family. Their family value is paramount. The stories that accompany them often include a statement that the object is scarce, one of only a few made, and, in some cases, a one-of-a-kind item. In ninety-nine cases out of one hundred, I have to grit my teeth, put on a diplomatic smile, and tell the homeowner that the object is extremely common or common and worth far less than they expected. Most take the news graciously.

A recent conversation with Bruce Greenberg, one of the nation's leading authorities on the toy train market and a personal friend, brought the "How common is it?" issue front and center in my mind. Bruce recently sold some the surplus items in his toy train collection on eBay. Knowing my strong interest in market trends, Bruce called to share his results. He also sent a follow-up e-mail

Bruce noted that extremely common and common items were selling at one-quarter to one-third less than book (price guide) value. The reason was twofold—the market was flooded and demand for new high quality trains had drawn customers away from the traditional secondary toy train market. Bruce found the trend applied to the pre-1942 and 1945-1969 toy train market. The market for post-1970 toy trains was very flat. The secondary market was often less than half of what the trains cost new. Today's toy train collectors would rather buy new than used. Bruce noted that following 1990 there was "a dramatic increase in supply due to new manufacturers. Since that time an increasing supply of high quality trains with new features have reduced the demand for used trains. Used train prices stopped rising and are now falling. The demand for new editions of our price guide books was predicated on rising prices."

[**Author's Note**: One measure of the strength of any collecting category is the copyright date of the most recent price guide devoted to it. When the copyright is five or more years old, the category is stable at best and most likely in a significant price decline. When the copyright is eight years old or older, the category has declined to a point where a very small number of old-time collectors are keeping the category alive. Few new collectors are attracted to the category.

Beware of false signals. Occasionally a dedicated collector or dealer, one whose desire is primarily to prop up the pricing in his specialty, can convince a publisher to issue a price guide in his specialty. The information that never appears in print on the copyright page is how many copies of the book were sold or printed. Learn to ask these questions.]

The more I think about the "How common is it?" issue, the more I am becoming convinced I need two, not five levels to adequately identify scarcity. Group extremely common, difficult to find, and half the extremely difficult to find objects in one unit. Put the balance of the extremely difficult to find and impossible to find objects into a second unit. Assume the value for the first group will either be stable or in slight decline over long periods of time, i.e., decades. Values for the second group will rise and fall depending on whether the collecting category is hot or not.

Today's market is trendy. Trendiness is one of the subdivisions in the desirability component of value. No antiques or collectibles category is free from the possibility of losing favor. However, in today's complex market, the effect of falling prices may be greater on the extremely difficult to find and almost impossible to find objects than on the more commonly found objects. Previously, I thought the commonly found objects were most influenced by trends and the very difficult to find and almost impossible to find objects were immune. Now I am not as certain.

Ego and Its Influence on Value

Recently I had the pleasure of doing a little antiquing with Brad Jones, an anchor/reporter for WGHP-TV, Fox 8, High Point, North Carolina. During our drive to Mebane to attend an auction, our conversation turned to factors that influence value. Brad commented: "The first five dollars is value. All the rest is ego."

My response was immediate. "What a great concept," I replied. "This is certainly fodder for a 'Rinker on Collectibles' column." I immediately wrote the quote on the back of one of my business cards so I would not forget it.

Ego and value are often directly related. Ego appears in a variety of guises. A few easily identified guises are: (1) no one outbids me; (2) I do not care what I have to pay for it, I need it to complete my collection; and, (3) my rival is only going to acquire that over my dead body. You should have no trouble thinking of others.

The January 12, 1999, Guernsey/eBay auction of record-setting home run baseballs is an excellent example to study ego at work. A Guernsey press announcement read: "MARK McGWIRE AND SAMMY SOSA 1998 HOME RUN BALLS TO BE AUCTIONED BY GUERNSEY'S IN ALLIANCE WITH EBAY / Items to be Auctioned January 12 at Madison Square Garden. / New York, December 8, 1998—Guernsey's, the New York auction house, in alliance with eBay (www.ebay.com), the largest person-to-person on-line trading community, announced today the sports auction of the century. The auction consists of seven famed baseballs along with other significant memorabilia from baseball's magical 1998 season, as well as other historical baseball items."

"The sports auction of the century!" Give me a break. Making such a claim in advance of the auction was based solely on ego and hype. Its goal was to artificially drive up the perceived value of the goods offered for sale. Truth rarely stands in the way of auction house pre-sale publicity, especially that generated by the New York establishment. They get away with these claims because reporters fail to call them to account after the auctions occur.

Guernsey's public relations people were telling the media that they expected the sale to exceed five million dollars, the record total for an earlier baseball auction. I was asked to comment about this possibility and other issues relating to the auction on CNBC-TV's *The Edge*, that aired on January 12 just prior to the auction. It probably comes as no surprise to learn that I was "Mr. Negative." Guess who turned out to be right? When the dust settled, Guernsey and eBay were the ones who struck out, not me.

Is or is not eBay an auction? Its sellers' agreement clearly states that eBay only provides a vehicle for the seller and the seller is the assumed auctioneer. Yet, eBay very much wants to establish itself on a par with the leading catalog auction houses such as Christie's and Sotheby's. eBay is not fooling anyone hiding behind its claim that it is a "person-to-person on-line trading community." It does not take a college degree to know when bidding is involved, an auction is taking place. How much longer will eBay be allowed to wear whichever hat—either the yes I am an auctioneer or no I am not an auctioneer hat—it finds convenient at the moment?

Pity poor eBay. When the auction was over, Guernsey received all the publicity. I could not find a report anywhere of how much was bid on the baseballs and other memorabilia prior to the beginning of Guernsey's Madison Square Garden auction. Is the reason for the silence the fact that eBay does not want us to know that it failed to generate substantial pre-auction bids?

There was plenty of "no one will outbid me" ego behind the $2.7 million plus buyer's penalty paid for the McGwire ball. It is the only way to explain the price paid for a baseball that has yet to stand the test of time. A Ruth/Maris signed ball sold for $50,000. The Hank Aaron 755th career home run ball, a feat that far exceeds the magnitude of McGwire's one season accomplishment, failed to meet reserve with an

$800,000 bid. There is a very transparent message here about the long-term investment potential in the McGwire ball. Further, even heaven will not be able to help the value of the McGwire ball if McGwire or someone else hits seventy-two or more homeruns in a future season.

Personally, I am surprised that neither eBay nor Guernsey failed to guarantee the owner of the Aaron the minimum reserve and shilled the auctioned until it reached that amount. Given their post auction media expectations, I thought their ego would have required it. The positive media publicity of two balls breaking the $1 million mark, especially from eBay's perspective, would far exceed the coverage of standard media advertising purchased for the same amount.

Bragging rights come with paying record prices. Some purchasers' egos are such that they point with pride to the fact that they paid record dollars. They feel it establishes them as kings of the hill. I refer to them as buyers of prestige. They fall into the same class as those individuals who only buy at New York auction houses or from high-ticket galleries and antiques show dealers and assume the fact that they do impresses people. The tragedy is that it does.

A perfect example of the "I do not care what I have to pay for it, I need it to complete my collection" ego value boost arrived on my desk as a January 4, 1999, letter from Myron L. Flaugher. In a previous column, I commented that I felt the book value of over $500 for a Dazey No. 1 butter churn was ridiculous. Flaugher responded:

> I am that "sucker." You're saying what? I am talking about what you wrote to KS of Appleton, Wisconsin, in *AntiqueWeek* December 7th edition.
>
> "I am speaking about the one-quart Dazey churn for $500 plus. I am that "sucker!" I will buy ALL the one-quart Dazey churn you can send me at $500. In good condition, of course!
>
> I have twelve churns, wood, stone, and glass. I do not have a one-quart Dazey because of the very high prices they sell for in my area. If you would give me KS of Appleton, Wisconsin's, address or phone number, I will give her $500 plus for her one-quart Dazey churn or anyone else who wants to sell.
>
> I have the Dazey two-, three-, four-, six-, and eight-quart churn. I only need the one-quart to complete my collection.

When God creates someone with an ego like this, who am I to pooh-pooh it. Opportunity knocks for those with a Dazey one quart butter churn to sell. I suggest a simple approach—kiss the hand and take the money. I also suggest being the first or second person to contact Flaugher. I strongly suspect that "ALL" does not mean a half dozen or more.

It is fun and amusing to attend an auction and watch two rivals bidding against each other with the end result of driving an object to three, four, or more times its value just to prevent the other person from buying it. This is all and only about ego. It has as much to do with not wanting the other person to have the object as it is with owning it one's self. This type of ego trip can be very expensive.

It also can lead to the acquisition of unwanted duplicates just to keep them out of a rivals' collection. Ego value disappears when a rival has what you have. Although this approach inevitably fails, ego generally requires that the attempt be made.

Ego is only one of may factors that can determine value. It ranks in the middle, not at the top. However, when it is in play, it is all-consuming.

There is little ego value in being the loser. Just ask Sammy Sosa. His sixty-sixth home run baseball sold for $172,000 plus buyer's penalty. The ball sold. Its owner was realistic enough not to allow his ego to dominate his expectations.

Some "Rinker on Collectibles" readers are probably thinking I have one hell of an ego saying this. If true, my congratulations, you have just hit a home run.

The Light a Candle Value

Collectibles do not have a fixed value. Every object has multiple values, e.g., auction value, book value, wholesale value, etc. Each value is equally valid. Value is time and place specific.

At the recent Great Eastern U.S. Antique Book, Paper, Advertising & Collectables Show, several sheet music devotees and I were swapping war stories. In the course of our conversation, someone commented on the outrageously high values asked and, in more instances than he cared to remember, paid for some collectibles. The prices realized at Sotheby's Jacqueline Kennedy Onassis auction added credence to his concerns.

As I considered his remarks, I suddenly realized that there is a value in the collectibles field that everyone knows exists but hardly ever discusses. Time to remedy the situation. The value in question is the "light a candle" value.

A light a candle value is that price at which a collectible is sold whereby the only honorable thing to do is to visit a church or synagogue and light a candle thanking the deity for delivering the seller a gullible fool as a buyer. Assuming this value is real and my premise correct, the churches in New York would have been ablaze with light following the conclusion of the Onassis auction.

A light a candle value is an extremely high value, totally out of touch with reality. It bears absolutely no relationship to what an identical object would sell for at any other time and place. It is a freak. Chances of it happening again are between zero and nil.

A light a candle value does not move a collecting category's pricing structure upward. In fact, its effect is more negative than positive. Light a candle values frequently are reported in public and trade media. Their size and ridiculous nature make them news. Tragically, media reports rarely put light a candle values into context. As a result, a public perception arises that these values do have real meaning relative to long-term pricing trends within the collecting category to which they apply. Nothing is further from the truth. A light a candle value is a once in a lifetime value.

Alas, try convincing someone who owns an identical object and wants to sell it that he should expect far less than the light a candle value that he read or heard about. If anything, he usually thinks he deserves more. In truth, the only time a candle will be lit for his object is if it is in his coffin when he is buried.

There are more light a candle values in the collectibles field than we realize or wish to admit. Think for a minute. What are the circumstances that lead to light a candle values? Once you turn your mind to the question, you will be surprised at how many situations you can identify. Here are a few of my candidates:

Two heirs are involved in a bitter dispute over an object in an estate. Unable to resolve their differences, the piece is sent to auction. Each relative is determined that the other will never own the object in question. The bidding quickly escalates until the value of the object is two, five, and ultimately ten times book. Eventually one of the two parties concedes. Neither party talks to the other for decades.

Forget the two heirs. What happens when two collectors lock horns at an auction, both equally determined to prevent their rival from adding an object to his collection? Does the word bloodbath come to mind? I have seen plenty of blood spilled at auctions. Alas, on occasion the blood was mine.

As a case in point, consider the $30,250 bid for a Jarvie Shop of Chicago catalog at Bruce Smebakken's Pioneer Auction in Amherst, Massachusetts, on March 23, 1996. Jarvie Shop is a major manufacturer of arts and crafts decorative accessories. David Hewett wrote a detailed story about the bidding war between two rivals that appeared in the May 1996 *Maine Antique Digest*. In summary, the general sentiment among those in the know is that the catalog's true market value is around $500. If true, this means that $29,750 of the $30,250 spent is funny money. Note the similarity to the sale of Caroline Kennedy's footstool that Sotheby's estimated between $100 and $150 and which realized $33,350. What is another $33,200 of funny money among friends?

Collectors covet. There are always one or more objects that they desire to own but do not. Their search already may have consumed years, even decades. The matter is made worse if their biggest rival already owns said object. Unfortunately, such individuals have difficulty keeping their desires private.

A dealer, fully aware of a collector's burning need, finds the collectible the collector most covets. What price do you think the dealer is going to ask? Rest assured, it will not be a bargain one. The dealer goes for the jugular. The dealer's only dilemma is deciding how high is too high. Whatever the final price, the dealer will have the funds to place a generous donation in the candle offering box in the house of worship of his choice.

I paid more than one light a candle price in my collecting career. I knew better, but I really wanted to own the piece. I justified my purchases by reasoning that since I had the money available to make the purchase at that specific moment of time God meant for me to own it.

As I have grown older, I have become wiser; at least I like to think I have. I can spot light a candle prices more easily; and, I have walked away on an occasion or two when I felt the price was too high. I also have learned that when forced to pay a light a candle price, I should always make a point after the sale is concluded to thank the seller and tell him how much more I would gladly have paid if I had to. You take the fun out of a dealer's triumph if you plant the seed of doubt that he did not get as much as he could have.

Perhaps the most frustrating light a candle value is the one resulting from the sale of a ridiculously priced collectible by a novice dealer to a neophyte buyer. New dealers are plagued by the fear of selling an expensive piece for too little. As a result, they overprice their merchandise, especially pieces about which they know very little. Neophyte buyers are embarrassed by their ignorance. They compensate by implicitly trusting what any dealer tells them. Ignorance selling to ignorance produces many record-setting light a candle values.

Finally, there are dealers fully aware of what they have and its value but who subscribe to the premise that there is a sucker born every minute. They frequently set up in malls. They are easy to spot. The merchandise in their booth and/or showcase is consistently priced three to ten times above book. They prey on and pray for the buyer whose purchase is nostalgia- or decorator-driven. They never see their victims. They should light a dozen candles at a time.

Light a candle value humor is the provenance of the seller, not the buyer. The seller never tires of passing along a good candle-lighting story. However, there is little humor when the realization hits that person who has been taken. It is a rare individual who can laugh at himself.

During the same conversation that led to my discovery of the light a candle value, another individual asked; "Are there collectibles whose real value is nothing?" I strongly support the premise that everything has collectibility. But, must it have value? Is it possible to collect something that has absolutely no value? What an interesting concept— something to think about. Maybe even a future column.

CHAPTER 5

Acquiring the Goodies

Becoming a smart buyer takes time. We all make mistakes. I call those mistakes the tuition we pay to become good collectors.

We begin collecting as wide-eyed optimists. We end as skeptics. I view this as positive rather than negative. A skeptical attitude makes certain we court an object before we fall in love with it. If you stop and think about this, such an approach is best applied to other areas of our life in addition to collecting. Skepticism forces us to ask questions rather than accepting everything on face value or the authority of the seller.

Inconsistency is one of the constants of the antiques and collectibles trade. The trade has no professional organization to impose a common set of professional standards. Everyone makes up his own rules. In many cases, one has to guess what they are because they are not shared openly.

While raising your defenses, hopefully this chapter will not turn you off from collecting.

Don't Buy What You Don't Know

Shortly after Christmas, I received a letter from John Bittence of Hiram, Ohio. Several of John's friends bought him Christmas gifts on the Internet. Alas, their good intentions have created a major problem.

> eBay is worse than I imagined! I now realize that it has become a dangerous venue for friends and relatives, well-meaning but short on knowledge, for purchasing gifts. And, a lucrative one for vendors wishing to unload low-valued merchandise at absurd prices.

I received four Christmas presents this year bought from eBay auctions. One was a fantasy item, one absolutely worthless, one a reproduction, and one inappropriate to my interests. Two were wrapped in their shipping boxes, so I was able to observe that the cost of shipping 'alone' exceeded the fair market value of the gift.

I was able to check back on the auction history of two of the items. They were maximum $12 items on the fair and open market, but purchased on eBay for $28 and $40! I do not know how much was spent on the 'worthless' gift, but the postage alone came to $14+, not counting insurance.

There are unfortunate consequences here. I regard myself as a hard bargainer and rarely pay market price for my collectibles, almost always less. The few times I have been bilked, I usually dispose of the item so as not to be reminded of the event. But now I am forced to recall that some scum bag collector somewhere in the world danced his/her way to the bank at my expense every time I gaze upon these gifts.

Obviously I need some way to discreetly display or otherwise explain away the absence of these items in my collection.

We all know about 'coffee-table' books, the perennial gift from our Aunt Minnies looking for 'something special' for that nephew with his strange hobby. We all have shelves full of these; and, we wink knowingly at each other when we spot one. But, the presence of a fraudulent, reproduction, or useless item in the midst of our pristine collection is another problem not so easily apologized away.

Sadly, I do not think eBay is going away, nor will the prices stabilize. It's too handy for amateurs seeking that 'certain something' for that collector without the need to leave the house to hunt the shops or research the subject. Most of these buyers would not care if they were bilked anyhow. They got their shopping done quickly and easily, well worth the price.

John's letter raises several concerns. It would be wrong to assume that the bilking of unknowledgeable individuals on the Internet is confined to eBay. It is a universal problem on the Internet wherever antiques and collectibles are sold. Buyers trust sellers to tell them the truth.

When lecturing about buying antiques and collectibles, I constantly tell my audience, "do not buy what you do not know." Do not assume the seller knows. When lecturing about selling antiques and collectibles, I urge dealers not to sell what they do not know. I believe the responsibility rests with the seller to properly represent his merchandise. I do not support caveat emptor (let the buyer beware), which places the burden of knowledge on the buyer.

David Lindquist, co-owner of Whitehall at the Villa in Chapel Hill, North Carolina, and a friend, argues with me constantly about giving dealers the benefit of the doubt when I discover an object that has been misrepresented. David feels dealers can be fooled themselves and make honest mistakes. I concede this is true. However, a seller that does her homework is going to greatly lessen this possibility, especially if she does not market items she is not certain about.

It is amateur night in the sticks on the Internet at the moment and likely to remain that way for years to come. There are experienced sellers on the Internet. Unfortunately, they currently are in the minority. Honest sellers are in the majority. It is the percentage that concerns me. I am not convinced it is over ninety.

John's need to check out the transactions that led to the receipt of his gifts reveals the ease by which information can be obtained on the Internet. A zealot might interpret John's research as an invasion of privacy.

The electronic trail is far more detailed and permanent than the paper trail. It takes only seconds to track a rival's purchases on the Internet or to find the selling and bidding information for any object on an Internet auction (there are ways around the thirty-day control). The day is not too distant when the individual doing the checking will work for a state sales tax collection department or the Internal Revenue Service. My guess is that less than 10 percent of Internet sellers report their profits as earned income on their tax returns.

However, I confess that the thing that has intrigued me most about John's letter is his plea for advice on how to rid himself of the unwanted gifts he received. A plea of this nature should not go unanswered.

Storing the gifts and putting them out only when the individual comes to visit is not the answer. Today, few individuals announce their visits in advance. The only solution is to make the objects permanently disappear.

Blaming it on the pet or the kids is the most obvious approach. "I'm just devastated. _____ (insert appropriate name of animal or child) knocked it off the shelf. It broke. I would have replaced it, but it just would not have had the same meaning as the one you gave me. Do not go to the trouble to replace it either. A replacement would only remind me of the one that was broken."

Here is my second effort. "A fellow collector, who is also a great friend, stopped for a visit the other day. You should have seen his eyes light up when he saw the gift you gave to me. He had been searching for it all his life. It was the one example he needed to complete his collection. Knowing this, I just had to give it to him. I made it clear it was a gift, but said I was sure you would feel exactly as I did."

The following is a variation on this theme: "I was visited the other day by a new collector. When he saw the gift you gave to me, he fell in love with it. You should have seen the emotion in his eyes. While I very much appreciated your kindness, I simply could not match this new collector's enthusiasm. I gave him the object in exchange for his promise that he would continue to collect well into the future."

I admit this one is a lame excuse, but it is worth a try if you are truly desperate. "A few months ago, I rearranged my collection. I even packed a large portion of it and put it in storage. When I realized that your gift was missing, I searched all the storage boxes twice. I am embarrassed to say that I could not find it. I know it is here. It is bound to turn up sooner or later. I did not throw it out. I will keep looking."

Know Who You are Dealing With

Trust plays a major role in the buying and selling of collectibles. The buyer trusts the seller to accurately represent the object he is selling and to price it fairly. The seller trusts the buyer to pay promptly with a valid method of payment.

In the vast majority of selling transactions that occur in the collectibles field, the buyer has little or no familiarity with the seller and
vice versa. In order for the process to work, a basic assumption is made
that both parties are honest. Fortunately, this is true more often than not.

Examine your own experiences. When buying at flea markets or
shows, how many times do you make a one-time-only purchase from
someone with whom you have never done business previously? If you
are typical, 75 percent or more of your purchases are from first-time sellers to you. How many sellers asked for your name and address? It is as
though sellers have no interest in selling to you again unless fate and
good fortune decide that your paths should cross a second or third time.

Although occasionally asking for identification when accepting a
check, most sellers never photocopy it for their records. They simply
deposit the check and assume it will clear. Regrettably, the buying and
selling of collectibles is very much an "over and done with" business.

Each year the percentage of collectibles buying transactions where
there is no face to face contact between the buyer and seller is increasing.
Historically, such transactions were limited to direct sale lists, responses
to classified advertising, and left bids at auction. In the 1980s, the arrival
of the co-op, antiques malls, and telephone auction bids increased the
physical gap between buyer and seller. All this pales when compared to
the Internet's potential to lengthen the gap even further. Do I foresee a
future when 50 percent or more of collectibles purchases will not involve
any physical contact between the two parties? Yes, I do.

I trust people, often to a fault. I can still hear my father saying
"Didn't you know who you were dealing with?" whenever I talked to
him about a transaction with which I was having trouble or had gone
sour. My father believed strongly in doing business only with people he
knew. We bought our suits from Refowich's, jewelry and gift items
from Ramblers, and cars from the local Ford dealer. Dad was a Ford
man for life. Mom shopped at Bush and Bull (Orr's), Hess's, Leh's, and
Zollinger's. Both parents believed in a bond of loyalty between buyer
and seller—a concept that has become virtually lost in collectibles selling transactions.

Every barrel has a few rotten apples. The only issue is the percentage. The business community accepts this and works to keep the
percentage low. Chambers of Commerce and other groups establish

selling standards and educate merchants about existing problems and how to combat them. What is so readily available in the business community is difficult to find in the collectibles trade. There are few groups that provide this service.

Recent stories reported in the national and trade media call attention to two growing problems in the antiques and collectibles community. First, Sandra Slack Hughes of Fort Worth, Texas, was found guilty in Iowa of writing bad checks for antiques and coin purchases. Charges are pending in other states. Payment using over-extended or discontinued credit cards currently is a bigger problem in the collectibles trade than bad checks. However, the auction community has seen a dramatic increase in bad checks during the past decade. Little wonder auctioneers now insist on two to three forms of identification before issuing a bidding number.

Second, Melissa Ann Stiver of Pensacola, Florida, has been charged with selling Beanie Babies over the Internet and not delivering the toys. She collected over $10,000 from trusting buyers. This follows a similar incident eighteen months ago when a person placed classified ads in several Barbie publications offering hard-to-find contemporary dolls at bargain prices. Collectors cast aside the "if it is too good to be true, it probably is" adage and bought heavily. In this case, the woman had collected over $30,000 before she was apprehended.

As the per unit value of collectibles has risen, the number of charlatans, crooks, and schemers attracted to the field has increased. The collectibles community's lack of business acumen, part-time nature, mobility, and blind trust of selling transactions combined with the unwillingness of local law enforcement to pursue, arrest, and prosecute offenders only enhances the appeal. Usually the amount of money involved is small, rarely more than $250 to $500. It is easier to absorb the loss than commit the time and money to seek legal redress.

In talking with a dealer who buys actively on the Internet, I inquired if he was experiencing any major problem. He informed me that he was having problems with one out of every twenty-five purchases. I was shocked. However, his attitude and approach to the problem was even more shocking.

"I have no problem living with the percentage," he explained. "I do so well with my other purchases that they more than make up for the money that I lose on the bad deals." The dealer had become so jaded that he was willing to accept a 4 percent loss.

Well, I am not. I am angry. I am committed to ending the problem, not settling on an acceptable loss ratio.

The above problems do not fall under the "ignore them and they will go away" category. Ignore them, and they only will get worse. The window of opportunity for taking action is now open. Quoting Barney Fife from *The Andy Griffith Show*, "Nip it, nip it in the bud."

How is this to be done? Buyers and sellers need to take a multiple approach. First become defensive. Learn about the person from whom you are buying or to whom you are selling. If the person is unknown, do not hesitate to ask for identification and references. If he refuses to provide a full name, address, and telephone number do not do business with him.

Second, go on the offensive. Report problems to the local police and trade periodicals. Demand action. Spread the word. Help drive the charlatans, crooks, and schemers out of the trade.

Third, do not be scared of the public's reaction to the publicity a crackdown will generate. Publicity turns up the heat on other charlatans, crooks, and schemers and discourages those who are considering tapping into the supposed golden opportunities the antiques and collectibles community represents. Publicity demonstrates to the public that we are aware of the problem and doing something about it.

Finally, the real solution begins with you. Make this pledge and stick to it: Know who you are dealing with.

Dating Objects: The First Step in Guaranteeing Merchandise

"Rinker on Collectibles" is a column about objects made after 1900. Occasionally, a topic arises that requires me to include comments on eighteenth- and nineteenth-century antiques to make my point. This is one of them.

Most sellers of antiques and collectibles do not assign a date of manufacture to the objects they sell. First, few see it as an added value factor. Second, most are unwilling to do the research, though it often involves merely locating a manufacturer's mark and/or copyright information on the object. Third, a select few realize that failure to date an object is protection against being charged with fraud.

If a purchaser pays $1,000 for object "x," described as "vase, pottery, handled, squat shape, blossom pattern, light green ground, partially glazed interior, marked Roseville," only to discover later that it is a modern reproduction costing less than ten dollars new, he has no legal recourse against the seller. The seller did not misrepresent the piece. He precisely described the object he sold.

There are no fixed prices in the antiques and collectibles trade. An object is worth what someone willingly pays for it. Further, value is contingent on time and place. Value is ever changing, not constant.

Regular readers of "Rinker on Collectibles" will find the above paragraph repetitive. I offer no apologies. This is something everyone in the trade should think about at least once a day, ideally more often.

If the seller had dated the object "circa 1920" and the buyer proved it was made in 1997, the sale is fraudulent. The seller misrepresented the object. The buyer has legal recourse if the seller refuses to refund the purchase price.

I am a strong advocate of the principle that sellers have the responsibility to guarantee the authenticity of the objects they sell. The burden of authentication should not fall upon buyers as it does under the principle of caveat emptor. I have no tolerance for any seller who hides behind the sin of omission, i.e., omitting the manufacturing date when describing the object being sold on the sales receipt.

When a seller indicates the date he believes an object was made during the course of the sale process, he demonstrates the depth of his knowledge, provides an unspoken guarantee that he stands behind what he sells, and exhibits a level of professionalism sadly missing throughout much of the trade.

How accurate must the date be? I offer the following table for consideration. In my view it represents the very minimum tolerance.

Date Object Made	+ / - Spread In Years
1700-1820	12.5
1820-1880	10.0
1880-1920	7.5
1920 to Present	5.0

In other words, an object made between 1920 and the present should be dated within a ten-year time span, e.g., 1920-30 or 1925-1935. Objects made in the eighteenth century or early nineteenth century should be dated within a twenty-five-year time span.

Dating an object as "eighteenth century" or "Victorian" is meaningless. There were six major design style changes in the eighteenth century and more than a dozen between 1837 and 1901, the reign of Queen Victoria. Terms such as first-half, second-half, middle-of, etc., are too broad to have precise meaning. Failure to date accurately indicates a seller's ignorance or laziness or both.

There is no requirement when dating objects that everything must fall within a specific quarter century or decade. 1840 to 1860 is just as valid a date period as 1825 to 1850. Actually, the latter example is five years over what I consider minimum standards. I find first-, second-, third-, and fourth-quarter nineteenth-century dating highly inaccurate.

Dating should be based on design style, not chronologically centered. Again, I have no tolerance for sellers who fail to educate themselves in the history of American design. Design styles do not follow neat chronological lines. Further, design styles overlap, especially in the nineteenth and twentieth centuries. The period when a single design style dominated ended in the 1780s/90s when Hepplewhite, Sheraton, Neo-Classicism, and Duncan Phyfe-style arrived on the American scene at approximately the same moment. Visit any store selling newly made furniture. Chances are you will find pieces in over a dozen different design styles, some inspired by eighteenth- and nineteenth-century design styles and others by post-1945 design.

How much dating error is tolerated before fraud is committed? If the seller is off by five or ten years, there is no fraud. When the error is more than twenty-five years, a good case for fraud can be made.

I have lost track of the number of times I have seen the Folgers Coffee advertising jigsaw puzzle, issued in 1981, offered for sale with tags containing dates ranging from the early 1950s through the 1960s. Unfortunately neither the puzzle nor its container is marked with a copyright date. I learned the correct date during a telephone conversation with the Proctor and Gamble archivist.

Part of the difficulty rests with the fact that some sellers see a relationship between age and value, i.e., the older an object is, the more it should be worth. When the Folgers Coffee advertising puzzle is correctly dated, it usually is priced between $8 and $12. When it is incorrectly dated, the value begins at $20 and can go as high as $40.

Age stopped being a major value factor in the antiques and collectibles trade over a decade ago. In the twenty-first century, condition, scarcity, and desirability are the main value factors. The principal value of age in today's market is as an authenticating tool.

This entire issue would be moot if sellers provided a money back, no questions asked guarantee for every object they sold, thus making customer satisfaction an important element of the buy-sell antiques and collectibles equation. Whenever I suggest this approach to sellers, I am immediately bombarded with questions such as how much time is reasonable for a buyer to request a refund. When the refund request involves authenticity, there is no time limit. Sometimes it takes years for a buyer to discover that a purchased piece is not what he or the seller thought it to be. The buyer should not be penalized.

The failure of buyers to insist that sellers date objects they offer for sale is probably the main reason sellers do not. The situation would change overnight if buyers refused to purchase any object offered for auction or sale that was not dated. However, it will not, primarily because of the overconfidence on the part of many buyers that they know what they are buying. Further, many buyers are too embarrassed to admit they make mistakes. They get angry at themselves instead of the seller. Problems are best corrected at the time of sale and not upon discovery of the fraud.

In most antiques and collectibles sales the seller provides the buyer with a receipt. When a receipt is issued, the description of an object rarely consists of more than three or four words. Rarely does the seller provide a description of an object's physical appearance and condition. Completeness, size, date, and repairs are conspicuous by their absence. Again, sellers see no need because buyers do not demand it.

If the antiques and collectibles field wishes to earn the same professional respect found in other mercantile enterprises, it has to clean up its act. Providing a manufacturing date for objects as a means of offering an implicit trustworthy guarantee that an object is what it is purported to be is an important first step. My concern is how many individuals in the trade are willing to assume this responsibility.

Search for a Universal Condition Grading Standard

When grading an object, what do the terms good, very good, fine, excellent, or mint mean? There is no correct answer because there is no universally agreed upon condition grading standard in the collectibles field. Each individual sets his own standards. Based on years of buying experiences and field observations, I have concluded that: (1) experienced sellers frequently over grade the condition of the objects they are selling; (2) seasoned collectors grade far too tough; and (3) individuals with little or no experience in the trade, buyers or sellers, almost always over grade an object's condition. As a result, opportunities for misunderstanding abound.

Condition and value are linked. The value of an object increases exponentially as its condition increases. At higher grades, e.g., near mint and mint, a jump in grade can easily double the value of an object.

When a sales transaction is direct, i.e., the buyer and seller are present and looking at the object, any question regarding condition can be immediately resolved. As the 1990s come to a close, the number of indirect sales transactions is increasing thanks in part to the growth of specialized trade periodicals and the Internet. More and more seller-buyer communication is in written form, either letter or e-mail. The buyer does not see the object until he has paid for it, his check has cleared, and the object arrives at his home or office. If a dispute arises over an object's anticipated versus actual condition, its resolution is time consuming, costly, and sometimes unsatisfactory. Smart sellers purposely under grade an object so that when the buyer receives it, he is pleased to find it better than expected.

I contacted an eBay seller about the condition of an object he was selling. The seller responded it was in good condition. Good condition means to me that an object has been heavily used and has noticeable damage on its surface. I e-mailed the seller asking if this was true and suggested he supply a telephone number so that we could resolve the issue. As a result, I determined the object was in very good to fine condition and willingly agreed to the asking price.

Not one to run from controversy, I offer the following condition grading scale for consideration in the attempt to establish a common condition vocabulary within the collectibles field. The scale is based on a unit of ten with one being the lowest grade and ten the highest.

Several ten-unit condition scales, e.g., the scales used by Richard O'Brien in his toy price guides and Ted Hake and Bill Bruegman in their collectibles mail auctions, already exist in the trade. My concerns are that (1) these scales are weighted too heavily toward the top end, i.e., they have too many grades above and not enough below very good and fine, the ideal mid-point, and (2) they are designed specifically to apply to a limited group of objects rather than the entire collectibles field.

There is a direct relationship between condition and completeness, just as there is between condition and value. An incomplete object should never be assigned a grade higher than good. This is especially true in today's market where buyers are condition crazy.

This is a controversial position. Some will argue that the loss of a minor piece should not result in such a severe negative assessment. They fail to take into consideration the cost to have an undetectable exact replacement piece made. A cost in excess of the final worth of the piece is far more common than they realize.

In respect to boxed objects, I view the object and the box as two separate entities. As a result, each should be graded individually. When an object is sold on a blister card package, the object and package are one single unit. Having clarified these points, my proposed scale is:

C1—Parts. A C1 object is an object from which parts can be salvaged to repair or complete the restoration of an identical object. A pocket watch that does not work or a boxed board game missing pieces are two examples of a parts object.

    I resisted the temptation to assign junk to a C1 object. Junk is junk. It belongs in the landfill. Junk is an object beyond salvage.

C2—Poor. This object looks as though it has been through at least one war. It shows extensive damage and/or wear. It is often missing major parts. The cost to restore it far exceeds the value of the finished product. It is an object that is teetering on the cliff above the landfill.

C3—Fair. An object that shows obvious signs of heavy use and
wear at first glance. It is often missing minor parts, usually not apparent at first glance. It is so bad that no serious
collector would consider displaying it.

The key to determining if an object is C4, C5, or C6 is known as
the arm's length test. Hold the object at arm's length and look at its visible surfaces. If there is noticeable damage, the object is C4 or below.
If there is slight noticeable damage, the object is C5. If there is no
noticeable damage, the object is C6 or above. Toy collectors differen-
tiate between C4 and C5 by noting that a C4 toy is heavily played with
and a C5 toy is lovingly played with. While this works for toys, it is
hard to apply to ceramics and glass.

Why an arm's length test? The answer is simple. This is the average distance from which one views an object on a shelf or in a cabinet.
Displayability is also a value key. Buyers place a premium on objects
that display well.

C4—Good. This object shows visible surface damage when
held at arm's length. It has minimal display value.
Restoration costs to bring it to fine or better condition still
exceed the value of the object after restoration.

This is the lowest collecting grade. Collectors purchase
examples of the scarcest objects (masterpiece and upper
echelon units) in their collecting category at this grade
with the intent to upgrade when a better example is found.
Commonly found objects in this condition have no value
appreciation potential.

C5—Very Good. An object that shows minor signs of use when
held at arm's length. Often one has to look two or three
times to spot the problems. The general assumption is that
the object has no serious defects, albeit "serious" is anoth
er term open to a broad range of interpretation. Repairs
and restoration are acceptable and usually detectable.

C6—Fine. An object with no detectable surface damage when
held at arm's length. However, problems associated with

wear and aging can be spotted when the object is examined closely. Any object with surface damage such as a minor chip or nick falls below this grade.

This is the minimum investment grade level for any antique or collectible made before 1970. While ideally this appearance should be achieved simply through the aging of a period piece, the field accepts objects brought to this level through repair and restoration.

C7—Very Fine. An object with no detectable surface damage; and, when examined closely, shows only the most minor wear and aging. Age and use have mellowed the object so that it no longer has its like new appearance. Bright and clean are often used to describe an object in this condition.

C8—Excellent. An object that retains its like new appearance. The slightest wear (usually confined to the edges) may be detectable on its visible surface but must not detract from the piece.

This is the highest grade that should be assigned to any object that has been repaired or restored. There is a quality difference between a restored object and a period object, i.e., an object as it left the factory.

This is also the minimum investment grade level for all objects made between 1970 and the early 1980s. The minimum investment grade level jumps to C9 for objects made after 1985.

C9—Near Mint. A period object that has lost a minute amount of assembly line luster, but retains a like new appearance. Very minor signs of wear may be detectable when examined very closely, but never on the visible surface.

C10—Mint. A period object that appears to have just left the assembly line. It is flawless on its visible and non-visible surfaces. It requires microscopic examination to determine that it is not new. Few surviving objects, less than one in a thousand, meet this standard.

My proposal for a universal condition grading standard is tough. I strongly believe these are minimum, not maximum criteria. Applying them involves using one's head, not one's heart.

Do I expect everyone to agree with them? Absolutely not! My goal is to encourage discussion of this issue. Judging from some of my recent attempts to achieve similar goals on other topics, I suspect I will not have long to wait.

Self-Evident Truths and Unalienable Rights

"We hold these Truths to be self-evident, that all Men are created equal, that they are endowed by their Creator with certain unalienable Rights, that among these are Life, Liberty, and the Pursuit of Happiness..."—Declaration of Independence.

The Institute for the Study of Antiques and Collectibles, which offers a series of courses designed to enhance the education of collector, dealers, and others in the antiques and collectibles trade, is alive and well. I have taught at Kutztown University in Pennsylvania, and Portland State University in Oregon. An antique dealer accreditation program in cooperation with the Antiques and Collectibles Dealers Association is one of the Institute's goals.

The Institute courses are taught with the underlying premise that selling antiques and collectibles at a profit is hard work. The approach is hard-nosed and realistic. The pluses and minuses of the profession are thoroughly discussed and analyzed.

One of the institute's core courses that I have taught is "Successfully Buying Antiques and Collectibles." During the course, I explored several business myths that I felt antiques and collectibles dealers assumed were self-evident truths and inalienable rights. The discussion began with the myth that every antique dealer deserves a profit on every item he sells. There is simply no truth to this statement. Before I knew it, I was on a roll. Thanks to a handy flip chart, I began making a list of these mythical self-evident truths and inalienable rights. When I was done, I looked at the list and thought—column!

I strongly suspect some in the trade will not find what follows humorous. So be it. I repeatedly tell the Institute students that my goal is to make them thinkers not robots. I want them to look in the mirror and ask tough questions of themselves in respect to their business practices, not blindly accept past practice because it is "the way things were always done."

The following antique dealer self-evident truths and inalienable rights are myths and not God-given rights. When confronted with them, do not accept them. However, think twice about arguing with their proponents. You will never convince them they are wrong. Just walk away and shake your head.

MYTH 1: My price is the right price. I set it.

There is no right price for any antique or collectible. All value is relative, subject to time, place, and a wide variety of other circumstances. Buyers are unaccustomed to questioning the price found on objects on the Internet, in an antiques mall, or at antiques show. They assume the dealer's asking price is correct and begin their purchasing consideration from that point.

The asking price is not right simply because the seller set it. It needs to stand the test against the prices on all similar pieces offered for sale in the current market. If a buyer does not have the knowledge to make that comparison, he is well advised to do his homework.

In the final analysis, the only right price is what the buyer is willing to pay. If the price does not reflect this amount, the buyer is well advised to walk away.

MYTH 2: I am entitled to the top price for every antique and collectible I sell.

Top price is the maximum that can be achieved for an object. It is the price a collector will pay who does not own the object and absolutely has to have it immediately. Less than one percent of one percent of buyers of antiques and collectibles meet this requirement. The remaining buyers are influenced by other buying considerations. They have little to no interest in paying top dollar.

Based on my observations, it is far more common to sell objects in the trade at high wholesale or low retail than high retail. If a dealer sells one-tenth of his inventory at top dollar, he should consider himself gifted.

MYTH 3: I am entitled to a profit on every item I sell.

Life would be idyllic if this were true. Every merchant knows this is a fallacy. Merchants would be thrilled if they could sell half their inventory for full price. Merchants live in a world of discounts and the harsh reality that there are times when you sell at a loss. Unsold merchandise is non-working capital. When necessary, you must sell at a loss to get back in the game.

The vast majority of antiques and collectibles are sold at discount. List price is a running joke in the trade. Every price is negotiable. The key question is—by how much? In today's market, some of the discounts are deep, i.e., over 30 percent.

MYTH 4: When a deal is done, I am the winner. Every sale is a contest between the buyer and me. No deal is a good deal unless "I made a killing."

The vast majority of sellers in the trade persist in making the selling of an antique or collectible a contest or, worse yet, a test of will. A sale is an epic battle in which there is a winner and a loser. No individual, no army, and no country ever won every battle.

Merchants know that a good deal is a win-win deal, a deal in which both parties go away happy and each feels it is a winner.

MYTH 5: God will provide a buyer for my things. If my object has not sold, it is because God has not yet sent me the right buyer. Because of this, I have absolutely no need for you as a customer. If you do not buy it, someone else will.

Is there a buyer for every object? The answer is no. If an object is in a condition that does not justify its price or it is priced right out of the market, it will not sell.

Few antiques and collectibles dealers take the time and make the effort to cultivate customers. Dealers do not ask buyers for their names, addresses, phone numbers, or e-mail addresses so they can contact their former customer when they find something else they think he might wish to buy.

Dealers will bring an object to a show for a favorite customer. However, few take the time to contact the customer and tell them they are doing this. If the customer shows, life is fine and dandy. If not, the dealer will add it to his display and offer it for sale to the general public.

In the antiques and collectibles trade, the best customer is not a customer that buys for a third or fourth time. The best customer is the one that has walked out of the blue, made a purchase, and disappears from the scene never to reappear again.

MYTH 6: I am entitled to always do better than my competition. If I have a good month, it is alright for someone else to have a good month. If I have a bad month, no one else is entitled to have a good month.

The green-eyed jealously monster is alive and well in the antiques and collectibles trade. Being happy and thrilled for a competitor, whether fellow collector or dealer, who has done well is the exception rather than the rule.

It is the individual dealer who controls whether he does well or not in a given time period. If he has not, the best place to find the reason is his mirror. Success in the trade has little to do with fate, and everything to do with hard work.

MYTH 7: How dare you question what I say? I am always right. I know everything. I am the authority.

Question all who profess to be experts in this trade, even the individual writing this column. The field is rife with inaccurate trade and research information. Opinions outweigh verifiable facts.

The wonderful thing about the antiques and collectibles field is that there is rarely one right answer. In truth, there are many right answers. The right answer for a person is the one that works best for him.

On the other hand, facts are facts. The problem is that so much information in the trade is regurgitated that facts become distorted. Writers borrow and rework information without ever questioning whether or not it was accurate in the first place. Original research in the antiques and collectibles trade is not standard. The key to survival is a mindset that questions everything.

Which, of course, leads to my final point—question and think about everything you have just read. If you do, I will have achieved my goal.

CHAPTER 6

Selling the Goodies— Heaven Forbid

Selling antiques and collectibles is an unnatural act. Collectors love every object they acquire. When I lecture, I sometimes note that I would sell my children into slavery before selling my favorite antique or collectible. Everyone laughs. They think I am joking. The laugh is on them.

When deciding what to include in this book, I originally had no intentions of including a chapter on selling. The concept is an anathema to me.

Unfortunately, necessity dictates that occasionally a collector must sell. The reasons are many, ranging from divorce to downsizing to financial hard times. It is a bullet I hope I never have to bite.

If collectors do have to sell, their expectations are clouded by the love they have for their possessions. Their expectations are highly unrealistic. Each object sold tears at their collecting soul and leaves a void in their heart.

Advice is easy to offer. If you do have to sell, my recommendation is to read this chapter over and over again until you understand it. Note, I said understand it, not believe it. I know not to ask too much.

The Selling Price

I have visited this topic in the past, and I try hard not to repeat myself. However, when a column has been around awhile—in the case of "Rinker on Collectibles" almost fifteen years—new readers may not have read or regular readers may have forgotten an earlier column.

Claudine Fuhrman of Bethlehem, Pennsylvania, wrote: "When a writer quotes an antiques and collectibles price guide reference source, how much of the quoted value can someone realistically expect to get if he or she sells that item? What percentage of that amount would be a fair price to expect upon sale if the object were in very good condition. I realize many factors enter in. I was just wondering about a ball-park figure. Judging from what I have read in your column, the stated value and resale value are not the same."

This is a timely time to revisit this topic, especially given the economic concerns facing America and the world as a whole. While the "r" word, recession, remains in the background, collectors have begun looking at what they might sell, ideally in hopes of raising capital to buy pieces they need, or, sadly, in order to obtain funds to survive the current economic upheaval.

There are no fixed prices for antiques and collectibles. Value floats based on time, place, and individuals involved. I have lost track of the number of times I have written this. I think of myself as a stuck record. Yet, it is essential to establish this point before proceeding further.

Price guide prices are merely a guide to retail prices—what a collector would pay if he (1) does not own the object and (2) desires to buy the object. If correct, price guide prices represent high retail. Further, they generally assume the object is at least in very good condition. Some price guides use fine condition as the condition basis for their values. Only a small number, my guess is between ten and fifteen percent at most, of objects in any collecting category meet this condition standard.

Further, experienced collectors question all prices, especially those found in price guides. Price guide prices should be field tested, i.e., prices found in the guide should conform within a narrow range, plus or minus 10 percent, to those at which identical pieces are selling at flea markets, antiques malls and shows, or on the Internet. Note, I wrote "selling" and not "listed for sale." Alas, some price guides are designed to prop a market rather than reflect realistic market prices. This is certainly true of a select few price guides focusing on a single collecting category. On the whole, the general market guides are relatively accurate. However, even these contain errors. Question, question, question.

In order to proceed, assume the value found in the price guide is a true reflection of the price at which the piece typically sells in the market. The price guide value is retail, not wholesale. As such, it reflects the profit expected by the seller and most likely the profits made by other individuals in a chain of buyers and sellers until it finally was removed from the market by a buyer who kept it for a period of time, usually several years.

Individuals understand if they buy something at retail and attempt to resell it within a short period following the purchase, they are not likely to recover anywhere near the initial purchase cost. Modern speculative desirables, such as Beanie Babies, are an exception. But, as Beanie Baby collectors discovered, speculative bubbles always burst.

Claudine is correct in assuming many factors determine the value of an object. However, individuals constantly ask me if there is a quick calculation method. There is, albeit I strongly suspect many individuals, especially dealers, will disagree.

It is necessary to make one more assumption before proceeding—the object in question is in very good or better condition. "Very good" means that the object has no visible defects when viewed at arm's length and is complete.

Perceived price guide value and availability are the two key elements that determine potential resale value. Further, they are closely related. Objects that are most available tend to have the lowest price point within a collecting category. The low price point is different in each collecting category. In the case of carnival chalkware it is around $25. It is around $4 for playing card decks and $500 for early twentieth-century cameo glass.

Here are the general rules that apply in attempting to determine (1) the likelihood that the object will sell and (2) at what value against price guide price, also know as "book price," it will sell. If the book price is $25 or less, it is best you place your desire to sell on hold and move on to something else. Objects valued below $25 tend to be extremely common, i.e., you are likely to encounter up to a dozen examples or closely related examples within a single sales environment, e.g., a flea market or antiques show. Sellers try to buy these objects at ten to twenty cents on the dollar. New dealers paying $10 to $15 for an object they hope to list at $25 is one of the primary reasons that many are out of the business in less than five years. After you factor in the time, energy, and costs you have to expend in hopes of receiving half of the price guide retail price, there is no way you can economically justify the effort.

Expect to recover between 25 and 35 percent of book price on objects valued between $50 and $250. These values still reflect objects that are readily available in the marketplace. Again, you may not receive adequate compensation for your efforts.

The percentage improves to 35 to 45 percent of retail book value for objects valued between $250 and $2,500. Because of the amount of money involved, there is sufficient incentive to do the necessary market research to determine where such objects are best sold. Also, the potential profit margin per piece is greater, enough to encourage a dealer to take a risk.

Increase the percentage to 50 to 60 percent for objects valued between $2,500 and $10,000. Scarcity now becomes a value issue. Objects in this value range are attractive to large auction houses. However, their commission rates range from 10 to 15 percent to the seller, something that can reduce the anticipated return if the objects are sold below retail book value.

Check the general price guides, especially those focused on twentieth-century collectibles sold at flea markets. What you will find is that the majority of the categories contain objects with values less than $250, many contain values primarily under $50. These are the value ranges where the selling price of an object is most volatile.

There are those private sellers who feel they are entitled to and, quite frankly, deserve book price. No problem. If you want book price, become an antiques and collectibles dealer. In doing so, understand you will now incur all the expenses involved, whether you sell at flea markets, an antiques mall, or on the Internet. My advice to private individuals wishing to sell collectibles is if someone is willing to pay 40 percent or more of book price, take the money and run.

Ask a dealer how often they get book price. If they are honest, it will be far less often than you imagine. Between haggling and everyone's desire to buy at a bargain, book price is just as elusive to some dealers as it is to private individuals.

Finally, the best selling price is one that makes you happy. If you never receive it, keep the object. I assure you that your heirs will not be as hard-nosed as you.

Where Can I Sell It?

When someone asks me, "What is my object worth?" he often continues by asking "And, where can I sell it?"

What he really wants to know is where he can sell the object for the amount I tell him it is worth. The simple answer is he cannot. While the reason for this discrepancy is evident to me, it often is not to the person asking the question.

When a person asks me to value an object, I provide the secondary market retail value, i.e., what it would cost to buy that object at an antiques shop or show. I often qualify my answer by providing a second value—the price at which the object can be bought on the Internet via direct sale or an auction site such as eBay. If the person inquires about the value of the object if sold at auction, I provide a third value.

Value is market dependent. The price of the same object can differ, and often significantly, depending on the market in which it is offered for sale. The concept of value in the antiques and collectibles field is complex. It is not easy to understand. All value is relative. There are no fixed values in the antiques and collectibles field.

Before discussing the sale venues for antiques and collectibles that are open to members of the general public, I want to propose a set of reasonable percentages against book value that the seller can expect. In this instance, book value represents the retail value found in an accurate antiques and collectibles price guide. Remember, not all price guides are accurate. Alas, far too many antiques and collectibles price guides, especially one-category or one-topic guides, are authored to support or, at worst, manipulate market prices.

Book Value	Seller's Percentage
Under $25	10%
$25 to $100	20% to 25%
$250 to $500	30%
$500 to $2,500	40%
$2,500 to $5,000	50%
$5,000 to $10,000	55%
$10,000 to $50,000	60%
$50,000 and above	65% to 75%

Based upon these numbers, here are a few rules to remember:

RULE #1: The higher the book value, the higher the percentage of return against book.

RULE #2: While there are many factors that influence value, availability (how many of the objects there are around) is one of the major ones. A low book value generally means that supply exceeds demand. However, it also can mean that the object is out of fashion and there simply are no buyers for it.

RULE #3: Selling objects valued under $100 is more likely to frustrate rather than satisfy the seller.

RULE #4: Personal attachment and family value do not translate into monetary value.

RULE #5: Dealers have to make a profit. Therefore, they cannot buy at book or close to book. Fifty cents on the dollar is extremely generous.

RULE #6: Collectors expect to pay book price when buying from dealers. They expect to pay the same percentages as dealers when buying from the general public.

What selling options are available to members of the general public who wish to dispose of their antiques and collectibles?

The initial reaction is to sell the objects privately. Personally, I like it when a member of the general public pursues this course. There is no better way to educate someone to the amount of work and expense involved with selling antiques and collectibles. If the seller keeps track of his time and expenses, chances are he will find (1) he is working for below minimum wage and (2) although he would have received less, he would have been far better off taking one of the other selling options.

The most obvious private route is to a collector. There are numerous sources to find buyers, both in print and on the Internet. However, most of the individuals listed are advanced collectors. They have no interest in buying commonly found items.

The best private source is family and friends. Make a list of those individuals who visit and say, "If you ever want to sell that, give me a call." Many times these purchasers' hearts, not their heads, govern what they are willing to pay.

When the vast majority of objects book for less than $50, consider renting a table or booth at a local flea market to sell the objects. Give it one shot. Box lot or junk the objects that do not sell. Do not frustrate yourself.

If the book value is less than $25 per object, a garage sale is the answer. Again, the goal is to dispose of the objects. At the end of the day, give away, bulk sale, or trash whatever remains.

If a single object has substantial book value or the seller has a large and highly diverse amount of objects to sell, my recommendation is to use the auction route. If the number of objects is limited and the person is computer literate, the obvious first choice is an Internet auction. If the objects are numerous and the per object value above $100, use a strong regional auction house. When the per object value is below $100, a local "box lot" auctioneer is fine.

When choosing the auction route, sellers should be aware of the cost of sale (percentage and other fees charged by the auctioneer) and the fact that most of the prospective buyers are dealers who expect to pay half or less of book value. The advantage is that the sale is a once and done proposition. Sellers should look at the final number and be happy.

Dealers buy privately. When selling in this situation, knowledge is power. If the seller has not done his homework, he is at a distinct disadvantage. Further, dealers often only want to buy the cream of what the seller is offering for sale. They do not want the junk, i.e., hard-to-sell items. Sellers who wish to dispose of a large block of items need to adopt a "take it all or not at all" approach.

When selling to a dealer, do a package deal. It becomes extremely confusing and time consuming when negotiating on a piece-by-piece basis.

Do not expect the dealer to make an offer. That is a free appraisal. If you ask the dealer to make an offer and then refuse it, you have utilized his expertise without compensating him for it.

It is the seller's responsibility to set the initial asking price. The buyer's responsibility is to say yes, no, or make a counteroffer. If a seller does not know what to ask or is unwilling to do his own homework, he should hire the services of an independent appraiser.

Finally, when the book value for a single object or group of miscellaneous objects is low, consider giving them away or sending them to the landfill. While the seller will not have money in pocket, with the exception of a possible tax deduction if the objects are gifted to a nonprofit organization that plans to sell them at a bazaar, he will have peace of mind. Never discount the importance of the latter.

CHAPTER 7

Period, Reproduction, Copycat, Fantasy, or Fake

How do I know that the object I am buying is what it is supposed to be? This question haunts collectors.

When I talk about this issue, I remind collectors that there are two critical questions about every object: (1) What is it? and (2) What is it worth? It is impossible to answer the second question without having a valid answer to the first.

Authentication is the process used to determine what an object is. In the past, collectors relied heavily on sellers' expertise to provide the answers. Today, due in large part to the tremendous lack of knowledge on the part of Internet sellers, collectors have learned that the burden of authentication falls entirely on them. Caveat emptor, *let the buyer beware, has never been more true.*

Authentication issues are many. There is no agreement on a common language. Value judgments are far more subjective than objective. Most collectors and sellers have limited or no training in the area of authentication.

What follows is only an introduction to the subject. Learning authentication skills is a continuing lifelong necessity. No one said collecting was easy.

What Are the Correct Terms?

You cannot tell a player without a scorecard. You cannot properly communicate about antiques and collectibles unless everyone is talking the same language. This is especially true in the area of authentication.

I want to discuss the incorrect terms before discussing the correct ones. Every time I hear the words old, genuine, real, original, unique, and rare I cringe. These are meaningless words in the antiques and collectibles field.

Old is a relative term. Let me explain this so you understand. When I was twenty, forty-year-old women were old. When I was batching it in my early sixties, forty-year-old women were just right, albeit I confess I found far more in common with the fifty-year-old women I dated. What is old depends entirely on how young you are. The 1950s is old to a person in their twenties. It is yesterday to a sixty-year-old like me.

Real and genuine are truly meaningless. If you are looking at an object, trust me it is real and genuine. Be honest. You never saw an antique or collectible marked unreal or non-genuine. Do not be deceived by these words.

Original is somewhat trickier. If a seller says this piece has the original finish, he means the finish that was first applied to the piece. If a seller says this piece has an original finish, it could have been applied yesterday. Learning to tell the difference between "the" and "an" is about as ridiculous as trying to separate "inhaled" from "did not inhale" when people try to justify their pot smoking. Why quibble when there are more appropriate words.

Rare and unique have become obsolete terms. Do an eBay search of "rare." You find tens of thousands of listings. It is the one time in the trade I almost died from laughter. We deal today with mass-produced goods, goods made in quantities of hundreds of thousands and millions. Their survival rate is high. There is nothing rare or unique about them. If you need further proof, check eBay. Rare and unique are merchandising, not descriptive terms.

I also want to talk about the style alarm bell before talking about proper terminology. Style means reproduction. It is a definition that is found in the glossary of most auction catalogs. A Sotheby's furniture catalog includes this explanation: "Chippendale Style Mahogany Chest of Drawers. The inclusion of the word 'style' in the heading indicates that, in our opinion, the piece was made as an intentional reproduction of an earlier style."

The problem with style is that it is often used to describe design characteristics. For example, a description that might read: "This chair includes elements of the Chippendale design style such as a wave crest, pierced splats, trapezoidal seat, cabriole legs, and ball and claw feet." When used to describe design elements, it is critical that the phrase "design style" be used rather than simply "style."

If the above terms are wrong, what terms are right?

An object that is correct is a period object. Period is used to describe an object that was made during the time when its design style was first introduced or during its initial period of manufacture. Once a design style enters the design vocabulary, it often continues for an extended period of time. You can find Chippendale style chairs made in the 1830s, 1880s, 1930s, and 2005. An American Chippendale period chair was made between 1750 and 1780, the period when the style was first introduced.

Period has many interpretations, especially when talking about objects made after 1945. It may refer to the first edition or period of initial release. Today, manufacturers save molds and patterns used to manufacture objects. If renewed interest occurs, they roll out these molds and patterns and reproduce exact copies of the period pieces. If they do not mark them properly, these later issues are virtually impossible to distinguish from their period counterparts. When I can identify them, I refer to them as restrikes, borrowing a term from print collecting.

Period also may refer to the lifetime of a personality or period when a group was together. Period Elvis ended on August 22, 1977. Or, did it? Is Elvis still alive? Period Beatles objects were licensed between 1964 and 1970, the period between the group's arrival in America and their break-up.

Reproduction is one of most misused terms in the antiques and collectibles field. When used properly, reproduction means an exact copy of a period piece. When a reproduction is placed side by side with a period piece, it is identical.

What then distinguishes one from another? The answer is twofold. The first is age and wear. If the reproduction is new, it will not have the same aging and wear characteristics as the period piece. However, if the reproduction is seventy-five years old or older, it may well have.

When this occurs, the saving grace is construction technique. The tools used to make reproductions often differ from those used to make period pieces. When one looks carefully, one finds construction variations, especially inside and on non-visible surfaces such as the back and bottom. It is these variations that are the authentication keys.

Copycats are what most individuals refer to as reproductions. A copycat is a stylistic reproduction, a "close but no cigar" object. When viewed from a distance, it appears to be period. When examined closely, it proves not to be.

Copycats abound. If placed side by side with a period piece, the differences between the two are obvious. Copycats vary over a wide range of areas, e.g., different size, color, pattern variation, composition, etc. Problems result when the collector does not have a period piece with which to compare.

Do not make the false assumption that copycats are poorly made. Many are made as well or better than the period pieces.

A fantasy is an object in an historical design style that did not exist when the design style was first introduced. This sounds complicated, but it is not. A few examples will clarify the picture. If you go to a modern furniture store, you will find coffee tables featuring Chippendale design styles and end tables featuring Hepplewhite and Sheraton design styles. Coffee tables and end tables are twentieth-century furniture forms. These forms did not exist when these design styles were first introduced.

Two other types of fantasy items are worth noting. Items licensed after a personality died or a group disbanded are correctly referred to as fantasies. The Elvis estate continues to issue licenses. Coca-Cola has no problem licensing its image to fantasy pieces in addition to authorizing a host of reproductions and copycats.

Items issued by fan clubs also are correctly labeled as fantasy material. Such material abounds at *Star Trek* and *Star Wars* conventions. Collectors' clubs often authorize special issue products as part of their annual conventions.

Reproductions, copycats, and fantasies appear in quantity. They are easy to spot when they first appear. Unfortunately, as time passes, memory of them fades. Subsequent generations of collectors can be confused. Further, reproductions, copycats, and fantasies can be collectible in their own right. 1950s and 1960s Fenton Burmese glass is a great example. It sells for almost as much as the period pieces from the end of the nineteenth and early part of the twentieth century.

A fake is an item that is deliberately meant to deceive. It is its deception that differentiates it from period pieces, reproductions, copycats, and fantasies. Fakes often are one-of-a-kind objects. They were made to be misrepresented and often sell far in excess of the piece's fair market value if properly represented.

Fakes also can be mass produced. Knockoff is the common term applied to these objects. Knockoffs usually occur during the initial period of popularity and manufacture. They sell for a fraction of the cost of the copied piece and are a deliberate attempt to defraud a licensing agency or manufacturer. Their appearance is often short-lived. However, they appear to have achieved a new sales source through Internet spam. Again, the problem does not rest in the immediate present but in the future. Knockoffs are poorly documented. One of the hardest things I ever had to do was tell a family that their mother's beloved Shirley Temple doll was a cheap knockoff rather than one of the properly licensed Ideal dolls.

Why do reproductions, copycats, and fantasies exist? The answer rests with the high cost of period pieces. Individuals looking for look and usability rather than authenticity find them perfectly acceptable. I have no problem with them either, provided they are sold for what they are.

Why do fakes and knockoffs exist and why are reproductions, copycats and fantasies passed off as period pieces? The answer is twofold. The first is greed. There are individuals who prefer the easy buck over an honest approach. The second is the pleasure some people get from deceiving others. These individuals should be drummed out of the trade. If you spot one, spread the word.

Ten Common Sense Rules To Determine if an Object Is Period, Reproduction, Copycat, Fantasy, or Fake

The hardest thing for me to convince the students taking "Authenticating Antiques and Collectibles" at my Institute for the Study of Antiques and Collectibles is that the same basic rules apply no matter what the collecting category. A student tells me he can authenticate furniture, but cannot authenticate ceramics, glass, metals, paper, etc. Another student tells me he can authenticate ceramics, but does not know glass, furniture, metals, paper, etc. I tell each of them that if they know how to authenticate one category, they can authenticate them all.

Authenticating is a state of mind. It can be learned. The learning process is slow at first. The person has to learn to follow the same mental exercise piece after piece. As the authenticator becomes more experienced, the process accelerates. The goal is to authenticate instinctively. It can be done.

In order to help students learn the authenticating process, I have developed ten common sense rules they need to follow. When I explain the process, I strongly suspect your immediate reaction will be, "I knew that." You might have known it, but did you think about it? Thinking is the key.

In the case of authenticating, thinking means questioning. Good authenticators are by necessity skeptics. They take nothing at face value. While such an attitude does not make them the most popular people in the antiques and collectibles trade, they are the least likely to make mistakes; mistakes that often can prove quite costly.

RULE 1: Assume every piece is a reproduction, copycat, fantasy, or fake until it proves otherwise. It is the French system of justice— GUILTY UNTIL PROVEN INNOCENT.

One of the biggest mistakes in the antiques and collectibles field is that we want to believe in an object rather than question it. We read a label and assume it is right. We accept what we are told as gospel, especially if it comes from a dealer or other authority figure in the trade. Bad mistake!

Do not be clouded by love at first sight. This is when the worst mistakes are made. Court an object before you fall in love with it.

Question everything about the object from its form, shape, construction, size, pattern, etc. Does it conform to what you expect? Flush the concept of one-of-a-kind from your memory bank. Almost everything you deal with is mass-produced. Everything about it should conform to the standards of the period in which it was produced.

This rule and the rules that follow are designed to set off alarm bells in your mind. An alarm bell rings when something does not conform to what you expect. Learn from the beginning to trust these alarm bells. When they go off, something is definitely the wrong.

RULE 2: If it looks new, it probably is. Look in the mirror and ask this question: "Do I look today like I looked twenty years ago?" You know the answer without me having to tell you what it is. You age. So do antiques and collectibles.

God did not put or expect objects put on earth to look new after twenty-five years, let alone one hundred or more years. Objects were made to be used. They should show signs of aging and wear.

It is important to understand the difference between aging and wear. Aging is the result of oxidation (the chemicals in the area) and patination (the dirt in the area). The trade uses the term patina to describe the overall effect of the two processes. As objects age, they mellow. Mellowing often produces a softer look than the object had initially.

Wear is what happens to the object when it is handled. The next time you pick up an object note where you place your hands. This is a location where you should expect to find wear. Get down on your hands and knees. No, I do not want you to pray. I want you to crawl around the floor examining the base of objects. Look for signs of wear such as scuff marks from shoes or pings and dings from vacuum cleaners and other household cleaning devices. The next time you sit in a chair, note where your back rests. This area should show more signs of wear than the area around it. Given all this, if you are asked to examine a hundred-year-old table and see no signs of any damage to the bottom of the feet, your alarm bells should ring.

If you want to become a good authenticator, you need to be constantly aware of your immediate surroundings. Every time you handle or see something is an opportunity to learn.

I am aware of the claims that grandmother received the object on the day of her marriage, put it in a chest or closet, and never used it. Objects age just sitting around. Textiles will have fold lines. Glass that has been exhibited in a china cabinet will show scratch marks on the base where it was dragged across the dust.

RULE 3: Whenever possible, examine all objects in natural sunlight. Light is your friend. It also is your enemy.

Many women readers will attest to the fact that they bought a piece of clothing in a store because they loved the color, but when they wore it outside, the color changed. Color is critical to authenticating and even value, in some cases. Artificial light of any type distorts color. Florescent light is the worst of all.

Try this experiment. Examine a wooden chair from a dining room set inside. Take it outside and look again. You will be surprised at how much more you see.

When using light to examine a piece, make certain to use raking light. If you stand directly under a light, glare bounces back in your face preventing you from seeing everything. Rake light in from the side.

Further, turn and angle whatever you are examining in the raking light. What you cannot see at one angle, you will be able to see from another.

Again, pay attention to how you normally handle an object. When held in a normal position, your eyes want the object to be whole. Your eyes often will deceive you by correcting any problems. It is not until you twist and turn objects so they are in unnatural positions that your eyes provide a true picture of the piece.

RULE 4: Examine all aspects and sides of an object. How many sides does a two-dimensional object have? If you remember your high school geometry, the answer is two. How many sides does a three-dimensional object have? The stock high school answer—top, bottom, front, back, left side, right side—is six. This is not correct in the antiques and collectibles field. What side is missing? The answer is the inside.

The inside is critical in the antiques and collectibles field. Restorers and fakers devote their attention to the visible surfaces, the surfaces that people see. They work on making these surfaces conform to what one expects. They rarely care about the inside. They assume no one is going to look inside. Do not fall victim to their assumption.

Develop a checklist mentality to make certain you learn to use this rule correctly. Every time you pick up an object, mentally check off a side. If it is two-sided, think front and then back. Do not forget to rake light over the object from several different angles. If it is three-dimensional, do top, front, left side, and right side. Then remove the object from where it is resting and examine the back. Turn it upside down and examine the bottom. Finally, look inside.

If an object comes apart, take it apart. This is the tricky part of this rule. First, do not take an object apart unless you can put it back together. I have done this more times than I care to recount. Second, do not take an object apart without the permission of the owner.

You cannot properly examine an object in a frame without taking it out of the frame. You need to determine if the object had been trimmed to be placed in the frame, whether mat or backing board is glued to the object, and whether the object is on the proper paper or printed with the correct technology consistent with its period of origin.

RULE 5: Check for consistency. Consistency is the key. Every authenticator needs to learn a series of historical period vocabularies—form, shape, size, color, pattern, construction, weight, etc. These provide the basis against which every subsequent object is compared.

Take color as example. If I say black and white, you think 1950s. If I say avocado, golden harvest, or rust, you think 1970s. Every time period has its favorite color combination. You can learn these combinations by paying attention when you handle an object that has been properly authenticated. When an object is stated to be from a specific period and the color does not match your expectation, off goes the alarm bell.

Color tone also changes over time. Pick a color and study it as well. Most authenticators chose blue or red. I prefer green. The tone of 1930s green differs significantly from 1960s green. Again, this is something you have to memorize. Developing authenticating skills is a continuing educational process.

Color is just a starting point. You have to develop the same skill set for form, shape, size, pattern, construction, weight, and whatever other areas apply to your favorite collecting categories. One of the easiest ways to see the shift in period shapes is to study creamer and sugar sets. Novice collectors often confuse late nineteenth-century creamers with small milk pitchers.

Consistency also applies to wear. Is wear where and of the type you expect to find? Fakers fake wear. However, it often is in all the wrong places. Make every wear mark explain itself. If you cannot explain the wear, ring the alarm bell.

RULE 6: Follow the Lindquist Apology Theory: "If a dealer apologizes for a piece more than four or five times or if you find four or five major things wrong with the piece, accept the inevitable conclusion that the piece has been highly restored, reconstructed, or is an outright fake." David Lindquist of Whitehall at the Villa, Chapel Hill, North Carolina, is one of the best authenticators I know. I had the privilege of teaching authenticating courses with him. As a team, I think we were unbeatable.

David's concept is that if a piece is wrong, it is going to be wrong in many ways, not just one. I agree. Once I discover one problem, I quickly find myself discovering more. While it might be possible to explain away one concern, it is impossible to explain away a half-dozen.

Alas, one's heart often tells you to continue in hopes that your concerns will be alleviated. Listen to your mind and not your heart.

RULE 7: Beware of bargains. If the price is low and the piece appears to be a tremendous bargain, be doubly alert. Every collector loves to find a bargain. A bargain sets off the alarm bell in the mind of every authenticator.

Reproductions, copycats, and fantasy items usually appear in the market at bargain prices. "You get what you pay for" is the adage that applies.

In fairness, every collector can regale you with stories about the bargains he found along the way. Yes, the antiques and collectibles field is loaded with bargains. Knowledge is power, and those who are knowledgeable can and do find bargains. However, they also know when to walk away. Sometimes the best bargain is the object you do not buy.

Fakes often appear on the market at, near, or even above bargain prices. Remember, they are meant to deceive. Hence, just because an object is fairly priced does not meant that it is authentic.

RULE 8: Develop a research file and study collection of reproduction, copycat, fantasy, and fake items in your collecting interests. Acquire catalogs from reproduction houses, save clippings on the subject from trade papers and magazines and collectors' club newsletters, and acquire examples that you can compare side by side with period pieces.

It is essential to remember that reproductions, copycats, fantasies, and fakes have been around for centuries. This is not a recent problem. While it is critical to keep current, it also is essential to backtrack. Be on the alert for out-of-print books and collectors' club newsletters.

Never assume you have found everything. Your search must be continuous.

RULE 9: Acquire these five books and read them once a year:

Chevenka, Mark. *Antique Trader Guide to Fakes & Reproductions.* Iola, WI: Antique Trade Books, A Division of Krause Publications: 2001. There are now several volumes in this series. Acquire them all.

Field, Rachael. *Macdonald Guide to Buying Antique Furniture.* London: copyright by Brooks Stephenson Publishing Ltd. 1986. Distributed in the United States by Wallace-Homestead Book Company. Out-of-print.

Hammond, Dorothy. *Confusing Collectibles: A Guide to the Identification of Contemporary Objects.* Des Moines, IA: copyright by the author, published by Wallace-Homestead: 1969. Revised printing, 1979. Out-of-print. Only buy the 1979 printing.

Kaye, Myrna. *Fake, Fraud, or Genuine?: Identifying Authentic American Antique Furniture.* Boston: copyright by the author, published by Little, Brown and Company: 1987.

Lee, Ruth Webb. *Antique Fakes & Reproductions.* Wellesley
   Hills, MA: 1950. Only consult the 4th through the 8th editions. Out-of-print.

You can purchase copies of out-of-print books on websites such
as www.abebooks.com and www.bookfinder.com. Make certain you
buy the appropriate edition.

Further, you also can ask your local reference librarian to obtain
copies of the books on interlibrary loan. Make photocopies of the pages
that apply to your collecting interests.

I read Field and Kaye once a year. I learn something new each
time I do. Remember, the key is to learn authenticating techniques and
apply them universally throughout the field. Most of the furniture
authenticating skills transfer to ceramics, collectibles, glass, metals,
paper, toys, etc.

RULE 10: Handle five hundred authenticated examples, and you
never will have problems spotting reproductions, copycats, fantasies,
and fakes again. Fred Weiser, an expert in Pennsylvania German fraktur, offered me this advice when I asked him how he learned his authenticating skills. I followed Fred's advice not only for fraktur but every
collecting category in which I had an interest.

Where can you handle five hundred authenticated examples? A
private collection, a specialized auction, a dealer's shop or booth, or a
museum are four obvious answers. I am fortunate. I receive dozens of
invitations to visit collectors each year. Whenever I can, I accept.
During my visits, I always ask them if their collection includes
reproductions, copycats, fantasies, and fakes. If they answer yes, as
they almost always do, I ask them to show me these items and share
with me how they knew they were not period pieces. It is a great
learning experience.

Likewise, I often visit museums to handle objects in their study
collections. Museums rarely display all their holdings. In fact, they
usually have more objects in storage than on display. With the right
approach, one can get permission to handle these objects.

These ten rules will give you a start on the road to becoming a
qualified authenticator. They only are a start. As indicated earlier, the
education process is continuous. Knowledge is cumulative in the

antiques and collectibles field. This is why old-timers, like me, are highly valued.

Finally, there are three other things I want to recommend. First, spread the word. Share your knowledge. Nothing destroys interest in a collecting category faster than reproductions, copycats, fantasies, and fakes being bought as period pieces. The faster the word is spread, the quicker the category can recover.

Second, consider subscribing to *Antique & Collectors Reproduction News* (PO Box 12130, Des Moines, IA 50312). The annual subscription is $32. Consider purchasing the back issues of this important periodical. For the latest information visit the website, www.repronews.com.

Finally, consider attending the two-day authenticating course offered by the Institute for the Study of Antiques and Collectibles. Information about the course's availability can be found on my website, www.harryrinker.com.

Reproductions, Copycats, Fantasy Items from the Past

For the past eighteen months I have been purchasing trading stamp redemption catalogs. My goal is to assemble a complete catalog run for Blue Chip, Gold Bond, Plaid, S & H Green, and Top Value trading stamps supplemented by samples from fifty or more additional trading stamp companies. Thanks to the Internet, primarily eBay, I have passed the halfway mark in achieving my goal.

In doing an eBay search several weeks ago, I found a listing for a lot of eight catalogs, one of which was a 1975 Top Value Stamps redemption catalog. I already owned a copy of that catalog. However, I will buy duplicates if the price is a bargain, i.e., cheap, cheap, cheap.

When I called up the listing, I was delighted, no ecstatic, to find it contained three catalogs from A.A. Importing—No. 37 (1978), No. 38 (1979), and No. 40 (1979). A.A. Importing was and remains one of the leading wholesalers of antiques and collectibles reproductions (exact copies), copycats (stylistic reproductions), and fantasy items (forms, shapes, colors, and/or patterns that did not exist in the past). I own a number of copies of previous A.A. Importing catalogs, but my collection is very incomplete. When I see them for sale at an affordable price, between $5 and $10, I buy them.

The seller of the catalog lot requested an opening bid of $4. I placed a substantially higher bid and made plans to be at my computer when the lot closed. I followed the lot for four days, nervously expecting someone to outbid me at any moment. I breathed a sigh of relief and thanked God when the lot closed at the initial opening bid of $4. After paying the postage, the average cost per catalog was under $1.

The catalogs arrived yesterday. Thus far, I have spent more than three hours studying them. As you probably suspect, I recognized a large number of items now in private collections or sold regularly at auction and antiques malls.

1978/1979 is only twenty-three/twenty-two years ago, not long by contemporary standards. It is more than sufficient time for a new generation of collectors and dealers to be completely unaware that these objects were made this recently. I confess that I will never look at a pinwheel overlay long stem goblet, wine, or cordial in red or blue the same way again.

The catalogs are fun because they provide three insights—first, A.A. Importing's marketing strategy; second, the range of objects being offered for sale; and third, how A.A. Importing adjusted to market demand. Both the 1978 and 1979 catalogs carry a front page banner reading "IN BUSINESS OVER 40 YEARS." This suggests a company origin dating back to the late 1930s. I would love to find a pre-World War II catalog, if it exists. I suspect the company did not begin issuing catalogs until the late 1950s or early 1960s.

A.A. Importing was located at 4244-48 Olive Street, St. Louis, Missouri, in 1978 and 1979. Time to bend over and ask someone to kick me in the butt. I was a student at Washington University in St. Louis from September 1963 until May 1966. During this period I attended auctions at Selkirk's, studied antiques under the tutelage of Charles Buckley at the St. Louis Art Museum, and visited antiques shops with my landlords, Charles and Ginny Boll. Alas, I did not visit A.A. Importing. I missed a great learning opportunity.

On the back of each of the three catalogs I acquired was A. A. Importing's "Traveling Road Show Schedule." The company must have had two crews on the road, since almost every weekend lists two different locations for the company's showrooms. The company used Holiday Inn, Howard Johnson, Ramada, and other local motels. A Plains-West Coast crew worked Dallas/Ft. Worth, Denver, Des Moines, Fullerton, Houston, Kansas City, Los Angeles, Portland, San Diego, San Francisco, and Seattle. An East-South-Midwest crew worked Atlanta, Cleveland, Columbus, Detroit, Hartford, Miami, Tampa, Pittsburgh, Richmond, Roanoke, Syracuse, and Washington, D.C./Baltimore. If you ever wondered why so many reproductions, copycats, and fantasy items exist in the market, A.A. Importing's aggressive marketing is one obvious answer.

I distinctly remember going into an antiques co-op in Toledo in the mid-1980s and seeing a Pony Express brass spittoon. Although being offered as period, I strongly suspected it was a fantasy piece. While not in Catalog No. 37 or No. 38, there it was along with the Union Pacific R.R. "Train" spittoon and the Redskin Brand Chewing Tobacco "Indian" spittoon. For late 1970s fantasy items, they were expensive at $17.50 each or $94.50 for six.

A.A. Importing carried a widely diverse line of reproductions, copycats, and fantasy items. Catalog No. 38 begins with "Victorian" étagères, occasional tables, rockers, and other furniture before moving on to metals, glass, ceramics, and dolls. I have been aware of the general store (octagonal calendar), regulator, and wall clocks. None would fool an experienced clock collector. However, they would fool many novices.

Many catalog items were designed for use as decorative accessories. The Dutch brass and copper helmet coal hods, "all hand-wrought and dove-tailed sections," umbrella stands, and planters are examples. The same holds true for the brass "taxi" horns.

I have seen more than my fair share of the simulated red cinnabar ($2.25 each, six for $12.50) and hand-painted ($4 each, three for $10.80) snuff bottles. I cringed when I reached the pages showing three silver-plated caster bottle frames and six different five-piece caster bottle sets (inverted thumbprint cranberry, clear fern, rose cut ruby overlay, clear grape, rose cut blue overlay, and clear wreath) for use with them. The frames cost $21.50 and the bottle sets either $16.25 or $18.75. Several times a year I have to tell an individual who brings one of these sets to a verbal appraisal clinic that its value is around $50 and not the several hundred dollars they paid for it at auction or an antiques mall or show.

The catalog is filled with numerous types of bells, cranberry glass, historical pressed and pattern glass, Mary Gregory glass, paperweights, and turn-of-the-century Austrian and Bohemian-type hand-painted ceramics, all of which were popular collecting categories in the late 1970s. The pages featuring bisque Romeo and Juliet (19" tall) and Cavalier and Lady (17¾" tall) mantel figurines, the kissing children vases (16⅝" tall), and fourteen different piano babies, several in pairs, started my stomach churning. I had the stomach acid under control until I turned the page and saw the wood block set featuring thirty rotating blocks that make six different "Victorian era" lithograph pictures of children playing. The box measures 10½" square. The set sold for $7.75. I see it everywhere, at prices ranging from $50 to over $100. I headed for the apartment and gulped down a few spoonfuls of Maalox.

Approximately two-thirds of Catalog 38 contains the same items found in Catalog 37 and in Catalog 40. Many items stayed in A.A. Importing's inventory for years.

A close comparison between Catalog 38 and 40 does indicate shifting collector trends. Catalog 40 contains some English formal "Wellington" pieces, indicating a shifting preference away from Victorian and toward the more formal Queen Anne and Chippendale styles. There is a page and a half devoted to Art Nouveau pieces. Art Nouveau enjoyed a major renaissance in the 1980s. The paperweight offerings increased as did their quality. The paperweights were now reproductions instead of the fantasy items and copycats in the earlier catalogs. In fact, my overall impression is that the majority of the pieces appear closer in form, decoration, and quality to period pieces, especially in the ceramics, than a year earlier.

Unfortunately, none of the illustrations show how the pieces are marked. Having handled many of these items, I am aware that several have pseudo-marks, especially the ceramic pieces.

I would very much like to assemble a full run of A.A. Importing catalogs. If anyone has examples they would like to sell, send quotes to Rinker Enterprises, 5093 Vera Cruz Road, Emmaus, PA 18049. Meanwhile check out my Internet site. I have posted several pages from the catalogs for your reference.

CHAPTER 8

Caring for Your Collection

Buying and displaying a collection is fun. Cataloging, storing, and caring for a collection is work. Therefore, most collectors ignore care issues. This often proves to be a major mistake.

Collectors hold objects in trust for the next owner. They are only temporary caretakers. They have a moral and ethical responsibility to pass the object on in as good or better condition than when they acquired it. Alas, some collectors achieve this better than others.

Collectors do not live in museums. They are actively involved in handling, playing with, and using their objects. If they are not, they might as well live in a museum. There is no fun in a "look but do not touch" environment.

Yet, the care needs experienced by collectors duplicate many of the concerns experienced by collection curators at historic sites and museums. It is for this reason that I highly recommend collectors acquire the appropriate pamphlets and books about object care published by the American Association for State and Local History (1717 Church Street, Nashville, TN 37203; www.aashl.org).

To Restore or Not To Restore—That Is the Question

What do you do with a collectible that is damaged or missing parts? Do you throw it out or repair it? What appears to be a simple question on the surface is horribly complex. The following will help you sort through the maze.

The first thing that you need to do is determine the classification of the object with which you are dealing. Is it a masterpiece (museum quality in design or extremely rare in survivability—known to some in the trade as the "ultimate unit"), hard-to-find, above average, common (core), parts piece, or landfill candidate (too far gone to be of any value)? If you make this determination only by looking at the object, you are deceiving yourself. The ability to properly classify an object within any collecting category requires years of experience and a continuing commitment to education.

Masterpiece objects constitute less than one-tenth of 1 percent of all items produced. This classification is reserved only for objects of exceptional design and beauty. These are objects that a museum displays, not as documents of their era but as expressions of the finest art and design form.

Since these objects enjoy a unique position among their counterparts, they also deserve unique attention if they are going to be repaired or restored. The goal of repair and restoration should be to stabilize the object with every original part preserved and nothing done that cannot be undone at a later date. Emphasis is on preserving the originality of the object, not returning it to an original condition through rebuilding, repainting, or replacement of original parts. The only person that should be allowed to touch masterpiece objects is a professionally trained conservator.

A restorer is not a conservator. Do not confuse the two. A conservator has both an undergraduate and graduate degree, often a dual degree in fine arts and chemistry, and has served an apprenticeship with another conservator. While not licensed, they can be identified by their membership in professional conservator's organizations. Their rates are not cheap. They charge as much as an appraiser, accountant, or attorney. However, they bring to their task a high level of technical competence, a commitment to minimalism (stabilize, rather than completely restore), and the highest ethical standards in terms of documenting what they have done.

An object that fits the hard-to-find classification is a judgment call. Approximately 1 to 2 percent of the objects in a collecting classification fit these criteria. Collectors planning to hold hard-to-find objects for an extended period of time (several decades) may decide to invest in the services of a conservator. In most cases the services of a restorer suffice.

Since the number of masterpiece and hard-to-find items is very small, you encounter them only rarely. The vast majority of items in the collectibles market are at best above average, in most cases common, and, more often than we like to admit, landfill candidates (junk).

There are two key factors at work in respect to these items—displayability and usability. If the principal role is display, only enough need be done to make the item presentable from arm's length. If usability is desired, enough must be done so that use will not cause further damage.

I am a minimalist. I believe in "originality," an object comprised of the same parts as when it first left the factory. New parts and especially new paint are detriments. They should reduce, not enhance value. Collectors of the 1990s are far too tolerant of replaced parts and repainted objects. It is time to raise, not lower, standards.

Nothing upsets me more than when a fifty- or hundred-year-old piece has all its signs of age removed. What is the fascination with an object made seventy-five years ago "restored" to look as though it just came off the assembly line? By the time some restorers have finished with a piece, you cannot tell it from a modern reproduction. My theory is, "If you have to err, be conservative." If it looks new, I am going to assume it is new.

Instead of restoration, which most individuals define as returning something to its original state, I would like to propose "presentable." Preserve the integrity and the pizzazz of a piece by retaining as much of the character and age as possible.

Of course, the major problem with restorers is that they are unlicensed. Want to be a restorer or refinisher? Just go to your local hardware store, buy the appropriate tools and supplies, and hang out a shingle. Restoration in America is amateur night in the sticks. The vast majority of individuals who hold themselves out as restorers have only a minimal amount of understanding of what they are doing, what the long-term consequences of their actions are going to be, and the unique properties of the objects on which they are working.

Not everyone buys objects for display. Many buy them, especially furniture, to use. A cane chair without a seat or back, a chest of drawers with missing veneer or a damaged foot, or a game board broken in half is useless. You cannot use an object unless it is in a good state of repair. Since pleasure comes from use, you have to take whatever steps are necessary to make them usable.

Restore objects as much as possible to their original appearance. I have no sympathy for the person who strips a piece of Mission oak and stains it walnut. This person has no respect for the historical integrity of a piece. This person is an uncaring idiot, a destroyer of an object's long-term value.

Since anyone can hang out a restorer's shingle, collectors must do their homework before entrusting an object to a restorer. Forget entirely turning your object over to anyone who bills himself as a "refinisher." First, visit the restorer's shop to (1) examine work that he has done, (2) examine work in progress, (3) check the cleanliness and order of his working environment, and (4) discuss the restorer's restoration philosophy. Second, ask the restorer to provide you with a list of individuals and/or institutions for whom he has done work. Speak with each reference. Obviously, the restorer is not going to provide you with a list of dissatisfied customers. Therefore, ask around. Question anyone who has utilized his services.

No restorer likes to have someone looking over his shoulder. However, it is critical that you have a clear agreement with the restorer of exactly what he is going to do and how before he begins to work on the piece. Have him put his restoration plan in writing. Ask to view work in progress. If something is not going as planned, you may still have time to reverse the situation.

Do not give the restorer a blank check. Restoration work has a bad habit of doubling and tripling in cost from original estimates. Get all estimates in writing. If possible, get the restorer to agree to these costs no matter what time and materials it takes that he has not planned upon.

A parts object has value only when the salvageable parts are in fine or better condition. Why salvage parts that have problems themselves? Replacing one rusted part with another that is not quite as rusted is a waste of time. Likewise, replacing a missing piece on a very good condition object with a mint condition piece, thus causing the new piece to stand out like a sore thumb is also not the best practice. Preserve the overall appearance of the piece whenever possible.

Document in writing and by photograph all work done to an object. Repair, restoration, or conservation is part of an object's provenance. You have a moral and ethical responsibility to reveal this information to the next owner. Alas, this trait is poorly practiced in the field.

Finally, remember that most of the collectibles about which I write in this column are mass-produced. Before you spend the money on restoration or conservation, ask yourself how hard it would be to find and buy a better example. When the cost of restoration or conservation is added to the initial purchase price and the end cost exceeds what it would cost to buy a piece in fine or better condition in the market, then money spent on restoration and conservation is not a wise investment.

As you have seen, deciding whether or not to restore an object is not as easy a decision as it first seems. The final decision rests with only one person—YOU. Good luck.

Appraising Collectibles

One of the questions most collectors never ask, let alone calculate, is: How much money have I invested in my collection? Ignorance is bliss. I doubt if one collector in ten has accurate enough records to determine exactly how much was spent in assembling his collection. Further, I would be surprised if one collector in one hundred has a current appraisal of his collection.

When you see a collection that numbers in the high hundreds, if not thousands of objects, it does not take a genius to figure out the collection's potential market value. Assume the collection has five hundred objects. At $1 each, the collection is worth $500; at $5 each, $2,500; at $10 each, $5,000; and at $25 each, $12,500. Now ask yourself: How many collectibles collections exist where the average price per object is under $10? NOT MANY. Where I grew up, five thousand dollars is a lot of money.

There are three primary reasons why collectibles collectors do not have their collections appraised. The first is they do not have an adequate list of what they own and do not feel that they have the time required to make one. The second is their Meineke muffler attitude when it comes to appraisals, i.e., "I'm not going to pay a lot for this appraisal." The incentive to do the first is the money that they save on the second. The third reason is they see no need for an appraisal. However, after a loss occurs and the collector meets resistance from his insurance company, he will wish he had.

Once a collection exceeds several hundred pieces and the average price per piece is $25 or more, the collector should discipline himself to have an appraisal done every two to four years. Easy to say. Difficult to do.

Many collectors feel that if they do not insure their collections, they do not need an appraisal. They are wrong. Collections are covered under most homeowner policies. Collectors have protection whether they realize it or not. An appraisal is an important document in proving ownership.

An appraisal forces the collector to pause and look closely at what he has. Properly done, it serves as a collection management document as well as a record of a particular moment in time. The appraisal process may be the first time the collector has seriously looked at his collection as a whole.

Finding an appraiser for a specific collectible category is not easy. While there are a wealth of generalist antiques appraisers trained both in appraisal techniques and object knowledge, their focus is primarily on those categories that comprise the antiques, not the collectibles sector of the market. No matter how skilled one's appraisal techniques, they are useless without the object knowledge necessary to perform competently.

There are two essential keys in picking an appraiser—knowledge and neutrality. The latter is the sticky point. If the appraiser is a dealer from whom the collector buys regularly, a serious question must be raised about the individual's objectivity. Will such a person put a lower price on an object that he sold if the market has moved downward instead of upward since the sale? I doubt it. He has an incentive to put higher prices on everything just to make himself and the collector look good.

I frequently am called upon by insurance claims adjusters and attorneys to review appraisals. The first thing I do is look at the qualifications of the appraiser and for any close relationship, other than friendship, with the person for whom the appraisal was done. There is nothing I love better than to smell a fix.

More often than not in the area of collectibles, the real expert is the collector himself. As a result, there is a need for a closer relationship between the appraiser and his client when doing the listings and the determining of values of collectibles than antiques. What the collector needs to find is an individual skilled in the appraisal craft with a working knowledge of their collecting field.

When working with individuals on appraisals of collectibles collections, I encourage them to do their own listing and pricing—ideally, on a computer. I provide a format they must follow. Usually, they make a list of forty to fifty items and submit it to me for review. Adjustments are made and then they proceed with the full listing.

This approach makes sense because a professional appraiser is paid by the hour. Appraisers earn the per hour equivalent of a local attorney or an accountant. In my area, this means $75 to $150 per hour. Few individuals can afford to pay someone these rates to do a listing of their collection.

Once the collector has finished listing his collection, I make arrangements to visit the collector and inspect the objects. Beware of any appraisers who claim they can appraise objects from a photograph or video. If there is a problem, one of the first questions an appraiser is going to be asked is: did you personally inspect each object? A statement to this effect must be included in the appraiser's appraisal cover letter.

Before my visit, I urge the collector to arrange the objects on a table, floor, or other surface in the order they appear on the list. This saves an enormous amount of time. My inspection focuses on two issues: (1) Is the description accurate? and (2) Is the condition report accurate? Price is not an issue at this point.

After noting any corrections on the computer print out, the collector turns over the computer disk to me. Now comes price and market research. With the collector's suggested pricing, I quickly can determine if the collector has accurately priced the objects or inflated them. I have yet to encounter a collector who has significantly undervalued his collection. Price adjustments are made.

Since the listing was done on a computer, recapturing the keystrokes on my computer is simple. No expense is incurred retyping the material. Like most appraisers, I have reached the point where I do all appraisals on computer. I also no longer do written appraisals for collectibles collections when the individual is not in a position to provide the basic information via computer disk. Times have changed. Indeed, they have.

Even with the time savings indicated above, appraisal costs for a modest collection begin at $500 and easily can reach the $1,000 to $1,500 range. Not everyone charges $75 per hour or more. Competition and the economy serve to keep the rates lower in many areas. However, before hiring the $25 per hour appraiser, remember the old adage—you get what you pay for.

One final note: Just like the attorney who has a fool for a client if he represents himself, a collector is not capable of appraising his own collection without outside help. The collector is not neutral. The values he assigns are "wish" prices, i.e., what he wishes the collection will bring when he is ready to sell it.

What are you going to do after reading this article about appraising your collection? The answer for more than 99.9 percent is absolutely nothing. To the one in one thousand who acts, congratulations. In life, big victories always are preceded by small ones.

Moving Your Collection

Over a decade ago, I was an expert witness in a court case involving damage done to a client's antique furniture and other decorative accessories by representatives of a moving company. My client argued that the movers damaged a number of his pieces to the point where he would still suffer significant loss of value even if the pieces were professionally restored. As is usually the case, I was hired to assess and appraise the objects after the damage occurred, not before.

The potential for damage and its accompanying loss of value is extremely high during any move. Far too many collectors fail to take the steps required to adequately prepare their collection for a move. This occurs through ignorance more often than neglect.

Preparing a collection to be moved involves careful planning, supervision during the moving process, and a condition check the moment the collection arrives at its new home. Each is essential to a good move.

There are several steps you need to take before contacting a moving company. The first is to evaluate and analyze your collection. Packing, weight, and distance are the major price factors in determining the cost of a move. The cost to move duplicates and triplicates of objects, secondary items, and non-related objects acquired along the way may far exceed their market value. When this proves true, it makes no sense to pay to move them. Sell them to obtain money to help offset the cost of the move.

Photograph or videotape your collection. Doing both makes even more sense. The key is to establish a permanent record of the condition of the objects in your collection prior to the move. A written appraisal by an independent appraiser is also highly recommended. This establishes the value of your objects prior to the move.

Many moving companies have little or no experience in moving collections. Others have specialist packers and drivers skilled in the task. When contacting moving companies for an estimate, ask specifically what their experience has been in moving collections and what special steps they take in handling them. I once interviewed several moving companies specializing in moving collections. When asking about the packaging approach used by one company, I was so upset by their answer that I immediately eliminated them from consideration.

Packing supplies and labor costs charged for packers are the highest profit centers in any move. Be prepared for a shock when you see the price a mover charges for a cardboard box.

The initial reaction by most collectors is to pack their own collections. They see this as a means of saving money as well as controlling the manner in which their objects are packed. This approach is fraught with problems.

There is a big difference between packing objects for a move in a large moving van and packing them following a purchase for transportation to the collector's home. Moving vans are generally stacked full. A box and its inside packaging must be capable of withstanding the weight of any boxes placed on top of it.

Wrapping and packing objects and properly placing and separating them inside a box is a practiced skill. About a year ago, I received a package containing more than a dozen objects that I had bought while on a personal appearance in Oregon. In the middle of the box was a plaster Doulton-like figurine. The person who prepared the objects for shipment carefully wrapped the figurine in bubble wrap and placed it in the center of the box, far removed from any of the box's six sides. Yet, when I unpacked the box, the head had broken off the figurine during shipment. Obviously, some sudden vehicle movement or shift of another object within the box caused a force strong enough to damage the figurine. Had the packer wrapped paper around the neck of the figurine before wrapping it in bubble wrap, the damage might have been avoided.

Most of the objects I purchase for my collection arrive via the U.S. Postal Service, UPS, or another carrier. Although most are inadequately packed, they still arrive safely. Having said this, I have had my fair share of crushed boxes (the shipper forgot to reinforce them from the inside with crumpled paper or tissue), bent envelopes and paper goods, and broken objects. My heart always skips a few beats when I open a box that contains Styrofoam peanuts or disks. These do not hold objects securely in place during shipping.

Make a detailed list of what goes into every box, whether you pack it or the moving company does. If this is not possible, rent a video camera and record the packing of each box. You need a record of exactly what was shipped.

One of the biggest concerns if you pack your collection yourself is whether the insurance you purchase from the carrier will cover any damage or loss. Even if it does on paper, you should expect the carrier to fight the claim from the moment it is filed, arguing that the damage occurred because of your packing negligence.

If you pack your collection, make certain you obtain your own insurance protection. The insurance program of the National Association of Collectors (PO Box 2782, Huntersville, NC 18070; 1-800-287-7127) includes coverage of a collection during a move.

If you decide to pay the carrier you select to pack your collection, be there looking over his employees' shoulders. This is not going to make you Mr. or Mrs. Popularity. Just keep in mind who owns the objects. Your very presence should be enough to impress the carrier's employees to take the time required to do the packing correctly.

Insist, no, demand that a detailed list be made of each object and box placed on the van for moving. Number each box. Make certain the list is detailed.

Hire a mover that plans to take your goods directly from the pick-up to the delivery point. Many people do not realize that household contents are frequently taken to a central warehouse location where they are off-loaded and reassigned. When this happens, the chances for damage and theft increase significantly. The waybill describes the contents of the move. Insider thieves keep a careful eye open for moves involving collections. Eliminate this threat by only hiring a firm that guarantees a straight-through delivery.

Make certain to be at the new location when your collection arrives. Do not be surprised to find a different crew unloading the van. Usually only the driver travels with the load. Loaders and unloaders are hired locally.

Obviously, the driver and unloaders want to get their job done as quickly as possible. Time is money. Time also is the enemy. When the unloading is done, the driver is going to ask you to sign a document indicating that you have accepted the load. The fine print generally contains a statement that you have made note of any damage that may have occurred during the move.

It is common for individuals to be tired and even irritable during the unloading process. They just want the move to come to an end. Avoid this pitfall. You need to be as alert, if not more so, during the unloading process as you were during the loading.

Inspect every box and object as it is unloaded. Do not give a damn what the driver and unloaders say. Check all six sides of every box. Make note of even the slightest dent. If the dent is serious, insist on unpacking the box and examining its contents in the presence of the driver.

Forget the Shakespearean admonition of "the lady doth protest too much, methinks." Point out everything of concern and make certain the driver makes note of it on the delivery sheet. Check and double-check to make certain that every item on the waybill has been delivered. If an object or box cannot be located, do not allow the driver to leave until it is. If the driver gives you a hard time, demand he call the local agent. Get your complaint on record.

Just because the outside of a box shows no damage does not mean there is no damage to objects inside. Ideally, you should unpack every box in front of the driver. Economically, you probably cannot afford to do this. Someone has to pay the driver for his time and that someone is you.

The solution is a commitment on your part to unpack all the boxes containing your collection within a three- to four-day period following their arrival. Carefully document any damaged objects and file a report immediately with the moving company. It is critical to save the box and the packaging for inspection by representatives of the moving company.

What happens if objects or boxes are missing or goods damaged? Call the local agent and get him to the site. Chances are you are never going to see the driver again unless it is in court.

Moving companies have learned that it is in their best interests to deny and fight claims. They have deep pockets. Far too many collectors settle for pennies on the dollar to avoid the hassle associated with dealing with a protracted claim. Every injured collector who does not push his moving company to the limit encourages this deny-and-fight policy. When a cause is just, it is worth a protracted fight.

Moving companies frequently want to send their own representative to repair damaged objects. Do not allow this. These individuals are fix and patch people. Demand that repairs done to damaged objects be performed by skilled conservators.

Has this column put the fear of God in you relative to moving your collection? Good! I accomplished my goal. The more scared you are, the more care and attention you will devote to doing the move right. I hope I scared the daylights out of you.

CHAPTER 9

Make Inanimate Objects Animate

I like to make objects come alive. Objects have stories to tell, and I want to learn as many of them as I can. So should you.

I own several Hopalong Cassidy cap guns. Which is my favorite? The pair accompanied by a picture of a young girl wearing them. The woman who sold them to me gave me the picture. She felt it was an integral part of the history of the guns. So did I. I am thrilled and honored to have it.

I do dozens of verbal appraisal clinics each year. There is nothing I love more than to have a person also present me with a picture of an ancestor holding the doll, teddy bear, or toy or wearing the piece of jewelry or watch they want me to appraise. Pictures help document age. The same holds true for old room or business photographs with the object pictured in the background.

Provenance is only one story objects have to tell. As a historian of science and technology, the story that most fascinates me is how the object was made. How the object was marketed is a close second. Every object I buy is an excuse to research these two questions. If brain inactivity is one of the major causes of Alzheimer's disease, I am never going to have this problem.

Getting intimate with objects is one of the hallmarks of a true collector.

How Did They Make That?

Collectibles are inanimate objects—just things to most people. It does not have to be this way. Animation lies just below the surface.

How do you make a collectible come alive? You ask questions such as: (1) How was it made? (2) Who made it? (3) How was it marketed?

(4) How was it used? (5) Why was it saved? and (6) What does the fact that it survived say about the person who currently owns it? These are only a few of the questions one can pose. The answers create a story. The story creates a unique personality for the collectible. The personality gives the collectible life.

Whenever I teach a seminar on a general collecting category, e.g., ceramics, glass, or furniture, I make a point to take time to talk about how the objects in that category are manufactured. Given the fact that I did my doctoral studies in the history of science and history of technology, this emphasis probably comes as no surprise. I focused on handcraft technology and how industrial technology eventually replaced most of it. I am fascinated by how things are made.

During my seminars, I urge participants to take one or two factory tours a year. It makes no difference whether the tour relates to their collecting interest. The object is to understand the abilities and limitations of the industrial process. I try to follow my own advice. I am not always as successful as I would like.

Whenever I visit a factory, I am astonished at the speed and the quantity at which things are made. My impression is that most individuals have no concept of how many objects an assembly line can create in the course of an eight-hour work day. With some exceptions—e.g., Harley-Davidson motorcycles—the number is in the tens or hundreds of thousands.

I am always impressed by how many individuals it takes to create an object. No object is the work of a single individual. During a visit to Dyersville, Iowa, to play a little pick-up ball on "The Field of Dreams," I also toured the Ertl factory. The tour guide took pride in the fact that over fifty people made individual contributions to the creation of a single Ertl truck. I kept count during my tour. The number is correct. Alas, Ertl toys are no longer made in Dyersville. Foreign ownership closed the Dyersville plant and moved the manufacturing abroad.

Factory tours constantly remind me of how much of the manufacturing process cannot be mechanized, a principal reason why I like taking tours. There are things humans can do better than machines. Nothing illustrates this better than a tour of the Fenton factory in Williamstown, West Virginia. There is far more hand labor than mechanized labor in the making of glass pieces, especially glass hollowware.

Do not limit your tours to industrial factories. Visit America's historic sites and watch the craft demonstrators. One of my earliest museum memories is seeing the papermaker at Colonial Williamsburg draw a screen through a vat of plant fibers and create a piece of paper. Last year I visited Seagraves, North Carolina, home to over a hundred potters, some of whom still fire their wares using a wood kiln. I had the opportunity to talk with several of them.

My only objection to historic site craft demonstrators is that they do not accurately demonstrate the speed of the individual craftsperson. Time is and always was money. The colonial craftsperson did not linger. The museum crafts demonstrator is charged with the responsibility of interpreting his craft for the general public. He does not live by the product he produces but by the information he dispenses.

The production rate of eighteenth- and nineteenth-century craftsmen is far greater than most realize. While it might take a weaver four to six days to rig a loom, he could complete between twenty and thirty coverlets in a day once he started the weaving process. A kick-wheel potter was capable of making hundreds of pots a day. Historical documents, e.g., trade ledgers, provide information about the quantity of goods manufactured by an individual craftsman. Unfortunately, this information rarely works its way into print in antiques and collectibles periodicals.

In spite of the limitations, I still recommend visiting, watching, and talking with the craft demonstrators at historic sites. Many local historical societies hold annual craft days, during which members demonstrate the "lost arts."

What happens if you cannot get to a factory? There are a number of alternatives. A surprising number of factory tour videos are available. The Fenton video is one of my favorites. I checked www.fentonartglass.com to see if the video was still available. I should not have been as surprised as I was to see there were CD, DVD, and VHS versions of the tour. Hurray for modern technology!

The Commonwealth of Pennsylvania sponsors a cable channel that features half-hour factory tours as part of its regular programming. I have watched dozens of factory tour programs from Just Born Candy to Zippo.

However, CDs, DVDs, VHS tapes, and television are poor substitutes for the real thing. They do not adequately convey the size of plant machinery, the sounds of manufacturing, and, in some cases, the smell.

Researching Collectibles

There are two key questions associated with every object: (1) What is it? and (2) How much is it worth? It is difficult, often impossible, to answer the second question without answering the first.

Misidentification of collectibles is a major problem. Examples abound at flea markets, antiques malls, auction and direct sale sites on the Internet, and even in antiques shops. In the vast majority of cases, the misidentification is not deliberate but the result of ignorance, lack of research skills, and/or the unavailability of research materials.

I recently was asked to authenticate a Beanie Baby being offered at auction on the Internet. The person did some research and concluded he had one of the first issues. He provided me with his checklist. Everything matched. However, one important piece of information was missing. The first Beanie Babies had a black and white tush tag. The example I was asked to authenticate had the second tush tag version that was red and white. Instead of being worth big bucks, the Beanie Baby's value was under twenty dollars.

Individuals selling collectibles must make a commitment to properly research and identify what they sell. I am a strong advocate of the position that responsibility rests with the seller, not the buyer to properly identify items offered for sale. I tell students at my Institute for the Study of Antiques and Collectibles, "Don't Sell What You Don't Know."

Identifying the correct collecting category or categories to which an object belongs, for example, whether a piece of glass is cranberry, pigeon blood, or just red colored glass, is merely the first of many questions that must be researched. Additional questions include: (a) Who made the object? (b) How was it made? (c) How was it marketed and used? (d) Why was it saved? (e) What does it say about the person who saved it? The answers to these questions make the object come alive.

Researching a collectible is fun. Many individuals have told me they find more enjoyment doing research than they do buying and selling. They love to learn.

Sellers rarely assign a value to the time they spend researching. If they did, they would find it all but impossible to recover the cost as part of an object's final selling price. Collectibles education is cumulative. Smart buyers and sellers make a commitment to invest in research now with the expectation that it will pay dividends in the future. I can attest that it does.

Numerous e-mails from individuals who tried to research a collectible on the Internet and failed is the primary reason that I am writing this column. The tone of most e-mails is "how dare the Internet not have the information I am seeking." I have designated these individuals silver platter researchers. They want the information they seek handed to them—NOW!

While it is true there is a wealth of information on the Internet, there are two others truths as well. First, there is a wealth of misinformation on the Internet. There is no screening agency for information offered on the Internet. Second, there are tremendous gaps in the information. Rather than turning to the Internet as my first research source, I use it either as my last or as confirmation for information I found elsewhere.

For the moment, a well-maintained antiques and collectibles reference library is the most reliable research source. The ideal situation is to create your own research library. This is expensive, even when the library is highly specialized. It costs well over $5,000 to 7,000 per year to keep a general collectibles library current. Few in the trade can afford this expenditure.

The key is to locate the best collectibles research libraries in your area. Begin by checking your public library. Books about antiques and collectibles fall into the "most requested" category. As a result, public libraries usually devote a fairly large section to this category. I know of several communities, e.g., Medford, Oregon, where local antiques and collectibles clubs provide funds and work with their public library to continually build and strengthen the antiques and collectibles section. See if this applies to a library in your area.

Do not even bother to check out the libraries at your local community colleges, colleges, or universities. Most devote little to no space to collectibles titles. The academic community as a whole looks down their noises at what they consider to be "amateur" researchers. Viewing us as scholars on their level is beyond their realm of comprehension. Having once had a foot in the academic camp, I assure you that many collectibles titles I have read written by "amateur" researchers put a significant number of scholarly PhD dissertations and university press titles to shame. What galls many of these ivory tower purists is these insignificant, inconsequential collectibles titles usually outsell their magna opuses by five-, ten-, and even fifty-to-one. Who said there is no justice in the world?

Collectibles researchers often overlook two obvious library resources in their community, the libraries of their local art museum and historical society. Large art museums maintain excellent research libraries. If the collection is comprehensive, it includes a wealth of twentieth-century material. Art libraries acquire the titles required to research this material. The lack of titles that are largely price guide driven is the major weakness of art museum libraries. Art museum purists consider value a non-discussible issue. Full auction catalog runs, with prices realized, from most major U.S. and some foreign houses are one of the strengths of most art museum libraries. Since price information occurs after the fact, it is seen as acceptable in this situation.

Spend time becoming familiar with the research libraries at your local and state historical societies. It is a mistake to assume they focus primarily on local documents and genealogical information. Most have extensive artifact collections. As a result, their libraries include titles useful in identifying objects. Again, they shy away from price guide titles, but not to the same extent as art museums.

If this column's emphasis was antiques, I would tout the research library of the Henry Francis du Pont Winterthur Museum in Winterthur, Delaware. It is without peer. I was first introduced to the library in 1963 and have been using it ever since. My only regret is that it is not closer to my office.

There is an equivalent library in the collectibles field, albeit nowhere near as well-known or acknowledged. If your travels ever take you to Rochester, New York, set aside a few hours and visit the Strong Museum. Resist the temptation to tour the exhibits and check out the library instead. It is wonderful. It is the only library to which I would entrust my research library and files should I ever decide to donate rather than sell them. This in spite of the fact that I can count the number of visits I have made on one hand. Alas, my travels rarely take me in that direction.

I have been pleased within the past decade to see the growth of antiques mall reference libraries. Many antiques mall owners are working with their dealers to create a major reference library. By pooling financial resources, these libraries can grow at a far more rapid rate than a private one. The vast majority are restricted to the mall's dealers. However, I have encountered a few that allow public access.

It is time to turn attention to the research procedures to follow once you have determined which facility you will visit.

The ideal situation is to walk over to your personal library and begin your research. Most collectors and dealers do not own an in-depth research library. They prefer to spend their money on a collectible rather than a reference book or document. I fully understand.

The telephone Yellow Pages' slogan, "Let your fingers do the walking," applies. Before driving to a research facility, telephone the librarian. Make certain they have the research sources you need.

I often do long distance research. If my questions are limited and I believe the information is easily found, I obtain the telephone number of the closest public library or historical society and call the reference librarian. I ask if they would be willing to check their records for me to see if they can find the answers I am seeking. Information about the history of a manufacturer and whether or not any catalogs exist are my two most popular requests.

If the librarian is willing to do research, I explain my needs. I take no offense if he asks me to put my request in writing. In fact, if he does not make such a request, I always ask if I can fax a hard copy of my request. I provide a telephone number where I can be reached if questions develop and encourage the librarian to reverse the charges.

Early in my conversation, I mention that I do not need the information immediately, even if I do, but would be happy to arrange a time to call back, usually later in the day or early the next day, to learn what progress has been made. The more pressure you exert, the less likely this approach is to work.

Many libraries now charge to make photocopies and send or fax them. The cost is always minimal. The price has never exceeded $1 per page. Given the amount of time I save, it is a small price to pay.

When researching an object, take it with you whenever possible. If it is too large, fragile to move, or too valuable, take along a picture or pictures. I have received excellent research suggestions from other researchers in the room who simply could not resist coming over and seeing what I had. This is especially important if you have a "whatsit," i.e., an object that you are trying to identify. Many individuals in the field lack the vocabulary to properly describe an object. Do you know what a cuneiform shape is? Pictures are a great help.

Your first research goal is to determine exactly what you have. This is easier said than done. Form (what the object is, e.g., biscuit jar, chair, sheet music, etc.), shape (what the object looks like), and general "what it is made out of" classification (ceramic, glass, metal, textile, wood, etc.) is not difficult. Identifying the specific type of ceramic, glass, metal, textile, wood, etc., requires much greater skill.

Heavily illustrated books, whether price guides or just plain reference texts, help. One often has to use the Superman reading method, i.e., flip through them one page at a time. A pox on those books lacking an easy to use format or detailed index.

I begin the research process by assuming that I will not find information about the exact object I am researching. This forces me to look for comparables right from the start. It also increases my delight if I do find the exact object.

My staff and I are trained to think of objects in terms of collecting categories. When looking at any object, the first thing we do is try to identify all the possible collecting categories into which an object fits. This creates alternate research avenues. For example, information about a 1949 Chesapeake and Ohio railroad calendar featuring an image of Chessie the Cat and her kittens might be found in books on advertising characters, calendars, cats, paper ephemera, or railroad collectibles.

Once I have answered the "what is it" question, I proceed to research the questions that breathe life into an object. Because of my history of technology background, I focus on learning how the object was made and used. In most cases, I already know the basic answers. I am looking for details associated with this particular object that I did not encounter previously.

Most researchers begin by seeking information about the manufacturer. When taking this route, pay close attention to the operating dates of the manufacturer, what products and lines were made during what period, and who the principal designers and distributors were. Make a note of any library, historical society, or private collector that owns one or more of the company's trade catalogs. These are invaluable resources.

Always check to see if the manufacturer is still in business. When checking, consider the possibility of a name change due to an acquisition or merger. If the company has ceased operations within the past few decades, some of its employees may still be alive. Consider placing an advertisement in the local paper asking them to contact you.

When I cannot identify a specific manufacturer, I concentrate on trying to determine the time period when the object was made. I consider a variety of factors such as shape, decorative motif, technique, and color tone. Once I have assigned a date, I draw up a list of six to twelve manufacturers who worked during that period making products similar to the one I am researching. I then begin the process of leafing through the reference books looking for comparable examples. Once in a while I get lucky and am able to attribute the piece to a specific manufacturer.

I maintain an extensive library of marks books. However, one needs to be aware, especially with the latest wave of late 1990s reproductions, copycats, fantasies, and fakes, that marks can be easily copied. The quality of the piece has to match the expectations associated with the mark found on it.

Collectibles collectors and dealers are basically trusting individuals. They rarely question the reliability of the information they find. This especially applies to pricing information. As much as I wish it were not the case, a skeptical attitude is wise until information has been confirmed by a second source. Beware. Misinformation is often copied from one source to another. Errors perpetuate themselves in the collectibles business.

The less thorough the information, the more skeptical I am about it. Weak caption illustrations, e.g., those missing vital information such as size or markings, set off my mental alarms. Minimum front matter, especially historical information, is another alarm bell. The absence of a detailed bibliography causes concern. Finally, I always make it a point to read the author's credentials when I am lucky enough to find them provided.

Make photocopies of the research you do. When the object leaves your possession, pass the information along to the next owner. It makes no sense to make the new owner repeat the research process.

This advice applies doubly to those individuals researching an object for the purpose of selling it. Collectibles no longer sell themselves. The seller now must play an active role in the selling process. There is an old mercantile adage—sell the sizzle, not the steak. The more one knows about an object, the more sizzle it has. An excited collector, one who is in a position to tout his collection, is a positive asset.

Finally, if you have uncovered new information in your research, consider sharing it with the rest of the field. Write an article for a trade periodical. Pass the information along to someone who is preparing a new or revised edition of a reference book. Send it to the editor of the appropriate collectors' club newsletter. Who knows? There may even be enough for a book.

Family Stories

"It belonged to my grandmother. She was in her nineties when she died in the 1970s. It has to be at least one hundred years old."

"It came over on the boat when my grandparents immigrated to America."

Appraising and family stories go hand in hand. Before I begin any verbal appraisal clinic, I tell my audience that an appraiser, in this case me, needs access to all the information available in order to make his appraisal as accurate as possible—the less he has to guess or assume, the better. I expect the person seeking the appraisal to honestly answer questions that include: how did you acquire the object; when did you acquire it; if you bought it, what did you pay for it?

The vast majority of objects I appraise at a verbal appraisal clinic are family pieces, i.e., they have been handed down from one generation to the next. As a result, I hear plenty of family stories. I would like to say that I believe all of them. The tragedy is that I question far more than I believe.

Family stories are wonderful, but they often are distorted. They contain kernels of truth, but the overall story is flawed. Based upon my observations, the more distance between generations the more unbelievable the stories become. For this reason, I am known to some as "The Great Debunker."

I cannot leave a flawed family story alone. I prefer truth over myth. It is my duty to correct the inconsistency. Those on the receiving end are not always grateful. In fact, some are downright resentful.

I remember playing "Pass It down the Alley" as a kid. You may know the game by another name—"Chinese Whispers" or "Whisper down the Alley." The game involves two or more teams. Each team is arranged in a row. A message is given that is to be whispered or passed down the line. The goal is to accurately send the message down the line as quickly as possible. If you have ever played the game, you know the end result. The message always comes out garbled, sometimes rather humorously, at the other end.

Family stories are oral history. Rarely are they written down. When they are, the writer usually is several generations removed from the initial storyteller. Unlike the game Pass It down the Alley where a phrase or story is transferred in a matter of minutes, family stories are transferred intermittently over decades and often centuries. Little wonder they are not as accurate as they first seem.

Family stories often contain faulty logic. For example, great-grandmother immigrated to America. This vase belonged to great-grandmother. Therefore, great-grandmother brought it over to America with her. Forget the fact that great-grandmother came from Germany and the vase is marked "Made in Japan."

I am continually surprised at how little people know about their ancestors. When I am presented with an object that "came over on the boat," I ask the current owner to provide me with the name of the person to whom the object belonged and the date he or she immigrated to America. I can understand the person not knowing the exact date of immigration. I expect a ballpark figure. However, most cannot tell me the exact name of the person.

Before you say hogwash, take a moment and do a quick genealogical chart that shows your parents, grandparents, and great-grandparents by name. Deduct points if you do not know the maiden names of your grandmothers and great-grandmothers. How did you do? Hopefully, you got the names of your parents correct.

When someone says "This belonged to my grandmother," my immediate reaction is to ask, "When did your grandmother die?" I am far more interested in when grandma died than when she was born. When she died is the last possible date that she could have purchased something.

It is a myth that grandmothers and mothers received everything they ever owned on the day they were married. Years ago, wedding anniversaries, especially those at five, ten, twenty-five, forty, and fifty years, were the occasion for a major exchange of gifts between husbands and wives. Other landmarks, such as birthdays, also were celebrated. As a result, grandmother received a great many presents during her lifetime.

Again, most individuals I query cannot tell me the dates of their parents' or grandparents' births, marriages, and deaths, if applicable. All these are key pieces of information to an appraiser when attempting to authenticate and value an object. How well would you do if I asked you these questions?

Allow me to share a few of my favorite family stories. I was asked to appraise a Philadelphia mahogany drop-leaf table that was accompanied by a story noting that an ancestor bought the table in the 1780s at a Philadelphia estate auction. The story included a further enhancement that the auction actually contained three drop-leaf tables, a matched pair and a single. Thomas Jefferson supposedly purchased the matched pair, and the ancestor of the current owner bought the other. The family provided me with a family tree. The dates of the initial owner made a 1780 purchase quite possible. I spent several weeks researching and authenticating the table. It was indeed a Philadelphia drop-leaf table made between 1750 and 1770. I contacted Monticello to see if the site contained a matched pair of Philadelphia drop-leaf tables. It did not. I also checked several years of Philadelphia estate inventories in hopes of finding an auction at which three drop-leaf tables were offered for sale. Again, I was not able to pinpoint a specific auction. On a probability scale of one to ten, I rated the family story an eight and a half.

During the taping of the third season of *Collector Inspector*, I encountered a signed Beatles album cover. It was in rough shape. I asked the owner how she acquired it. She informed me that her father was a chauffeur in Las Vegas when the Beatles appeared there. Another chauffeur, his friend, was assigned to drive the Beatles. This friend had the Beatles sign several albums which he gave away as presents. The owner was quite young at the time and was only interested in the music. She played the record and kept the album in her record stack. As a result, the cover became scuffed. It was not until more than thirty years later when her daughter was her age that she remembered the signed cover and was fortunate enough to find that she still had it. I rate this family store a nine and a half.

I have seen my share of signed Babe Ruth baseballs over the years. One individual came to me with a story that grandpa was sitting in the bleachers at Yankee Stadium when the Babe hit one of his home runs. Grandpa caught the ball and took it to the clubhouse to have it signed. He told the doorkeeper how he acquired the ball. The doorkeeper took it inside and returned a few minutes later with it signed by the Babe. I gave this story a one and a half rating when I first heard it. Alas, it was and remains a common practice for doorkeepers, batboys, and publicity agents to sign balls for players. A comparison of authentic Ruth signatures quickly showed that the Babe did not sign the ball.

I saw another Babe Ruth signed ball during my *Collector Inspector* taping. This owner's story said that when her uncle was a young boy, he lived near the Babe. He took ill. Family friends who knew the Babe suggested a visit by the Yankee slugger might cheer up the boy. Babe visited and signed the ball. The ball was accompanied by a letter and picture of the young boy. Unfortunately, it was not a picture of the young boy and Babe standing side by side. I rate this family story at seven and a half. I liked the story and documentation. I did not have my reference books to do a signature comparison.

Appraisers, collectors, and dealers love to tell war stories, i.e., stories about their experiences in the field. Recounting some of the more unusual family stories they encounter is generally part of any conversation.

Family stories are important. They deserve to be preserved.

Start by writing them down. Then do your homework. Put the story to the test. Do genealogical research about the original owner and the generations through which the object passed. Research the object itself and make certain it dates from the time period assigned to it by the family story.

Do not be discouraged if the facts do not fully support the story. The good news is that you own the object and it came down through the family. When you pass it to the next generation, your written documentation will keep the story straight.

This is something to shout about, not whisper.

CHAPTER 10

Things You Just Need to Know

If you read this book from cover to cover, you may never have to say "if I had only known that" again.

Assumption is a problem in collecting. Long-time collectors assume novice collectors know certain things. As a result, they never take the time to tell them.

Further, there are dark secrets collectors would rather not share with other collectors. Not me. I am for getting everything out in the open—good, bad, or indifferent.

Just remember, laughing, especially at yourself, is an essential element in collecting. It is time to have a few laughs on me.

Sneaking Collectibles into the House

Several years ago I bought a local tall case clock. When delivered and set into place, it would be my third area tall case clock, joining one my mother had purchased in the early 1970s and another I had purchased shortly before. I forgot to mention the purchase to Connie, my wife.

I arranged a delivery date with the dealers who purchased the clock on my behalf. There were two problems. I ran late that day; and, Connie was home when I did not expect her to be.

The dealers arrived, unloaded the clock case sans the works, walked to the front door, and rang the bell. Connie answered, a surprised look on her face.

"Where do you want the clock?" the dealers asked.

"Put it on my side of the bed," was Connie's reply. Connie could tell by the look on their faces that they did not fully understand what she had said. She repeated herself. "Put it on my side of the bed. He is sleeping with it tonight."

Now they understood.

Every collector I know has faced the problem of incorporating a newly purchased item, especially when it was expensive, into his or her collection without a spouse's knowledge. No matter how much the spouse purports to understand and support the collector's addiction, there always are purchases that push that understanding and support over the edge.

Why the need for sneakiness? The reason is those dreaded questions no collector wants to hear or answer from anyone, especially a spouse: What do you need that for? How much did you pay? Where did you find the money? Don't you have one of those already? I thought you promised me you were not going to buy anything more for a month? What are we going to give up for THAT?!

Never question the inventiveness of collectors, especially when it comes to sneaking something new, i.e., old, into the house. Unfortunately, the very nature of this sneakiness means that proven techniques rarely are shared among collectors.

Time to remedy this oversight. What follows are a few techniques used by collecting addicts. Obviously, I have never had to resort to any of them since my own spouse is totally understanding and supportive of my collecting habit. YEAH, RIGHT!

Many collectors use the "united they stand, divided they fall" approach. The technique necessitates displaying as much of the collection as possible in as small an amount of space as possible. If shelves are used, objects are several units deep. When a cabinet houses the collection, cram in so many examples that the door cannot be opened without risk. Are these collectors related to the telephone booth and Volkswagen people stuffers of the 1960s?

The theory is that the number of objects is so great that the entire collection blends together and appears as a single unit when displayed. The piles of stuff are so mind-boggling that individual identification of pieces is impossible. All that is required to incorporate a new purchase is a slight rearrangement, known officially as cramming in another.

Personally, I admire the out-in-the-open collectors. They constantly test their wits—a survival-of-the-fittest struggle between collector and spouse. Darwin was right.

A much more conservative approach is sneaking in the purchase and immediately putting it into a storage box or drawer. While slipping in new items appears easy, one has to remember the ingenious ability of spouses to notice when a preset order has been disturbed. Collectors' boxes of goodies weigh a fair amount. They make indentations and other marks in the carpet. Put a box back into place incorrectly, and, BINGO, the evidence is indisputable.

Further, few collectors can simply put an object into a storage box or drawer. The order of the entire storage unit must be rearranged. This takes time, time that can result in discovery. Think of all the times that your spouse magically appeared behind you while you were working on your collection. A collector's hearing is dulled significantly when fondling his objects. Learn to lock the door.

"This room is off limits" is one of the safest approaches. Every collector dreams of having a room of his own, one to which the door remains closed to whomever he does not want to enter. Spouses forbidden. It is a shrine to the collector, a hell on earth to the spouse. I have lost count of the number of times I have heard spouses tell me that their burial plan for the collector is to have him or her stuffed, placed in the infamous room, and the door bricked shut. Sounds great to me.

Any off-limits room should: (1) have a private entrance from outside, (2) be over the garage or in the attic, or, better yet, (3) be located in another building, preferably on site. Further, if the collector can park his car in its accustomed place when entering the off-limits room, life is ideal. You would be amazed how quickly spouses notice when a car is parked somewhere other than normal. It always raises questions.

Of course, the real problem is not what to do with the new purchase once it clears the door, but how to get it undetected through the door in the first place. Forget the unmarked, plain brown bag or package. No spouse is that stupid.

Have you ever watched spouses at flea markets, malls, or shows? They are constantly observing how their spouses' purchases are packaged. After one or two visits, they can identify a new purchase package just from its look.

The automobile industry is not the collector's friend. Cars, even vans, have limited places to stash purchases until the coast is clear. The options are the trunk, under the seat, and the glove compartment. Most of my purchases do not fit into the last two. The sound of a trunk opening upon the return from a flea market, mall, or shop is one of those sounds that a collector's spouse hears no matter where she is in the house or on the property. Oiling the hinges does not help.

Many collectors drop their purchases off with a friend until a convenient time can be found to slip them into the house. This works well only if the two spouses do not speak to each other. More do than collectors realize. Birds of a feather stick together.

A few collectors have a shed by the parking area, thus providing a temporary home until time is advantageous. This is viable if the door is kep locked and the only person with the key is the collector.

One of the reasons so many collectors collect smalls is that they are easier to slip into the house than large objects. The only recourse for the large-object collector is to face the music and perfect the "there is no way I could live without it" justification arguments. A preliminary softening based on flowers, candy, and other customary gifts is doomed to failure. Either talk the object into the house or forget it.

Some collectors first take their new purchases to their office. After a few months or years have passed, the objects arrive at home under the guise of "this no longer fits the new office decorating scheme and I like it too much to get rid of it." This approach is cowardly; but, not every collector is a superhero. The field has wimps.

You Can Tell a True Collector by His Underwear

After several years of continuing hints from Connie, my wife, about the increasing deterioration of my underwear, I finally bit the bullet, went to a store, and purchased replacements. Even I had to admit that I let things go a bit too far. I could read a newspaper clearly through the cloth of my undershirts. It is amazing how well things last when you take good care of them.

Parting with old friends is difficult. When faced with a crisis of this nature, I have discovered that the only way to preserve one's mental health is to take an "out with the old, in with the new" position. As I entered the store, I had made the decision to purchase a totally fresh supply of underwear.

When it comes to clothing, I fall into the thrifty class. I see no reason why I should not wear a ten-year-old sport coat as long as it still fits and wear is minimal. If the fashion industry had to rely on individuals such as me for its well being, there would be no fashion industry. I wear my shirts until the elbows wear through. I used to ask Connie to iron on a patch so I could stretch the wearability a littler longer. She did it once and then watched horrified as I wore the shirt at one of my public appearances. Now she refuses. How inconsiderate.

I am fully cognizant that another interpretation of my thriftiness is that I am cheap. This may well be. There are individuals who wear the cheap label with pride. Thrift and cheap—they are one and the same to me. Given this fact, it will come as no surprise that I waited to buy my new underwear until one of the major department stores was having a 25 percent discount sale.

My clothing life works on the "ten-day" supply theory—five pairs of white socks and five pairs of dark blue socks, ten sets of underwear, and ten favorite shirts. Recycle them regularly and carefully. When I do, they last, and last, and last, and last.

The problem is that most basic white undershirts and shorts are sold in packages of three. You already know that I would never waste my hard-earned money on overpriced designer anything. What to do— buy twelve or nine? Yep, Mr. Thrifty bought nine.

The final bill for my purchases was under $75, not bad for a once every five to seven year expenditure. I should have felt good when I left the store; but I did not.

All I could think about was the fact that I had spent $75 on something that would eventually wear out and that I would have to spend the same amount or more to replace them at some point in the future. $75! Do you know how many goodies I could have added to my collections if I would not have had to spend that money on clothing? It was all I could think about. I felt victimized.

A question that I am often asked is: "What characterizes a true collector?" My stock answer is that a true collector is an individual who plans to die owning everything he ever collected. He never sells or trades. Each object he acquires is so precious that parting with even one is enough to drive him to the edge of insanity.

Since few questions in life have a single answer, my stock answer may be too simplistic. Consider as an alternative the concept that a true collector is someone who sees every expenditure on something other than his collection as a waste of money. Sound ridiculous? It is not. I know people like this. I am one of them.

I have not reached the point where I deny myself the basic necessities of life—shelter, food, and clothing—in favor of yet another goody for the pile. Occasionally I even give in to excess, especially when good food is involved. I do not have a weight problem for nothing.

However, in reflecting upon my personal experiences and talking with other collectors, there is one inescapable fact. The definition of what constitutes a basic necessity differs significantly between a collector and a collector's spouse and, in some cases, society as a whole. Could this be one of the reasons why so many individuals view true collectors as eccentrics?

For example, consider ties. Ideally, I would own only one tie. Actually, if life were truly ideal, I would not own any ties. I hate ties. I view ties as a total waste of money. I have never understood why men have to wear ties. Whenever I try to make one useful either as a handkerchief or bib, people get upset. The only reason I own a tie is for public appearances. Television show producers and individuals who hire me to speak feel more comfortable if I show up wearing a tie. A good tie is capable of lasting a lifetime. I still have several ties from the 1950s that are as good as new. I would love nothing better than to select one and wear it forever.

On the other hand, Connie feels quite differently. She thinks that I should own a number of ties. She buys me several each year. Her selections are stylish and trendy, her attempt to keep me fashionable. Inside I know that I should deeply appreciate both her generosity and caring, BUT... The ties that she buys are expensive. There rests the problem. All I can think about is how many collectibles that money could have bought; and, it is not even my money. Try as I might (and, believe me, I have tried), I cannot get past this problem.

"Rinker on Collectibles" is written from the personal perspective. However, it would be wrong for my readers to assume that the above is a male-related collecting problem. Rest assured, I know a large number of female collectors whose mindset is very similar to mine.

As a means of opening the door to greater understanding between true collectors and their (spouses, significant others, companions, partners—pick a term with which you can identify), I offer the following list of what true collectors question as basic necessities: anything gourmet or with a designer label; articles of clothing exceeding ten in number; a new car or appliance unless the previous model is older than ten years or repairs occur at a rate greater than once a week; dining out more than once a month; anniversary or holiday gifts that are not collectible-related; flowers; and, vacations, especially those involving family or travel greater than fifty miles.

The list that I drafted prior to beginning this column was far longer. No purpose is served by making true collectors look like ogres. Deep down inside, true collectors are really nice people once you get to know them.

Shortly after my underwear purchase, I was sharing my experiences and thoughts with the Rinkettes, the Rinker Enterprises staff. One of the women was extremely surprised at the longevity of my underwear. Her family's last less than half that long; but she adds bleach to her whites. When I went home that evening, I hid Connie's bottle of bleach—no sense taking chances.

I realize that among a select group of moderns the no underwear approach is quite popular. I tried this for a day; but quickly found it was not my thing.

In the final analysis, I doubt if my contention that you can tell a true collector by his underwear will ever be tested. No government or private foundation is likely to provide a grant for this purpose. It is questionable how many true collectors would cooperate. Be that as it may. They know. And, now you know.

Neither a Borrower nor a Lender Be

The following telephone conversations are true. The names have been changed to protect the innocent. Any similarities to persons living or dead are purely coincidental.

[Ring, ring, ring]

"Hi, Ed."

"Harry, how's it going?"

"Not bad."

"What can I do for you?"

"Well, Ed, I was at the Allentown Toy Show this past weekend. It was great. Added a few neat things to my jigsaw puzzle collection."

"Wait a minute. Are you telling me you need to borrow money, AGAIN?"

"Ed, you're a prophet. There were a couple of things I simply couldn't resist. Top of the line items. Must haves. You know how it is. Too good to pass up. They kept saying 'buy me' every time I looked at them. I tried walking away. I really did. Unknown forces kept pulling me back. The temptation was simply overwhelming. I had no choice but to give in."

"How bad is the damage?"

"How does a thousand sound?"

"Harry, you haven't paid off the loan we financed last February."

"I realize that, Ed. But, listen. The loan was for twenty months, right? I just made the eighth payment. At two hundred a month, I've paid the bank over sixteen hundred dollars. All I want to do is borrow back a thousand. It doesn't take a genius to see I'm actually ahead."

"Ahead! You haven't been ahead on your loans for over ten years. The minute you even come close to paying off a loan, there's always something that comes along you can't live without."

"What do you want me to do, Ed, become a monk? I have to go to the shows. It's my job. Buying is an occupational necessity. They trust me because I buy. Besides, you know I'm good for it. Have I ever failed to make a payment?"

"Yeah, yeah. You've sung this song so many times it sounds like a stuck record. When do you need it?"

"Well, errr...(cough, cough), I kind of ran out of cash the first hour of the show. Fortunately, I had my checkbook. Is today too soon? If you're busy, tomorrow is fine, just call the main office and tell them not to bounce any checks between now and then."

"Just a minute while I check your file. Harry, where's your personal financial statement? If I remember correctly, it was missing the last time, too. You took a form along and promised to send it to me the next day."

"Ed, you know how busy I am. I intended to fill it out and send it to you. Really. Filling out forms and me, well, you know. I've dealt with your bank for over three decades. That has to count for something. My payment record is solid. I'm a no-risker."

"Harry, the bank has requirements. I really need that form."

"Fine. Send me a copy; and, I'll fill it out."

"What do you mean send? If you want money, you'll have to come to the bank and fill out an application."

"Fill out an application! Listen, Ed, nothing has changed since the last time. Make a photocopy of the old form and change the date."

"Harry, banking has changed. We have procedures that we have to follow."

"I know, I know. Can't you just fill out the application form for me? I'll sign it when I stop in to pick up the money. Better yet, deposit the money directly into my savings account. I'll stop by in the next day or two and sign the papers."

"No way, Harry. Things aren't done that way. Besides, there's the application fee."

"An application fee? I never paid an application fee before."

"I know you didn't. I waived it in the past as a courtesy. The only problem is I can't keep waiving it. Your borrowing frequency is such that the bank loses more than a hundred dollars a year in waived fees for you alone."

"But, I'm a good customer."

"I admit that—always good for a laugh. By the way, what are we financing this time?"

"I found this great wooden jigsaw puzzle. It's a Bildajig. You build several layers of wood jigsaw puzzles and then stack them on top of each other to make a three-dimensional wooden cargo ship. English. From the 1930s. Very hard to find."

"This is a step up for you. [**Author's Note:** The fictitious character who is the focus of this story borrowed money in February to finance the purchase of a dark blue, Historical Staffordshire chamber pot featuring Erie Canal transfers. The object and amount involved was the subject of snickers, laughter, and disparaging remarks among members of the Lehigh Valley, Pennsylvania, banking community for several months.] The problem is my superiors. When they look at the loan and see that it is secured with a jigsaw puzzle, they are going to think I've lost my mind. What am I going to tell them?"

"Tell them I got a bargain."

"There's no way on God's green earth I am going to persuade my loan reviewers that a thousand dollar jigsaw puzzle is a bargain."

"Ed, everyone has to pioneer new ground. Remember, the Hopalong Cassidy bedroom suite?"

"Remember! They still think I was crazy."

"Yeah, I know. But, the bank did loan the money. In fact, if I remember correctly you and several members of the bank visited my office to inspect the bedroom suite."

"Harry, every bank checks the property securing its loans from time to time."

"True, Ed. But, the guy who wanted to lie down on the bottom bunk. Really!"

"Harry, I want you to make me a promise."

"If I can, Ed."

"I want you to promise me this is the last time you'll ask me to do this until your loan is paid in full."

"I can't do that. If I keep the payments at the current level, the loan will be for at least eighteen months. Asking me not to make a major purchase during that period is inhuman."

"Well, you might try limiting your spending to money you have on hand."

"Ed, there are things you simply have to buy when you see them. You may never have another chance. You cannot say no."

"Harry, I'm sorry. No promise. No money."

"Ed, I've already written the checks."

"Sorry, Let me know if you change your mind."

[Click]

[Ring, ring, ring]

"Hi, Diane."

"Harry, how's it going?"

"Not bad."

"What can I do for you?"

"Well, Diane, I was at the Allentown Toy Show this past weekend. It was great. Added a few neat things to my jigsaw puzzle collection."

"Harry, NOT AGAIN!"

Why Do I Have to Remember All Those Damned Dates?

Pop quiz time. Do not panic. There are only eight questions. Write your answers on a separate piece of paper. You only need to get four right to pass. To save embarrassment, grade your own paper.

Question #1:   The United States Postal Service introduced Zip Codes on July 1st of what year?

Question #2:   The United States occupied Japan from September 9 of what year to April 28 of what year?

Question #3:   In what year did Congress pass the McKinley Tariff Act?

Question #4:   The first telephone area code was instituted in Englewood, New Jersey, in what year?

Question #5:   According to the United States government, a firearm has to be made on or before what date to be considered "antique"?

Question #6:   The three western zones of occupied West Germany combined as the Federal Republic of Germany on September 21st of what year? [Note: East Germany became the German Democratic Republic on October 7th of that same year.]

Question #7:   The U.S. government decreed that "Nippon" was to be replaced by "Japan" on goods imported into the United States in what year?

Question #8:   In what year did NBC's New York City station, WNBT, start regular network service to Schenectady, NY, and Philadelphia, PA?

The answer to Question #1 is 1963. One of the surprising pieces of information that is missing when twentieth-century collectibles are sold is the date or period when the object was made. The appearance or lack of a zip code in the manufacturer's address on the box or instruction sheet helps place the object before or after 1963. While this does not solve the specific date problem, it does provide a point of reference.

America occupied Japan from September 9, 1945 to April 28, 1952. Americans love to collect by category. It is extremely hard to justify collecting Occupied Japan material from an aesthetic point of view. Not all goods manufactured during this period were marked "Made in Occupied Japan." Some were simply marked "Made in Japan" or "Japan." For Occupied Japan collectors the key is "occupied." Without "occupied," collectibility drops considerably.

Congress passed the McKinley Tariff Act in 1891. The act is important to collectors because it required that goods imported into the United States had to be marked with their country of origin. Read the previous sentence carefully. The act did not state that the goods had to be marked with a non-removable mark; paper labels were adequate. Likewise, only one object in a set had to be marked, not every piece.

There is a false assumption made by many sellers that if no country of origin appears on an object, it must have been made before 1891. Not true. It could be an unmarked object from a set or an object from which the paper label has been removed. Further, some manufacturers, especially the English, marked their export goods with the country of origin long before the McKinley Tariff Act was passed. During the Victorian era, individuals of means preferred European objects based on a prejudice that European goods were of better manufacture and design than American pieces.

Unlike the Zip Code, the use of telephone area codes did not happen simultaneously across the country. The first area code was instituted in 1951. Area codes were introduced as regional telephone companies purchased and installed equipment to handle the new system. It took several decades before the process was completed. An attempt to locate a list of the various area codes and when they were first used proved futile. Because of the extended rollout, the use of area codes as a dating key is difficult.

We should know better than to trust anything involving the antiques and collectibles business to the federal government. According to the Bureau of Alcohol, Tobacco, and Firearms regulations in Title 27 of the code of Federal Regulations, an "antique" firearm is "Any firearm (including any firearm with a matchlock, flintlock, percussion cap, or similar type ignition system) manufactured in or before 1898..." So much for the one-hundred-year rule. Where the government came up with 1898 is beyond my wildest imagination. The date remains fixed. Weapons collectors are stuck with 1898 until Congress decides to change it. Attempting to regulate when anything becomes an antique is the height of ridiculousness.

There already are collectors for goods made in the western zones of occupied Germany. Again, I question the raison d'etre, but what the heck. There is no accounting for reason or taste in collecting. The Americans, English, and French combined their German occupation zones and created the Federal Republic of Germany on September 21, 1949.

I have to wonder how many of the twentysomething, thirtysomething, and even some of the younger fortysomething generation recognize the word "Nippon." It was the term used to describe Japan during the early part of the twentieth century. In 1921 the federal government (don't you just love how they interfere?) decided that "Japan" should replace "Nippon." Therefore, Nippon pieces usually will date between 1891 and 1921.

Network television provided the framework for large-scale star endorsing. The Hopalong Cassidy phenomenon would never have achieved the level that it did without television. The first regular network service was introduced in 1946. By the late 1950s network television was king. The golden age of television is the Age of the Big

Three (ABC, CBS, and NBC). Fox, a host of other independents, and cable have sounded the death knell for the big three. TV will never be the same.

As a bonus question, which early television network was poised to be the third of the big three, but did not make it? The answer is DuMont, which set up a national network in 1946/1947.

How did you do? You only had to get four right to pass. My bet is that you failed.

The simple truth is that in order to survive as a collectibles dealer or collector, you have to know history—not just American history, world history. Dates are important. It is not enough to date something as twentieth century or post-war. We have to be specific.

Between undergraduate and graduate school, I spent nine years in college studying history, ranging from general history to the history of science and history of technology. Hardly a day goes by that I do not draw upon this background in the collectibles field. I have learned the hard way that I must pay attention to what happens around me and more importantly when it happened.

If someone asks you where you were when the *Challenger* spacecraft blew up, chances are you can tell them. However, if asked the month, day, and year, how would you do? If you are lucky, you will get the year right.

The sadistic side of me says to end the column NOW. Do not give the answer. Make the curious look it up—first, to see how much time it takes and, second, to penalize them for not remembering something that they witnessed. I am too nice to leave them hanging. The correct date is January 28, 1986.

CHAPTER 11

Collectiquette

Until now, you could not find this information in any book about collecting. Yet, every collector assumes everyone knows, understands, and practices Collectiquette. I make it mandatory reading before anyone views my collections.

The Etiquette and Protocol of Collectors

The best museums in America are not found in marble-faced buildings with column entrances nestled in urban park settings or in the homes and workshops of hundreds of well-known historic sites. This nation's best museums are located in modest inner city and suburban dwellings, largely indistinguishable from those of their neighbors. These inconspicuous edifices house collections ranging from fine American colonial furniture to twentieth-century lunch boxes assembled by thousands of private collectors. Their owners are the real preservers of this nation's heritage.

Never turn down an invitation to "come see" a private collection. It is a privilege and opportunity that is too good to miss. Most collectors are extremely selective when issuing such invitations.

Implied in the invitation to view a private collection, but not always understood by the visitor, is a series of dos and don'ts called Collectiquette. Private collectors automatically assume individuals invited to view their collections know and adhere to Collectiquette's prescribed rules. Unfortunately and often with tragic consequences, many visitors are completely unaware that such rules exist. Collectiquette is not covered in etiquette books.

While Collectiquette involves more than common sense, applying common sense is a good place to start. If time permits, do advanced homework—both about the collector and his collection. If you are unfamiliar with the type of objects in the collection, read one or more books on the subject, especially if one is written by the person whose collection you are visiting. Collectors come alive when their visitors can "talk their language."

Turn your invitation to view the collection into a learning opportunity. The primary reason you received an invitation is the collector's assumption that you have some interest in what you will be seeing. Collectors have little tolerance for gawkers and starers.

Set some goals for your visit. What would you most like to learn? Share your goals with the collector. Most will quite willingly alter their usual tour approach to accommodate a visitor's wishes.

Do not talk about your upcoming visit to anyone. Respecting the privacy of the collector and his collection is perhaps the most violated rule of Collectiquette.

Even if they have a sophisticated security alarm system, most collectors are paranoid about theft and extremely sensitive about the general public and rival collectors knowing exactly what they have in their collections. These are primary reasons why collectors severely restrict the number of individuals they allow to view their collections. They do not want a security leak.

Everyone loves to brag. Couple this desire with the competitive nature of most antiques collectors and problems arise. He who tells the best war stories, i.e., has the best bragging rights, is a hero. It requires a major effort to refrain from talking about a visit to the home of a collector and describing in detail what you saw.

Never accept an invitation to visit a private collection if you have time constraints. Assume a minimum visiting time of two to three hours. Collections are meant to be enjoyed and savored, not gulped. If you only have limited time available, tactfully explain your situation to the collector and ask if you can reschedule or only see a part of the collection with the opportunity to return later to view the rest.

Never hesitate to ask the collector in advance or upon arrival how much time he has set aside to spend with you. Even if you have allotted more time than this, accept this time limitation without question. Extending it rests with the collector, not you.

Resist being nervous. Relax. You are not visiting Mecca, Valhalla, or the heavenly kingdom. More likely than not the objects in the collection were mass produced and utilitarian in origin. There is no need to treat them as religious objects and worship them.

Socializing before viewing a collection is common. It gives the collector a chance to become comfortable with his visitors. This is an excellent time to discuss your goals and expectations if you did not do so in advance of the visit. Consider yourself lucky when you encounter a collector who postpones socializing until the end.

There are a few collectors who socilize in advance to heighten the anticipation of their guests, especially when the guest is a rival collector. They love milking the candy shop syndrome. There is a special place in hell for them.

Allow the collector to set the pace. Some collectors have a fixed routine for showing their collections. Their tours are carefully planned. They become uncomfortable if this routine is broken. When you encounter such a collector, hold your questions until the end.

DO NOT TOUCH ANYTHING WITHOUT THE COLLEC-TOR'S PERMISSION. An invitation to visit is not an invitation to touch. This is a courtesy that can only be extended by the host. Being granted permission to touch an object is not blanket permission to touch another. Assume, until told otherwise, that permission to touch is granted on an object by object basis.

Never handle an object unless in the direct view of the collector. If the collector leaves you alone for any reason, keep your hands in your pockets or at your sides. Look but do not touch.

How you handle the first object will determine whether or not the collector will grant you permission to handle additional objects. Watch the collector's eyes. They will indicate to you how you are doing.

Follow these simple rules: (1) use two hands; (2) always support the object from the bottom; (3) if an object has parts, e.g., a lid, handle them one unit at a time; (4) do not move around while holding an object; (5) if something is in the way, remove it before picking up an object; (6) put the object back in the same location and facing in the same direction as it was prior to your picking it up; (7) indicate that you have hold of an object securely when passing it to or accepting it from another individual; and, (8) if your hands are dirty or become dirty during the handling of objects, excuse yourself and wash them.

Asking questions is a standard part of the learning process. The collector expects you to ask questions. He uses them to judge your interest and the depth of your background knowledge. Hopefully, you did your advanced homework.

Resist the temptation to ask too many questions, especially during the first moments of the tour. If a collector proves responsive to questions, keep them object focused. Let the collector share his knowledge and experiences. Keep your personal stories and thoughts about the collector and his collection to yourself. This is the collector's moment in the sun.

There are some questions that you should never ask, e.g., how much did you pay for that and where and from whom did you buy it? Do not be surprised if the collector quips, "none of your business." This is the correct response.

Often a collector's spouse will accompany the tour or be within earshot. All too often, objects are not brought into the house openly. Many collectors are very secretive concerning their acquisitions, especially with their spouses or partners.

If you see something in the collection that you would like to own, is it proper to say something to the collector? The answer is a guarded yes. Be highly selective. I usually say, "if you ever plan to sell 'x,' I would very much appreciate it if you would give me a call." I usually try to make such statements when the spouse or partner is present. I know it sounds callous, but if something unfortunate happens to the collector, I want the remaining spouse to remember that nice man who visited and wanted to buy a few things.

Permission to visit is not permission to take photographs. This is a very sensitive point. I recommend no camera during an initial visit. If you do see an object of which you would like a photograph, make your wishes known to the collector. Many collectors have photographs of the objects in their collections, especially the important ones. State specifically why you want the photographs and how you plan to use them. Collectors are far more tolerant when the photograph is for personal reference and not to be shared with someone else than they are when the photograph might appear in print. If studio shots are required, this is best done during a future visit. Do not be surprised if the collector says no. Most will.

Avoid talking about your collection. This is neither the time nor place. You are on tour, not involved in a game of one-upmanship. If the collector does ask you about your collection, keep your answer brief.

Eventually, the formal tour ends. If time remains and the collector is amenable, now is your opportunity to ask to examine some of the objects or a specific portion of the collection in more detail or inquire about things you thought you would see in the collection but did not.

Have specific goals in mind when asking to handle a group of objects. You might inspect a few objects to learn more about how they were manufactured or examine in detail that portion of the collection that crosses over into your collecting focus.

Two areas generally not included by most collectors in a general tour of their collections are secondary support literature, ranging from advertising to trade catalogs, and reproductions. Today's collectors are sophisticated. Collections are much broader in scope than in the past. Most collectors buy anything related to or picturing their collecting theme, e.g., an automobile collector with an extensive collection of car-theme postcards.

Reproductions (exact copies), copycats (stylistic copies), fantasy items (later items made in the same fashion as period pieces), and fakes are a fact of life in every collecting category. Collectors acquire examples for study purposes. Knowing what objects exist, how they were made, and how they age helps collectors avoid buying mistakes. These pieces provide the collector with the ideal opportunity to showcase his knowledge. Handling and discussing reproductions, copycats, fantasy items, and fakes with a collector more often than not is the highlight of the tour.

Forgetting to say thank you is a major problem in the antiques community. Do not make this mistake. If you consult Miss Manners, you will find that a handwritten thank you note is proper. It certainly does not hurt. Thanks at the door and a telephone follow-up call a few days later expressing your gratitude serves just as well.

Do not be surprised if you find yourself making one or more promises to your host. A tremendous sense of sharing takes place during the viewing process. If you make promises, write them down and honor them. Collectors always remember these promises, especially if they relate to providing them with information they do not have.

There is one last unwritten Collectiquette rule. If you are a collector, the person whose collection you are viewing assumes you will reciprocate his generosity by extending an invitation to visit your collection when he is in your area. Do not fight this. The collector will call when he is in your area whether you formally invite him or not. Extend the invitation.

When extending the invitation, do not hesitate to establish a few conditions. "I would like to invite you and your spouse to see my collection whenever you are in my area. However, because of my spouse's and my busy schedule, I need a few days advance notice. I hate to have you come only to find that I am not home or have insufficient time available to show you my collection properly."

Horror stories and collecting go hand in hand. One of my worst involves a "come see" invitation. After viewing a private collection several years ago, I invited the couple to stop by and see my collection when they were in the area. About nine months later at 8:30 on a Sunday morning (a rare Sunday off for me), I received a call from the couple.

"We are in the area. Could we stop by and see your collection today?" Although my wife was shaking her head no, I told them to stop by around one in the afternoon.

Our peaceful Sunday morning was spent cleaning and straightening the house and preparing light refreshments to be served after the tour concluded. Sure enough, a car came down our lane at one o'clock. Then another car, and another. The couple had invited every friend they had in the area to come on the tour.

My wife was furious. She exited out the side door telling me I was on my own. I suppressed my anger and gave the group a very fast fifteen-minute look. I should never have let them in the door.

Now I am very specific when inviting someone to view my collection. When he calls, I ask exactly who is coming. If he says he is staying with friends, I make it quite clear that the invitation is limited to him and does not include friends. I will never win the Mr. Popularity award; but my sanity is preserved.

Writing about Collectiquette is easy. Practicing it is very difficult. Most collectors violate the rules, especially those relating to privacy, before they realize it. Mistakes happen. The key is to keep trying. You will know you are on the right track when the collector you are visiting ends your visit by saying, "I would love to have you come back."

CHAPTER 12

The Internet

Each day the percentage of antiques and collectibles bought and sold on the Internet increases. While the Internet will totally replace the traditional selling sources—auctions; antiques flea markets, malls, shops, and shows; and collector-to-collector and dealer-to-dealer sales—its growth potential is still in infancy.

The Internet is more than eBay. Search the Internet and you will find dozens of stores, and thousands of individual sellers, information resources, and auction Web sites devoted to antiques and collectibles. Having stated this, eBay is the place everyone goes to buy, sell, or do research.

Only a few of the "Rinker on Collectibles" columns that comprise this book were written before the Internet arrived on the scene. It is impossible to write about any aspect of the trade today without considering the impact of the Internet. As a result, you will find references to the Internet and eBay everywhere. The index provides their locations.

This chapter is a catchall for information that applies primarily to the Internet.

Retail Value—Is a New Definition Required?

The first three paragraphs of the "Price Notes" section of the introduction to *Harry L. Rinker The Official Price Guide to Collectibles, Third Edition* (House of Collectibles, 1999, $19.95) read: "The values in this book are based on an object being in very good to fine condition. This means that the object is complete and shows no visible signs of aging and wear when held at arm's length....

"Prices are designed to reflect the prices that sellers at an antiques mall or collectibles show would ask for their merchandise. When an object is collected nationally, it is possible to determine a national price consensus. Most of the objects in this book fall into that category. There are very few twentieth-century collectibles whose values are regionally driven…

"There are no fixed prices in the antiques and collectibles market. Value is fluid, not absolute. Price is very much of the time and moment. Change the circumstances, change the price…."

It is impossible to discuss the value of an object without considering its condition. Most price guides use "very good condition" as the standard. A few use "fine condition," one grade above. In reality, less than a third of surviving objects, especially those from the post-1945 era, meet or exceed "very good condition" criteria. Far too many objects offered for sale at flea markets, malls, shows, and on the Internet should reside in the local landfill.

I have examined the condition issue in past columns. This column explores how the Internet is forcing a redefinition of retail value. Until the arrival of the Internet, the price placed on an object by an experienced dealer selling at a mall or show was accepted as the standard for retail value. The general assumption was this was the price an experienced collector would pay for an object he did not own and wished to acquire. Almost no one questions a dealer's price. Heaven forbid a dealer would incorrectly price an object. Given the large amount of material that remains unsold at malls and shows, it is time to question the validity of these prices. Within the past year, there is a growing sentiment in the field that mall and show prices are too high.

A few market reporters have suggested that prices realized on the Internet should become the new retail value standard. Used in this context, Internet is synonymous with prices realized on eBay. If eBay becomes or is the standard, reality suggests that a viable definition for "retail value" is no longer possible.

In the middle of the twentieth century, prices realized at auction, especially catalog auctions, were considered an accurate reflection of retail value. This holds true only if two key criteria are met. First, the final buyer is a collector. Second, the collector competed actively against one or more additional collectors, each of whom shared a strong desire to own the piece.

In reality, dealers purchase more than half the lots sold at a typical auction. They are buying inventory for resale. Most will double or triple the initial purchase price. For these lots, the auction price is not a valid reflection of an object's true retail price.

Ebay is an auction. Actually, it is only the auction vehicle, providing a venue for the seller and bidders to interact. As at a live auction, determining if the final eBay buyer is a collector or seller is almost impossible. I have lost track of the number of dealers who have told me, "Ebay is a great place to buy, but a very difficult place to sell."

I have no statistics to support the following assumption, only a gut feeling. I believe less than half the goods purchased on eBay are bought by sellers seeking merchandise for resale at shows and malls. Collectors, individuals purchasing for nostalgic and decorating purposes, and individuals buying for reuse are making the majority of the purchases on eBay and the Internet. There are two basic reasons. First, the Internet offers a far higher level of availability than any other selling venue. Second, bargains abound.

Ebay and other Internet prices have to be carefully and correctly interpreted when being used to determine an object's value. For the vast majority of objects, Internet prices appear to follow a specific pricing cycle. When first offered, an object, especially if it falls into the hard to find, top echelon (top 100 to 150 objects in a collecting category), or masterpiece level (top five to ten objects in a collecting category), usually achieves a very strong price. Potential sellers surfing the Internet take notice. Within a short period, a second or third example appears. Once again, these attract strong prices, albeit the number of bidders decreases. As additional examples appear, the market bottoms out. Experienced Internet auction buyers know that if they are patient, they usually can buy the fifth, sixth, etc., example at one-third to one-half the price realized for the first object.

Ultimately, the market floods. There is nothing I love more than to track an object during its duration on eBay or another auction site and find that it failed to attract a single bid. If I would like to purchase the object, I do not hesitate to e-mail the seller and make an offer, sometimes significantly below the asked opening bid. I am successful more often than I fail in reaching an agreement with the seller to buy the object.

There are many categories and subcategories where less than half the objects offered actually sell. While a myriad of reasons from poor condition to an unrealistic opening bid or reserve are possible explanations, oversupply and fulfilled market is the most common explanation. The Internet has caused every buyer and seller to rethink scarcity. The Internet has shown that objects are far more common than most buyers and sellers are willing to admit.

Joe Pizzo, the new Soakie advisor for the 2001 edition of my *The Official Price Guide to Flea Market Treasures,* published by House of Collectibles, wrote: "The prices listed are lower than those on similar items from your last edition and also lower than the prices in the Bubble Bath book by Greg Moore and myself. This is due to the influence of the Internet—particularly eBay. Internet auctions have exploded in the past year or two, bring more supply of collectibles onto the market than there is demand for. For example, in the mid-1990s I searched for years for a Little Orphan Annie container from Lander Co. and finally found one for $60. Now the same bottle is offered for auction on eBay at opening bids in the $10 range and will usually not receive any bids.

"You may receive letters from people telling you that they can get one or another particular soaky for less on the Internet than I have listed in your book. However, the book is a price guide for flea markets, and collectors are willing to pay more at a flea market or antique mall where they can handle the item, pay no shipping charges, and receive instant gratification. Therefore, I have established values in the middle ground between prices realized on Internet auctions and recent guide values of the past two years."

Is there a middle ground? Is this the answer? If the answer is yes, the answer is temporary. Price is a factor of supply and demand. It is also a factor of access to that supply.

The Internet is not a good barometer at the moment because it is still a long way from reaching its access potential. As the number of users increases, the fluctuation in prices realized will also increase. Value will become even more fluid than at present. Once liquid starts to flow downhill, it becomes difficult to reverse. Many are concerned that the "turn around point" for Internet prices is already past.

What is the current percentage of difference between prices realized on the Internet and asked at malls and shows? The difference appears to be somewhere between times two and three at the moment, higher in some collecting categories and lower in others. It is only recently that these differences are being openly discussed in the field and print.

I noted earlier "there are no fixed prices for antiques and collectibles." This is more true in 2005 than it was in 1995.

The consequences are significant. Price guide authors are finding it increasingly difficult to establish standards that can be used to create meaningful prices. Some are hiding behind ranges, but this is the coward's way out. More than ever, price guides are merely guides.

More and more buyers are recognizing the savings they can achieve by comparison shopping. They want bargains. Chances are that they will only buy one out of ten items at price guide retail. The rest will be bought near or far below price guide retail.

Sellers are accustomed to maintaining a large inventory, often keeping objects in inventory for years until a buyer surfaces. This is a big mistake in today's trendy collectibles market. Like regular merchants, they are discovering the "take what you can and move on" sales approach makes more sense than holding long-term.

Until the Internet matures, a firm definition for what constitutes an object's retail value will remain elusive—a frightening concept for some, a sense of excitement for others.

The Costs of Doing Business on eBay Can Add Up

New Orleans was the site of eBay Live!, eBay's annual convention. "Leap to New Heights" was the theme of the 2004 convention.

I spent the morning and most of the afternoon of Friday, June 25, at the convention. I learned a great deal, albeit not as much as I would have learned had I been present for the full three days, June 24 to 26.

Before talking about specifics, it is again worth emphasizing the declining importance of antiques and collectibles in the overall eBay revenue stream. Once king-of-the-hill, antiques and collectibles now represent a very small portion of eBay's revenue. The good news is that eBay remains committed to the antiques and collectibles trade. eBay has no intention of forgetting its roots.

When I entered the antiques and collectibles trade in 1981, I wanted to make a living without selling antiques and collectibles. As a result, I created an antiques and collectibles education and information service. Today's business analysts would describe my approach as "thinking outside the box," hopefully something I still do.

My business is service. The same is true for dozens of new "outside the box" businesses participating in the tradeshow portion of eBay Live! This column focuses on four key areas: (1) photography, (2) international trading, (3) audio, and (4) bonding. Many of these services are designed primarily for other eBay divisions, especially those selling contemporary merchandise. However, the services offered have application to the antiques and collectibles field as well. All have one element in common—utilizing them increases the cost of doing business on eBay.

Photographs are essential to selling objects on eBay. Quality photographs are few and far between. I continually make great buys by bidding on objects where the photography is so fuzzy that it is impossible to see the detail. When I am familiar with an object and there is an accurate condition report in the listing, I do not need a sharp photograph to know what I am buying. The same is not true for novice and less experienced buyers.

[**Author's Note:** All the following quotes are from the Community Conference Guide, the program guide for the 2004 eBay Live! convention.]

Three companies offered photograph lighting packages. Cloud Dome, Inc. (P.O. Box 9, Lafayette, CO 80026; www.clouddome.com) is "a studio-in-a-bag. It's the simplest way for anyone to take professional-quality photographs without complicated lighting. Made of high impact, non-yellowing acrylic, Cloud Dome evenly diffuses ambient light over the surface area of the object being shot as well as stabilizing your camera."

Litestage Lighting Systems (904 Fairway Drive, Bensenville, IL 60106; www.litestage.com) has a "complete, self-contained, do-it-yourself product photography lighting system. Litestage eliminates shadows, hot spots and reflections providing consistent controlled lighting...Comes with integrated strobe (flash) and tungsten lamps. 30" x 30" x 24" inside."

Ortery Technologies, Inc. (7 Chrysler, Irvine, CA 92618; www.ortery.com) specializes "in the creation of color-managed, digital photography studios that can be used by anyone, regardless of photography experience, to create (in seconds) SHADOW-FREE, professional images ideal for eBay auctions and business communications." I saw Ortery's Coloreal (www.coloreal.com), a turnkey digital photography studio. I was impressed. When Rinker Enterprises was actively engaged in preparing black and white and color images for the trade, we used a special bottom- and back-lit photography table. Coloreal's box measures 24" x 24" x 28", so its ability to photograph large objects is limited. However, it is ideal for small objects. I am seriously thinking of acquiring one just to photo document Linda's jewelry collection.

I offered a series of Institute for the Study of Antiques and Collectibles courses at Kutztown University (PA) and Portland State University (OR). I repeatedly urged my students to think globally. Many raised concerns about doing business globally, especially in the areas of shipping and customs. Recognizing this growing market, several companies now have programs designed to answer these issues. The two companies below offer services for large scale importers and exporters. It will not be long before a company arrives on the scene designed to service the one-at-a-time eBay seller.

A & A Contract Customs Brokers (#101 120-176th Street, Surrey, B.C. V3S-9S2, Canada; www.aacb.com) helps "you save time and money with all your cross border and distribution needs. Customs? Duties? Taxes? Warehousing? Shipping & Distribution? A&A has been providing solutions for small, medium and large importers and exporters since 1979. They are also eBay users themselves and understand the unique challenges of the eBay community."

Borderfree (20 Eglinton Avenue West, Suite 600, Toronto, ON M4R 1K8, Canada; www.borderfree.com) "allows sellers to easily reach international buyers without changing existing fulfillment practices. Simple, easy-to-use tools provide your buyers with international cost information directly from your listings, low-cost global fulfillment services are available through a domestic shipping address, and robust order management tools assist in processing and tracking orders."

How do you close a sale? It is a problem when you cannot converse with your customer. Adding audio to your listing just might be the answer. Three companies think it is.

3cim, Inc. (46560 Freemont Blvd., Suite 406, Freemont, CA 94538; www.slidetour.com) is a "leading web imaging solutions provider. 3cim's patent-pending technology allows eBay users to upload and create interactive slide show presentations for their auctions. 3cim, Inc., products allow the user the ability to add audio narration to the auction listing from any phone and manage their data online."

Auction Video.com (51 West Center, Orem, UT 84057; www.auctionvideo.com) provides a "simple and innovative way for all eBay sellers to include AUDIO and VIDEO in their eBay listings, through Patent Pending Technology."

TalkinAuction.com (3038 Smith Lane, Franklin, TN 37069; www.talkinauction.com) is a service that "enables eBay sellers to add the power of the human voice to auction listings. TalkinAuction.com links your custom audio message to your eBay auction, and your TalkinAuction.com message begins to play automatically."

I saw several of these audio systems in action. I was impressed. Pressed for time, I did not investigate the costs.

The business community and auctioneers within the antiques and collectibles trade are familiar with bonding, a service that guarantees the integrity of a seller's performance. Its time has arrived in respect to eBay sellers. BuySAFE, Inc. (5350 Shawnee Road, Suite 302, Alexandria, VA 22312; www.buysafe.com) is an "online auction bonding service. Buyers can have peace of mind because their transactions are guaranteed up to $10,000 at no cost. Surety bonds provided by The Hartford allow sellers to gain a powerful competitive edge that attracts more bidders and turns shoppers into buyers."

As I indicated earlier, all these services cost money. In the antiques and collectibles business where sellers are reluctant to incur any extra costs, their initial appeal will be limited. However, eBay sellers doing volume business should find them attractive.

Finally, these additional expenses are add-ons to the basic costs of doing business on eBay: (1) an Internet provider, (2) photography and photography Internet storage costs, (3) eBay fees, and (4) auction management services. I tell my Institute students to take the time and calculate their costs of doing business in each selling venue in which they participate. Much to their surprise, the costs of doing business is much higher than they thought.

[**Author's Note:** Internet companies come and go. Some of these companies may no longer be in business when you read this book.]

Shilling—Moving to the Internet

A shill is a person who acts as a decoy. At an auction, it is an individual whose role is to run up bids, i.e., force one or more bid jumps before the auctioneer hammers the item as sold. The goal of the shill is to never buy anything. An experienced shill seems to have a sixth sense that enables him to determine exactly how high he can drive a bidder.

The good news is that most auctions are free of shills. The bad news is that not every auction is free of them.

Not every shill at an auction is in league with the auctioneer, a commonly held belief. Consignors often ask friends or relatives to "bid up" pieces on their behalf. Most auction contracts prohibit the seller and members of his immediate family from bidding. Private collectors, dealers, and dealer pools (a combination of dealers) frequently drive up competitors in hopes of exhausting their money early in the auction process. Pools bid up competitors either to force them into the pool or to discourage them from competing when a pool representative is bidding.

Whenever I have a client who is selling at auction, I strongly recommend that he does not attend. Even when the final payment is greater than expected, I find clients only remember the things that brought less than they expected and not those that sold for two to ten times more than the client anticipated.

One of my worst moments at an auction occurred when a client began bidding in order to buy back her items because she felt they were selling too cheaply. She was not bidding the items up. She was actually buying them. Since everyone at the auction knew whose material was being sold, this had a negative effect on all bidding. The auctioneer stopped the auction and asked me to talk with my client. I was able to convince her to stop bidding. The auction continued. The sales total did exceed the initial estimates.

Spotting a shill or shills at an auction is not that difficult. As bidding proceeds over a wide variety of objects, keep track of the underbidders. When the same person is the underbidder time and time again, chances are he or she is a shill. When I spot a shill, I like to play the "make him buy it" game. The goal is to end your bidding before the shill expects, thus causing the auctioneer to sell him the piece.

The use of a shill is an illegal trade practice. If it can be proven, legal action is possible. I have the highest respect for auctioneers who either ask individuals they believe are shilling to leave or refuse to take their bids.

Rumors abound about the use of shills on Internet auctions. Many sellers openly admit that they use friends to shill their merchandise. If the shill is the successful bidder, the consequences are minor. The cost to relist the piece is negligible.

In many cases, the shill is used to create a hidden reserve. Since the cost to establish a minimum reserve is low, I fail to see the merit of using a shill. Simply set a reserve.

Many Internet sellers appear to believe that starting an item at a low opening bid will promote bidding fever, thus driving an object to its reserve and higher. When no bids are received or bidding slows, the shill is called upon to move the process forward.

I have been the victim of a shill in an eBay auction. I was bidding on an advertising skill puzzle on behalf of an English dealer. It is not something I normally buy. As the final hours neared, an individual who is a prominent collector of this type of material topped my bid.

Anyone who tells you that there is privacy and anonymity on the Internet does not know what they are talking about. Everything that happens on the Internet is public knowledge. Buying and selling handles can easily be deciphered.

The advertising skill puzzle upon which I was bidding was fairly common. I was astonished to find the prominent collector bidding on it. Surely, he must have one or more in his collection. The piece was in exceptionally fine condition, so I gave him the benefit of the doubt and assumed he was upgrading. This legitimized his bid in my mind.

I was the successful bidder. In contacting the seller, I nearly fell off my chair when I discovered it was a very close personal friend of the prominent collector, a friend who is constantly in the field searching for material for the prominent collector's collection.

I am not dumb. It does not require a college education to realize what had happened. The prominent collector was acting as a shill for his friend.

I was sorely tempted to check out the selling and bidding record of these two individuals over the past month to see how many times the prominent collector assisted his friend, either in driving up bids or preventing a piece from selling too cheaply. I was mad and prepared to be vitriolic. I prefer the high ground. However, since I know both of these individuals, I decided that perhaps I really did not want to know how often they were in cahoots. The high ground is often not as high as one thinks.

As I stated earlier, there is little privacy on the Internet. I am familiar with most of the bidding handles used by rival collectors. Many collectors use more than one handle. Many collectors also sell. In essence, they are collector dealers.

I was checking the multiple handles of a rival when lo and behold I discovered him shilling the merchandise he was selling through his second handle. The object offered for sale had no reserve. The collector seller obviously was making certain that if it did not reach the price he wanted, he could buy it back to protect it. He was more than willing to pay the Internet auction the modest listing and sales fee.

Internet selling sites prohibit shilling, but they are powerless to enforce it. I doubt if any take the time to try to identify individuals involved in the practice. Some encourage users to report shills. My concern is who is checking the accusers.

Identifying an Internet shill is a time-consuming process. Fortunately, some sites allow the viewing of an individual's selling and buying record. If you feel you have been the victim of shilling, check the buying record of the shill's handle. If they have lost the vast majority of the lots on which they bid, it is time to check further. The diffi-

culty is establishing the link between the shill and the seller. Review
the closed auction page for each of the lots they failed to win. If the
same seller appears over and over again, chances are strong you have
found a shill.

Sometimes a suspicion proves negative. I bid on an item and lost.
Within days, the same listing reappeared. The listing and picture were
identical to the one on which I bid. I suspected that I was shilled. I e-
mailed the seller to ask if the initial bidder did not pay for the object. If
so, why did he not contact me as the underbidder and offer to sell
direct. The seller had a hoard, preferring to sell the multiples individually rather than through a "Dutch" auction. He did not feel it necessary
to do a new photograph each time he listed another example. Based on
this I bid and bought the item for a quarter of what I had bid during the
earlier auction.

There is no agency that appears capable of enforcing commercial
laws on the Internet. The Internet appears to be above the law.
Municipal, state, or national governments have largely been unsuccess-
ful in finding ways to apply their laws to transactions on the Internet.

With prices dropping in many collecting categories on the
Internet, the problem of shilling is going to increase rather than
decrease. Greed runs rampant over ethics and the law on the Internet.
The mindset seems to be: "If I can get away with it, I will do it."

The only defense is for a buyer to determine what he is willing to
pay, bid that amount and no more. Do not become caught up in auction
fever—easy advice to give, difficult to follow.

CHAPTER 13

The Next Generation of Collectors

The basic rules of collecting never change. What is collected most certainly does.

The future of collecting rests with the coming generations. Once a collector is hooked on collecting, the field owns him for life. While it is important never to ignore the established collector, it is critical to develop the collecting skills of the next generation. There is no future to collecting without them.

Which torch is to be passed is the critical question. I am concerned only about passing the "love of collecting" torch. I have little to no interest in seeing that a specific collecting category torch is passed. I do not care if future generations collect Hopalong Cassidy memorabilia or Depression glass. All I care about is that they collect.

Each generation has the right to determine what it collects. It owes no obligation to past generations of collectors to collect and love what they did. Today's younger collectors are highly resistant to the dictates of older collectors. My hat is off to them. Keep up the good work.

Grandfatherly Advice—The Parents

Antonio Joseph Vogt, my first grandson, was born at 2:29 a.m. on Sunday, December 17, 1995, in the Howard County Hospital in Columbia, Maryland. Connie, an operating room nurse by profession, and Rick, her son, were present throughout the birthing process. I gladly accepted the hospital's limit of two individuals in the room during the final birthing stages and dutifully waited in the waiting room.

The event was videotaped in its entirety; and I mean in its entirety. It is as explicit as any educational Lamaze class video. I have not viewed the tape and most likely never will. Some things should remain a mystery. Besides, it is the product, not the process that interests me.

My exact relationship with Antonio falls into the twilight zone, an all too common occurrence today. I am related to Antonio through marriage, not blood. I have become his grandfather by default. I am married to his paternal grandmother, but I am not his father's father. Does this mean I can opt out of any grandfatherly responsibilities? Technically, I suppose it does. But I am hooked. Antonio is a keeper.

I knew from the moment I saw Antonio that he was born to collect. He arrived wide-eyed and curious. He constantly lifted his head on his own and looked around. His tiny hands grabbed and held on to things. These are very good signs.

It is impossible for me to resist the urge to provide Ellen and Rick Vogt, Antonio's parents, with some grandfatherly advice about developing Antonio's collecting gene. Everyone has a collecting gene. They were born with it. It is fully developed in some, hardly in others. Hopefully, Antonio's collector gene will be a dominant one. I am going to do my best to see that it is.

Far too many parents neglect their child's collecting gene. They assume that it will mature on its own. This is not the case. The gene needs plenty of help. Those surrounding Antonio will exercise a great deal of influence relative to his collecting gene. Decisions made during the next ten years will be critical. Here are the guidelines about which I talked with Ellen and Rick:

Encourage Antonio to collect. Do not be concerned about what he collects and never negate or look down upon what he collects. Collecting is highly individualistic. If Antonio is typical, he will change his collecting interests dozens of times throughout his life. While this may bother you, it will not trouble him. The greatest joy of collecting is the act of collecting. Collecting is action-focused, not object-focused.

The encouragement of collecting is a delicate process and must be handled carefully. When Antonio shows a collecting interest in something, resist the temptation to rush out and buy him dozens of examples. Beware of creating collecting overload. It has the potential to turn the child off to collecting.

Let Antonio decide what he wants to collect. Of course, it will take several years before he is making his own decisions. In the interim, you will collect for him. Collect something for Antonio that you do not collect or covet. Collecting competitiveness within a family is not a key to family harmony. You might start his collection with material associated with his birth month.

Collecting is contagious. It will not take as long as you think for Antonio to develop his own collecting interests. Chances are they will differ from what you acquired. Accept this. Each collector is different. I hesitate to use unique, but I think it applies. Your primary goal is to trigger Antonio's collecting gene and then step back.

The moment he is able, let Antonio do his own collecting. Resist the temptation to do it for him. He will never experience the work and joys involved in the hunt unless you allow him. Keep your assistance to a minimum. The quicker Antonio learns to rely on his own judgment, the better a collector he will become. Yes, he will make mistakes. However, keep two points in mind. First, right and wrong in collecting is cloudy at best. There are few absolutes. All you want to see in Antonio's eyes is a love for what he has acquired. If it is there, no acquisition is ever a mistake. Second, collectors learn from their mistakes. It is one of the best teaching aids that they have. Use Antonio's mistakes to educate, not to chastise.

Show Antonio how to collect, not what to collect. Teach him to hunt. Share your techniques. Explain his options. However, be pleased and not upset when he ventures out on his own. The best collectors constantly seek new collecting options. Learning to collect remains very much a "by the seat of the pants" educational experience.

Most important, teach Antonio to be patient. Set a course that will show Antonio that collecting is a lifetime experience. There is no joy in rapidly assembling a collection only to discover in a few years that there is little or nothing left to collect.

Support Antonio's collecting. In this case, support means providing Antonio with opportunities to collect and learn about his collection. Take him to garage sales and flea markets. Take him places where he will meet other individuals who collect what he does. Encourage him to see that the individuals one meets along the way are another of collecting's joys.

Work hard at teaching Antonio that inanimate objects can live. They live via the stories associated with them, stories about the individuals and techniques involved in their making, distribution and use, and perhaps most important, the tales involved in their acquisition. Do not hesitate to invest in the books and trips that will allow Antonio to learn about what he collects. Collecting broadens one's horizon.

Whenever possible, make him spend his own money on the things he wants. Hopefully, it will be money he earned and/or saved. I know he needs to save for a college education, but there is a middle ground. It is critical that he learn early that collecting is best done with discretionary income and that buying opportunities always exceed purchasing ability. Collecting involves budgeting and discriminating. It also involves desiring and coveting. Learn to view these latter two as positive rather than negative attributes.

I am concerned that I have waxed a bit too philosophical. Time for some immediate and practical advice. While the chances are minimal that he will remember or desire objects associated with his infancy, selectively set aside a few remembrances, e.g., nursery decorations, crib quilts, and a few favorite toys.

No matter what Antonio collects as a child, what he mostly likely will collect when he reaches twenty-five and beyond are those things that he grew up and played with during the ages of seven to fourteen. You need to recognize Antonio's favorite things and save them for him. If you have the funds available, buy a duplicate item, keep it in its original box, and store it. Most fifty-year-old collectors would kill to have their fondest childhood memories in mint-in-the-box condition.

Plan to store Antonio's personal things until he is in his late thirties or early forties. This is when he will rediscover his childhood. It is a mistake to hand over childhood treasures to a male immediately after his graduation from high school or college, or shortly after his first marriage, purchase of a house, or birth of his children. Twenty- and early thirty-year-old males have insatiable appetites for income. They frequently sell off their childhood treasures for something that fills an immediate desire but that does not maintain its value. Ten years later they deeply regret their actions because they (1) sold something that meant a lot to them and (2) sold it at a bargain price. It takes deep pockets to buy back one's childhood in one's forties.

Finally, be Antonio's bridge to the past. I am thrilled that some of Antonio's nursery furniture is recycled. There is something solid and comforting about an old wooden crib. I am extremely proud that the bassinet in which Antonio sleeps is the very one in which I was carried home from the hospital.

Antonio will receive a great many new things during his childhood. I look forward to working with the two of you and Antonio's relatives and friends to ensure that he receives a great many things from the past as well. We will make Antonio's traditions multi-generational. Together we will give Antonio a great gift—the skills and loves of a collector.

Grandfatherly Advice—The Grandchild

Earlier in this chapter I offered advice to Rich and Ellen Vogt, Antonio's parents, concerning the development of Antonio's collecting gene. This column's advice is for Antonio.

Yes, I know that it is several years premature. Few children collect before their fourth birthday. Serious collecting commences once a child reaches seven or eight. Developing collecting skills rather than lifelong collecting interests are the focus of the formative years between four and eight.

Caught in the euphoria associated with Antonio's birth, there is no way I am going to wait four, let alone seven or eight, years to write this column. His parents, concerned and responsible adults that they are, are just going to have to salt away a copy and give it to him when he is old enough to read and understand it.

Antonio, my first piece of advice is: COLLECT. Individuals who do not collect are incomplete as human beings. They are missing out on one of the greatest joys of life. Collecting will provide you with a wide range of experiences from the sense of discovery to understanding what you have collected and why. You will find that the lessons you learn through collecting are applicable to all aspects of your life.

It makes absolutely no difference what you collect so long as you are fascinated by it. Collect for yourself, not to please others. You will be surprised by the pressures associated with what you collect. There are traditionalists who think only they know what is worth collecting. Peer and social expectations will point you in directions that you may not wish to take. Resist these pressures. The only collecting path that counts is the one you want to travel.

Collecting is not a religion. Worshipping what you collect or how you collect is wrong. Chances are you will collect utilitarian objects designed for everyday use or play. If you put them on a pedestal and worship them, you deal with them out of context. Work hard to keep a sense of perspective. Understand the economic, technological, and social importance of the objects that you collect. Make the objects in your collection come alive by what you learn about them.

Likewise, resist any temptation to view the objects in your collection as works of art. Some will have great design. Utilitarianism and ugliness are not synonymous. Do not allow an object's design to overshadow its utilitarian function. Toys are toys, not museum masterpieces. Never inflate the value or importance of what you collect.

I challenge you to surround yourself and interact with what you collect. Use or play with the objects in your collection. What is the fun of having a fine vase if you do not occasionally put flowers in it? Toys and games were designed for play, not to be displayed on a shelf. Use your things as they were meant to be used. Remember, there is a difference between use and abuse.

Pooh-pooh those naysayers who warn: "Be careful; you might break it." So what. The objects in your collection are probably massproduced. You have no need for a one-of-a-kind worry. If misfortune strikes and you break something, replace or repair it.

If you find you have difficulty with this point, I recommend a simple solution. Buy duplicates and play with them. There is no rule that a collection has to contain only one example of each object. There are hundreds of duplicates in my collections. You will be surprised how your attitude toward an object changes when you acquire a second example. You will be far ahead of most collectors if you apply this same attitude toward the single items in your collections.

Take time to be a child. Resist the pressures to become an adult too soon. Adulthood is not all it is cracked up to be. Collecting helps. Collecting keeps alive the joys of childhood. True collectors are really kids at heart. There is a strong similarity between how a child reacts on Christmas morning and how a collector reacts when visiting a mall, shop, or show. I very much like being a fifty-four-year-old kid.

As early as possible, you need to make it clear to your parents, relatives, and friends that the appropriate gifts for your birthday and holidays are playthings and objects associated with learning. Clothing is not an appropriate gift on these occasions. I have far too many unhappy Christmas memories involving tearing the wrapping from a box only to discover that it contained shirts, pants, underwear, or socks instead of something I really wanted. I am working hard to ensure you do not suffer a similar fate.

Collect selectively and with a definite purpose. This advice falls into the do-as-I-say-not-as-I-do class. I am an accumulator. I collect almost everything. Saying yes is far easier than saying no. Collecting is a natural act. Accumulation is a sickness. My problem is that I have no desire to be cured.

Never collect for investment purposes. Collecting for monetary gain is collecting for the wrong reason. Collecting is about falling in love with the objects you collect. Investors keep objects inanimate and remote. Their commitment is short-term, not long-term. There is far more joy within an object than the pleasure derived from selling it at a profit. In fact, experience shows that antiques and collectibles are extremely risky investments. The possibilities are far greater that an object will be sold at a loss than at a profit. There is little joy in discovering you made a mistake.

Bond with your objects for life. Make collecting a lifelong experience. The real investment value of antiques and collectibles is the pleasure of ownership they bring on a continuing basis. True collectors die with their collections intact. Every object proved too precious to part with while they lived.

Does this mean that once you lock into a collecting interest, it can never change? Absolutely not! Expect your collecting interests to change several times. This is normal. Continually discovering new categories to collect is one of the great joys of collecting.

A new collecting interest does not mean that you have to lose interest in what you collected previously. If you are a typical collector, you will collect dozens of categories. Some collections will spin off from existing categories. Others will develop independently—something you found that was neat or just fun to own.

Do not allow collecting to dominate your life. Years ago, collecting was a hobby, something done with one's spare time. Alas, I know far too many individuals for whom collecting has become an obsession. I have been accused of being one of these on more than one occasion. There is more to life than collecting. Find and take the time to enjoy life's other pleasures.

Never allow collecting to be a financial burden. Collect with discretionary income, not income needed for your home mortgage, credit card bills, or children's education. When you can find money for objects and not for essentials, you have crossed the line. Every collector has to face the fact that there are some things he will never own because he cannot afford them. When an object's price is beyond your financial means, you must walk away.

Finally, I encourage you to include things from your parents', grandparents', and nation's past among your collections. When a nation's past resides only in museums, the nation's pride is lost. The link with the past needs to be personal.

Antonio, I look forward to assisting and guiding the development of your collecting skills. However, I think it fair to warn you that I plan to put special emphasis on this last point. If all goes well, my greatest contribution will be to instill in you a collecting love for those objects with which you did not grow up. I want you to be a collector who bridges the gap between collector generations, not one who increases the separation as is so prevalent among today's young collectors. By the way, Antonio, that bridge I am writing about starts with me.

[**Author's Note:** Alas, as all too often happens, Antonio's parents divorced, and Connie and I divorced. My present contact with Antonio is limited. Hopefully, he will rediscover this grandfather when he gets older and I will have the opportunity to fulfill the promises I made to him.]

Redefining "Boomer"

The standard definition of a baby boomer is someone born between 1946 and 1975. There was a baby explosion following the end of World War II. 1947 marked the greatest single-year population increase in United States history.

I was born in 1941. Technically, I am not a member of the boomer generations. Yet, why do I feel as though I am? I identify more with individuals born in the late '40s than I do with those born in the late 1930s. Those who know me well will argue my ambiguity has much to do with the fact that I refuse to grow up. I believe otherwise.

The years in which one grew up rather than when one was born should be the determining criteria in defining who is and who is not part of the boomer generations. Note I wrote generations, not generation. Three very distinct generations grew up in the period between 1946 and 1975. Lumping them together into a single era is incorrect.

I have long advocated that what an individual collects is influenced by his childhood experiences between the ages of six and fourteen, i.e., between second grade and the time he discovers the opposite sex. There are exceptions. There always are. Yet, if you consider collectors as a whole, my proposition is correct more often than incorrect.

Ignoring birth date and using the age six to fourteen principle, I divide the boomer era into three time periods, 1945 to 1955, 1956 to 1962, and 1962 to 1970. A person born in 1975 grew up in the early 1980s. The 1980s were the Reagan years. I challenge you to find anyone who views these as Baby Boomer years.

What solidified my thinking was the "You know you're a boomer if…" list that appeared, courtesy of *The Baltimore Sun*, in *The Morning Call*, April 8, 2001. The list began: "As boomer author Michael Gross points out, a generation defines itself not by what the Census Bureau says, but by shared experiences, beliefs and cultural references. In his book, *My Generation*, he suggests defining boomers as people born between Pearl Harbor Day and the assassination of JFK. Are you are boomer? Answer yes if you…"

Michael Gross and I are in total agreement as to the key criteria for dating the era. However, we disagree on its homogeneity.

His questions included:

"Owned a copy of *Jonathan Livingston Seagull*...

"Remembered when the Dodgers were still in Brooklyn...

"Know exactly where you were when President Kennedy and Dr. Martin Luther King Jr. were shot...

"Had original Elvis records..."

While I had memories associated with every statement Gross proposed, I quickly realized that I did not answer yes to every one of them. I never owned a copy of *Jonathan Livingston Seagull*. I married a woman who did, but that does not qualify. Elvis records? I owned Glenn Miller records.

Do my "no" answers disqualify me as a boomer or, even worse, make me less of a boomer than others? I do not accept either possible conclusion. I am a boomer. I know it in my heart.

Television is the defining element that determines whether one is or is not a boomer. It is possible to divide the entire world in to the generations that grew up listening to the radio and those who grew up watching television. The transitional generation is the boomers who grew up between 1945 and 1955. They have a foot firmly planted in both camps. I know. I am one of them. I remember life before television, back when dinosaurs roamed the earth.

When one was exposed to television had much to do with where one lived. I was one of the lucky ones. I lived in the East Coast corridor between Philadelphia and New York. The first television arrived in my neighborhood in either 1949 or 1950. I do not remember the exact date. By the time of its arrival, the first national network, Philadelphia-New York-Schenectady, was in place. It took more than a decade for television to reach the country as a whole.

The first of the boomer generations, 1945 to 1955, witnessed television in its infancy. Television experienced its youthful exuberance during the second generation, 1956 to 1962. It reached maturity in the third generation, 1962 to 1970.

If you grew up, i.e., between the ages of six and fourteen, with television and were born by 1960, you are a boomer. If you grew up remembering only color television and more than thirteen channels, chances are you are not.

Are there key events that define each of the three boomer generations? I believe there are. Here are my questions. Remember, base your yes answer on whether or not you remember the events as happening between your sixth and fourteenth birthday.

Generation 1945 to 1955:

1. Did you ride a balloon tire bike without a gear shift?
2. Do you remember watching *Hopalong Cassidy*, *Flash Gordon*, and *Tom Corbett Space Cadet* on television?
3. Did your parents own a car without fins?
4. Did you own records by Pat Boone, Perry Como, Doris Day, Eddie Fisher, Dean Martin, or Dinah Shore?
5. Did you see *The Greatest Show on Earth*, *On the Waterfront*, *The Thing*, *Twelve O'Clock High*, *Shane*, or *Stalag 17* during their initial movie theater runs?

Generation 1956 to 1962:

1. Did you ride a bike with a gear shift?
2. Do you remember watching *Gunsmoke*, *American Bandstand*, and *Disneyland/Walt Disney Presents* on television?
3. Did your parents own a car with fins?
4. Did you own records by Chubby Checker, Elvis, Fabian, Ricky Nelson, or Marty Robbins?
5. Did you see *Giant*, *Pillow Talk*, *Psycho*, *South Pacific*, *The Alamo*, *The Guns of Navarone*, or *West Side Story* during their initial movie theater runs?

Generation 1962 to 1970:

1. Did the bike you rode have more than three gears?
2. Do you remember watching *Bonanza*, *Car 54: Where Are You*, *The Jetsons*, and *Lost in Space* on television?
3. Did your parents own a Corvair, Mustang, or Volkswagen?
4. Did you own records by the Beatles, Monkees, Peter, Paul & Mary, Rolling Stones, and Supremes?
5. Do you remember seeing *Bonnie and Clyde*, *Goldfinger*, *The Planet of the Apes*, *The Dirty Dozen*, *The Great Escape*, *The Nutty Professor*, *The Pink Panther*, *The Sound of Music*, or *Yellow Submarine* during their initial movie theater runs?

Obviously not everyone is going to fall neatly into one category or the other. You belong in the category where the majority of your memories are found.

Is there a lesson in all this? The answer is yes. 1970 was thirty-five years ago. If you were six in 1970, you are now forty-one. If you were fourteen, you are now forty-nine. With each passing year, the 1960s is becoming more distant. Forget the 1940s and 1950s. They already are ancient history. Maybe this explains why so many boomers are having sleepless nights these days.

Do the Math

I asked Dana Morykan, senior researcher on my staff, to review one of my television appearances. She cast a quizzical glance when she heard me say: "Twenty-something and thirty-something collectors grew up in the 1950s and 1960s."

"Harry, do the math!" Dana exclaimed.

I did. The results made me feel old—really, really old. Today's twenty-something and thirty-something collectors did not grow up in the 1950s and 1960s. They grew up in the 1970s, 1980s, and early 1990s. They missed the initial telecasts of *The Monkees* (1966-1968) and *The Munsters* (1964-1966). Only the thirty-somethings could have watched *Charlie's Angels* (1976-1981) and *The Six Million Dollar Man* (1974-1978). Their knowledge of the 1950s, 1960s, and much of the 1970s comes from history books.

The problem with growing up in the late 1940s and early 1950s is that one thinks of anything occurring after that time as recent. The assassination of President Kennedy occurred yesterday, not over forty-two years ago. Age adjustment is extremely difficult.

This point was driven home even more by a series (Monday through Wednesday) of "Zits" cartoon strips. The Monday strip shows Jeremy talking with his mother:

Jeremy begins, "Wow. Look at the Moon."

"I remember where I was during the first lunar landing."

"You were ALIVE when they landed on the MOON??"

"Alive? I was fourteen!" "We watched it on my family's black-and-white television."

"YOU HAD A BLACK-AND-WHITE TV?"

"If you're trying to make me feel old, it's working."

"Would you consider speaking to my American history class?"

The theme continued on Tuesday:

Jeremy states, "I can't believe that you were alive back when they landed on the moon!"

"Jeremy, the first moon landing was in 1969! That was only..." The next panel shows Jeremy's mother using her fingers to count. "...Thirty-three years ago."

"That's what I'm saying! You're an historical artifact!"

Wednesday's strip concludes the theme.

Jeremy asks his mother, "(Gasp!) You were alive when Woodstock happened! Did you go?"

"No."

"GAAA! WHY NOT??"

"Jeremy, I was only fourteen! I didn't even know it was happening until I heard about it on Walter Cronkite."

"You were alive when Walter Cronkite—"

"Oh stop it. You never even heard of Walter Cronkite!"

What I found especially significant in the "Zits" strip was the choice of the moon landing and Woodstock rather than the Kennedy assassination as the pivotal date in the strip. Mathematically there is little difference between 1963 and 1969. Generation-wise, the difference is astronomical.

The mid- to late 1960s was America's psychedelic period—the Beatnik and Hippie era, the social cause period from Civil Rights and Women's Liberation to Ban the Bomb and Save the Whales. It was a time of turmoil. The mid-1960s drew a clear line of distinction between the first generation of Baby Boomers and their reincarnation as Yuppies and Dinks.

Over time, events condense. Memory clouds. Events that occurred decades ago seem as though they occurred only years ago. This is why people use defining events, from personal events such as graduation, marriage, or the birth of a child to national events such as the Kennedy assassination, the moon landing, or 9/11, as reference points to determining occurrences within their own lives. As the "Zits" cartoons strips show, even this is not foolproof.

Your response to key questions reveals your age and generation. Name two or three key television news anchors. If someone asked me this question, I probably would reply John Cameron Swayze, Chet Huntley, and David Brinkley. I strongly suspect the majority of my readers have never heard of them.

I have not given the matter a great deal of thought, but suppose one clear indication of old age is when most of your personality memories are associated more with the dead than the living. If asked to quickly list major movie stars, the first names on my list would be Clark Gable, Cary Grant, and Marilyn Monroe. They are dead, and they did not die yesterday.

In truth, I would have far less trouble making a list of movie stars from the 1940s and 1950s than I would from the 1980s and 1990s. I am not a hermit. I see dozens of movies each year. As I have grown older, I find I concentrate more on the movie's theme than the movie's stars.

What interpretation should be assigned to the above? Is it possible that a disproportionate share of one's memories is formed during one's juvenile period, i.e., between ages six and twenty? The answer is yes.

Further, these memories become even more intense as a person grows older. The norm is to cling to the past. Little wonder gaps occur between generations. Most individuals find they are not able to assign an equivalent memory importance to recent experiences compared to that assigned earlier childhood memories.

This explains the growing collecting gap between what appeals to twentysomething to fortysomething collectors versus what appeals to fiftysomething and sixtysomething collectors. While the love of collecting passes from generation to generation, the love of a specific collecting category does not. This is why many traditional antique collecting categories and even some post-1945 collecting categories have fallen on hard times. The next generation of collectors simply does not care. As old collectors die off, new collectors are not replacing them.

Collecting is driven by memory. No one is going to buy a John Cameron Swayze, Chet Huntley, or David Brinkley collectible if they do not remember watching them on television. The same holds true for *Charlie's Angels*, *Dukes of Hazzard*, and *The Six Million Dollar Man* collectibles.

It is easy to watch memories fade. It takes time, work, and intense effort to keep up with the times. It is even more difficult during this first decade of the twenty-first century when one not only has to keep memory current but also adjust to a wealth of new technologies.

I work hard at doing both. Yet, there are days when I feel that I have simply reached memory and technological overload. There is simply too much data. It is impossible to be an antiques and collectibles generalist, i.e., have a competent level of knowledge in all collecting categories. The twenty-first century is an age of specialization. Specialize and survive. Generalize and die.

If it makes Jeremy's mother feel any better, I was twenty-seven when Woodstock occurred, and I did not go either. I did not learn about it until I read about it in *Life*. I was deeply entrenched in my museum career track.

By the way, where were you when you watched the moon landing? If you can answer this, do not tell anyone unless you want them to know that thirty-nine is your fictional age.

Who Are the Young Buyers?

I love getting letters from Arlene Rabin, a show dealer, collector, and astute observer of the trade. Arlene's letters always contain several comments that stimulate my gray matter. Her November 3, 2002, letter is typical. I want to share it with you and then comment on the points she raises.

> I am sensing changes in the attitudes of the younger customers. It seems related to age and generation. The older collectors (our age and older!) keep on buying and buying until every variation of their widget has been consumed. They will make their living quarters accommodate the growing volumes. It is a lifestyle: a serious quest for every one, for better ones, and for all the information, ad infinitum.

I own 850 enamel mesh purses, and no two are alike. Variations keep on appearing. My mother, of course being one generation more advanced, has about 1,500 hatpins. At this point, both of us have attempted the 'ONE IN, ONE OUT' rule. Financially, it hardly works. The $300.00 one goes in, and the $22.00 one gets weeded out. But spatially it makes sense. Do we really 'need' these over the bed and in the bathroom?

The changes I sense are from younger show goers—although there are not enough of them. This alien life form comes into my booth and says, 'wow, these are beautiful. I could hang six of these in my hallway,' as if she just had a revelation. I saw the woman three shows later and showed her some great pursues. She replied that after three shows, she purchased all six, which is what she had space for.

I am baffled….Are these not as strong as heroin as we once thought.

'Don't you have to have more?'

'No, they collect dust.'

A young man bought an antique toothpick holder from me recently. The conversation centered happily on his grandmom's toothpick collection, which numbers in the over-500 league. He said he likes them, but he is too busy to dust or to research. He has no free time. He has a little curio cabinet that can shelter twenty or so toothpicks. That is it. It is finite.

These people are not dedicated, not addicted. They will not compromise their living space or busy lifestyles to accommodate antiques. But, they do like them.

Perhaps we need to do what the cigarette manufacturers have admitted to: beefing up the 'nicotine delivery system.' So, how should we get the young ones hooked?

Well, have to go. We are building a ledge around the bedroom to hold my husband's collection of figural product ashtrays. They have filled all the windowsills so we cannot crank open the windows.

I agree with Arlene. There is a major difference in attitude between today's young collectors and those who began collecting prior to 1985. Like their predecessors, today's young collectors are hooked on collecting. Collecting is still addictive. However, it is the concept of collecting that has them hooked and not a specific collecting category. In the course of their collecting life, they will change their collecting focus six to ten times, even more for some. They assemble large collections in years, not decades. When they become bored or fashion dictates another course, they willingly change their collecting focus. The collectors of the 1990s and the first decade of the twenty-first century are "The Trendy" generation.

Arlene views most buyers as "collectors." For over a century, the antiques and collectibles market constituted of two principal groups: (1) dealers, a.k.a. sellers, and (2) buyers. This approach is no longer valid if one wishes to understand today's market.

The collectors to which Arlene refers in her letter are not "true" collectors. They are decorator/nostalgia/feel-good buyers; an entirely new buying group that began having a major impact on the antiques and collectibles trade in the early 1990s.

In the early 1980s, the professional interior decorator, whether representing a private client or a restaurant chain, was a major player in the antiques and collectibles marketplace. The decorator was purchasing a look, sometimes stylist and other times nostalgic. These individuals paid exorbitant prices for ordinary, second-level pieces without blinking an eye. They simply passed along the cost to their clients.

Professional interior decorators fled the antiques and collectibles market in the late 1980s, largely in response to the economic recession. They re-entered the field in the late 1990s, largely through "decorator malls." However, their importance to the market's strength is far less than during the glory days of the early 1980s.

Do-it-yourself decorators are currently the major decorating force in the antiques and collectibles community. These individuals gain their decorating prowess through mass market periodicals and the numerous lifestyle television cable channels.

Just as with young collectors, they are trend motivated. They want the latest, the hottest, the most "in" objects available. If one of their gurus says black instead of white, as Mary Emmerling did recently, they toss their cans of white spray paint into the trash and head to the local home improvement store to buy black.

Decorator/nostalgia/feel-good buyers are space focused. They buy with a specific space in mind. When it is filled to their satisfaction, they stop buying. They visit auctions, flea markets, malls, shops, and shows with tape measure in hand. When they find a piece they like, they measure it to see if it will fit. They will not move existing furnishings nor enlarge a space to make room for an oversized item—no matter how much they might like the piece.

Decorator/nostalgia/feel-good buyers move around and in-and-out of the market quickly. As trends change, they change. Little wonder antiques and collectibles dealers are frustrated. What sells well one moment is unwanted merchandise the next.

What percentage of the younger (under forty) buying public at antiques and collectibles flea markets, malls, shops, and shows do decorator/nostalgia/feel-good buyers represent? While I cannot provide statistical support for my guesstimate, my gut feeling is that the number is between 75 and 80 percent. Collectors stopped being the dominant market buying force by the mid-1990s.

The antiques and collectibles market has survived the current economic downturn thanks largely to the decorator/nostalgia/feel-good buyer. The national periodical and television pendants no longer validate the use of antiques and collectibles in decorating schemes. The consequences are dire.

I am extremely concerned. Cable television is rapidly replacing periodicals as the major decorating influence among the general public. Take the time and watch several of the home decorating shows. When you do, you will notice how few members of this new group of pontificators incorporate antiques and collectibles in their decorating schemes. Where is Martha Stewart when we need her?

Selling into decorating trends is the key to short-term survival as an antiques and/or collectibles dealer. Rebuilding a strong collector base is the key to long-term survival.

CHAPTER 14

Harry at His Wildest

I am a passionate guy, especially when it comes to collecting. There is nothing neutral about me. Collecting is part of my daily life.

I have been blessed with the ability not to take myself too seriously. When collecting becomes serious, the fun disappears. I am never going to allow this to happen to me.

I still have problems realizing that some professional people envy what I do for a living. What they do is work. What I do is fun. I constantly tell people that I have never worked a day in my life. Truth be known, there have been a few bad days, but very few. My life is a hoot!

When Susie Barbour, a very good friend and host of a weekend radio show on KDKA in Pittsburgh, learned that I had signed a contract to appear on Home & Garden Television's Collector Inspector *television show, she was concerned that I would have a problem if the show failed. Susie also has a Type-A personality. We assume success. Failure is not an option.*

Susie called and talked to me. She encouraged me to approach the first session of Collector Inspector *as an adventure with no concern about the potential consequences. I took Susie's advice. It was not difficult. My life is an adventure.* Collector Inspector *was just another chapter.*

During the initial taping of homes for Collector Inspector, *Home & Garden Television (HGTV) instructed 44 Blue Productions, the show's producer, to allow Harry to be Harry. 44 Blue did. When HGTV saw the results, they immediately called 44 Blue and told them to put the clamps on me. Harry at his wildest is something that should never appear on television, and I have a few roles of outtake footage to prove it.*

I am at my best when I am at my wildest. I hope you agree.

You Do Not Want To Collect What I Collect

While visiting a fellow collector recently for the purpose of selecting some of his toys for use as illustrations in my *Collector's Guide to Toys, Games, and Puzzles*, I could not help but notice a newly acquired wooden jigsaw puzzle that I am absolutely convinced would be much better housed in my collection than his. By sheer coincidence (cough, cough) it was located behind some of the toys that I wished to consider. Checking the urge to kill, I put on a happy face and complimented him on his latest find.

Although the collector had acquired a number of wooden and cardboard jigsaw puzzles as part of his collection over the past decades, he had never fully realized the potential of jigsaw puzzles to supplement his collection until I made the mistake a year ago of showing him the puzzles in my collection that related to his approach. Before I knew it, his classified advertisement was competing with my advertisement in trade papers. Since his advertisement focuses only on one specific type of jigsaw puzzle, sellers with an example will respond to him rather than to my general wants advertisement on the assumption that the more specific the request, the better the chance of a sale.

In the course of our conversation, I mentioned to my toy-collecting friend that I was considering buying several tin lithographed toys that had been offered to me. That caught his attention.

"Are you planning to start collecting toys in addition to puzzles?" he said, somewhat taken aback and astonished. "You do not really want to do that." Talk about the pot calling the kettle black. What is good for the goose, etc.

There is something that you have to understand at this point. The toy collector and I are friendly rivals. We enjoy competing with each other, sometimes rather fiercely, but never lose sight of the fact that it is just a game. We share war stories, hunt for one another once our own needs are filled, and find plenty to laugh about in the trade.

Immediately after the toy collector made his remarks, we both looked at each other and broke out in smiles. No collector relishes a rival. Yet, a collector's enthusiasm for his collection is contagious. Ask any collector to talk about his collection or show his collection to you.

You will see firsthand. Before a collector knows it, his very actions have created the thing he least desires—a rival collector.

What do you do when a prospective collector asks your help to get started? Help or tell him to get lost? It is a tough pill to swallow when a budding collector who you have helped finds something for which you have searched for years, tells you that he has become enamored with it, and although he bought it with the idea of selling or giving it to you, he now plans to keep it. I have been on both sides of this equation during my collecting career. While I realize the noble thing is to help a prospective collector, the older I get the more I favor the "get lost" approach.

It took only a few seconds for me to suggest to my toy-collecting friend that what we really need is a checklist of approaches to tell a prospective collector for the express purpose of diverting his collecting interests into a non-competing area. Do not do as I do, do as I say. My toy-collecting friend loved the idea and made a number of suggestions. I told him that I would mull them over, add a few of my own, and pass them along in a column. For what it is worth, here are some of the approaches that we thought of:

1. It is not right for you. Although it is obviously right for me since I own a pile already, your personality traits suggest that you will not derive any long-term collecting enjoyment. Forget your enthusiasm of the moment. You will never be able to sustain it over the long run.

2. It is not from your generation. True enjoyment only comes from collecting what you remember owning in the past. Since you did not play with or use these items as a child, you will never achieve the same thrill as collectors who grew up with them. Collect something from your own childhood. Leave mine alone.

3. It is far too expensive. The best pieces are through the $1,000 barrier. Even the common forms are expensive. You will be lucky to get twenty examples for under $10,000. Few collectors are satisfied with owning just a few examples. I do not think you will be either. I bought the bulk of

my collection years ago when prices were cheap. Now I am lucky to add one or two examples a year. Of course, if you have an unlimited pocketbook, go ahead.

4. All the good examples are in the hands of collectors already. People have been collecting and hoarding for decades. The chances of any major collections coming on the market soon are minimal. You will have to search long and hard for the few examples that you will find. Even when you do find something, it is likely to be in poor condition and expensive. It is a lot of hard work for very little reward.

5. The existing collectors are cliquish. They have not welcomed a new member into their inner circle for over a decade. Do not count on them sharing their collections or information with you. You have nothing to offer in exchange. Better people than you have tried to crack the group and failed. Unless you are a glutton for punishment, try another area.

6. It is a lousy investment. Prices are high. It is true that some examples are sold every year. However, prices are confined to a narrow price range. They are basically the same today as they were five years ago. I do not see any change in the short-term future. Of course, if you do not want any return on your money, you might want to get involved.

7. Do you know what it costs to maintain a collection of this type? You have to put in a security system, buy specially lighted and humidity-controlled storage units, and invest heavily in insurance. You will be spending one dollar on other costs for each dollar you spend on objects. I accept this. Are you certain that you can?

8. Collecting this type of material will change you life. You will have to start screening the guests who come to your home. Theft is a major problem. You will not be able to talk about your collection outside a narrow group of collecting friends. Once you start spending big bucks, you can expect trouble from your spouse. Each object you buy will be viewed as a vacation that you never took together.

9. If all of the above fail, the final approach is to divert the prospective collector's focus to another collecting area. Think. Have you met a collector who is collecting in an area that you wished that you had the time and resources to collect or one who enjoys a lack of competition in his collecting area that has turned you green with envy? Now you know where to point the prospective collector's attention.

I think you should collect (blank). It is not hard to sing the merits of this collecting field. Just reverse all the arguments provided above. If you are going to help a prospective collector by revealing inside sources and trade secrets, this is the ideal opportunity.

My Kind of Vacation

My ideal vacation is a place where I can spend every waking moment immersed in the study or purchase of collectibles. In my mind, a flea market, shop district, show, or auction that I have never attended is an exotic place that easily surpasses the mysteries offered by a foreign land. Spending sixteen hours in the pursuit of something one loves is not exhausting. It is relaxation.

I keep asking myself—why would anyone want to go to a place where all you do is sleep late, lie around, and gorge yourself on large quantities of food that normally would be avoided? Spending money to produce mental memories has never done it for me.

I stopped taking my camera on vacations over fifteen years ago. I also swore that I would never attend another showing of vacation slides no matter how much I cared for the relative or friend who inadvertently planned to subject me to this modern-day torture form. I have stuck to my promise. My life is richer for it. Further, can you think of anything less likely to be saved from an estate than vacation slides, 99 percent of which are found without labels? They are the finest trashcan collectible that I know.

I like vacations to produce tangible memories, i.e., information that I can publish and goodies to add to my collections. If you accept the premise that part of each collectible's history is its acquisition story, I have far more and better vacation memories than any slide of an African elephant or a food banquet table in Scandinavia can produce. When was the last time you looked at your vacation slides of ten years ago? I see the things that I acquired during my vacations every week.

Put me at a resort, near a beach, or on a cruise ship for a couple of days and I experience withdrawal symptoms. Instead of relaxing, I become unpleasant—in fact, downright irritable. I need a daily collectibles fix. Why is it that non-collectors' and a fair number of collectors' spouses have absolutely no ability to understand this?

A Colonial Williamsburg, Virginia, television commercial is responsible for starting me thinking about past vacations and what I have really gained from them. Visiting commercial and non-profit historic sites concentrating on the Colonial period and nineteenth century for the purpose of "going back into history and discovering how our ancestors lived" has always been viewed as a socially proper thing to do, an indication of one's good taste. I must confess that I have spent more than one winter weekday (summer and weekend crowds are not my version of a vacation) in Colonial Williamsburg enjoying a fire in a guest cottage on Duke of Glouchester Street, a hearty breakfast at Christiana Campbell's, and evening gambols at Chowning's Tavern. Trés romantic—BUT!

No matter how hard I work, I am never going to be in the financial position of affording period colonial furnishings, especially now that quality furniture pieces are in the half-million-dollar-plus category. I think this is true for most collectors who visit sites such as Colonial Williamsburg. Colonial Williamsburg's holdings represent the candy we cannot eat because it is behind a window in a closed shop, Antiques appraisers and "upscale" dealers can justify time spent at these sites. For the vast majority of us, all we can do is look, appreciate, and dream.

I reached the conclusion that I derive much more enjoyment spending time related to things I can or do own. As a result, my vacations tend not to follow the normal pattern, whatever that may be. Try some of the following suggestions. I think you will be surprised.

First, visit all the local historical societies within a two-hour drive of your home. Instead of concentrating on their eighteenth- and nineteenth-century holdings, only look at objects made after 1900. You will be amazed at how many collectibles were made in "your backyard." Avoid most museums. The twentieth century is too new for them.

Second, plan a research trip to the location where your favorite collectible was manufactured. Find the factory, visit the public library and area historical society to see what information they have about the manufacturer and its products, locate and talk with former employees, and track down local collectors and visit with them. Plan to stay a few days. Detective work takes time. Whenever I have tried to do this on a "few hours" basis, I have become frustrated because I simply did not have enough time to follow up all the leads that I uncovered.

Third, visit museums that have specialized collections relating to your collecting field. If you collect dolls and have never been to the Margaret Woodbury Strong Museum in Rochester, New York, you have not lived. While most glass collectors are familiar with the Corning Museum, far too few have visited the Bennington Museum in Bennington, Vermont.

One of my specialized collecting interests is the American mule-drawn canal era. Do you know how many canal museums there are scattered across the United States? The answer is over ten. I have been to them all—from Lockport, New York, to Lockport, Illinois. A few years ago I subjected Connie to a night at the Lock 7 Motel on Canada's Welland Canal instead of a honeymoon suite in nearby Niagara Falls. I went to bed by midnight. It was Connie who stayed up into the early morning hours watching the lake freighter lock through.

Be careful about museum names. Whenever I head west on Interstate 70 through Ohio, I always allow time for a visit to Cambridge, site of several glass museums and manufacturers. I avoided the Degenhart Museum during my first several visits on the premise that I had seen more than my share of Degenhart glass at flea markets and shows. Finally, I decided—what the heck. Time for a visit. Was I surprised! The museum was not devoted exclusively to Degenhart glass. It was Mrs. Degenhart's glass collection. The museum display on glass reproductions, copycats, and fakes was excellent. I learned a good lesson. Visit a museum before you write it off as useless.

Fourth, head for that legendary flea market or show you have always wanted to visit. At my age, I am no longer big on denial. If I want to do something, I am going to do it. No collector worth his salt collects regionally any longer. It is time to think nationally, better yet globally. One can spend a week in London going to a different flea market each morning, museum each afternoon, and theater each night. Forget the Tower of London—the jewels belong to the crown.

Fifth, plan to visit all those collectors that you have met along the way who have invited you to view their collections. Nothing better expands your horizons and understanding of your collecting category. Whether you spend the evening exchanging information, engaging in collector one-upmanship, or simply sharing war stories, it will most likely be memorable.

Finally, be honest with yourself. Give some thought to your long-suffering, tolerant spouse. Occasionally, you have to indulge her in a vacation that fits her expectations. Connie enjoys traveling by herself. She really does.

When Harry Wasn't Cool

I was spending a pleasant afternoon working the antique malls in south-central Illinois with Don Johnson and Connie Swaim of *AntiqueWeek*, when I saw "it." Destiny was on my side; God provides.

Normally, I am a cautious and practiced buyer. Over and over again at seminars I tell participants to keep a stone face so they do not tip the extent of their interest to the seller. I stress that the best collectibles purchases are made when you use your head, not your heart. I practice what I preach—most of the time. This was not one of them.

I advocate covetousness. No, not your neighbor's wife—the best pieces in a rival's collection. The only thing that I love more than seeing a rival's collection is duplicating her prime pieces in my collection. To state that this desire motivates me is an understatement. Once I have identified pieces that I do not own and made the conscious decision that life will not be complete until I do, I am obsessed, possessed by the collecting devil. If you know a good exorcist, Connie, my wife, would like to hear from you. My staff has offered to help pay the costs. There is no sense writing to me; I am not seeking a cure.

Of all the jigsaw puzzle types, the advertising jigsaw has most captured my soul. Although I have only been collecting advertising jigsaw puzzles for a few years, my collection numbers in the middle hundreds. An offer of a treasure that I do not own is a command from on high to buy. Thus far, I have avoided paying what I consider to be "ridiculous" prices. Those surrounding me are not as convinced on this point as I am.

Over the past several years, I have been privileged to view several major jigsaw puzzle collections. In every case, I have been exposed to puzzles that I COVET! Like a disease, these puzzles are a virus in my brain. The only known cure is adding one to my collection. I am sick most of the time.

While not every collector will admit to having a "hit list" of examples they covet, I think we all do. I do not have a hit list; I have hit lists—an avocational hazard when you collect more than one thing.

Meanwhile, back to south-central Illinois. As I was casually meandering through one of the malls, I spied one of the advertising puzzles on my hit list. Actually, it was more than just "one" of the puzzles. It was the puzzle at the top of the list.

I wanted to touch it, hold it, caress it—make it mine. The damn case was locked. I threw my body on the case, determined to shield the puzzle from prying eyes until I could arrange to have the case opened. I tried to act casual, but I started to sweat. My body got the shakes. I told myself, "Thank goodness it is a mall. The piece is priced. There is no seller who obviously would know by my actions that he had a sucker on the line."

Don volunteered to go to the front desk to ask a mall staffer to bring the keys. Why is it that every time I am anxious to buy something at a mall, all the staff is busy? No one came. Hours passed—actually it was only a few minutes. I panicked. Don had wandered off. What was I to do?

I knelt down, the reverential position seemed appropriate, to gaze at the elusive prize. At that moment, another individual who recognized me looked over my shoulder and said, "That's been sold." I could not believe what I heard. I jumped up. "When, who bought it, impossible, show me the bum" (not the actual word that I used, but one that I have to use if I want this column printed) issued forth from my mouth as a single sentence. If looks could kill, the offender was already dead and buried. Somewhat startled, the individual said, "Just kidding." Who said there was no humor in the collectibles field?

I confess that one of the things that excited me was the price—$10. I will not tell you what I was prepared to pay for the puzzle, but it was more than that. Not only was God kind, he was generous.

At long last, Don returned, surprised that the case was still not open. Assuming the protective position in my stead, Don suggested that I go up to the front desk to determine the delay. Patient is not the word that best describes the mood that I was experiencing. After extracting a promise that the case would be opened in the next five minutes, I beat a hasty return. My treasure was still there.

Upon returning Don had a big grin on his face. "Notice that sign over there?" Yes, Virginia, there is a God. Everything in the booth was 25 percent off. The puzzle was not going to cost $10. The final figure was $7.50.

When a mall employee finally appeared upon the scene, I did not wait until she opened the case to make a firm point that I wanted the puzzle. "I WANT IT; I WANT IT," I shouted. I was under the impression that I made the statement in a rather mild voice, but other observers at the scene assured me that I was shouting.

Finally, I held it. It was mine. When the mall employee asked if she could take it up to the front desk, she had to pry my fingers from it one by one. I had touched the Holy Grail.

The puzzle was in its original box. I had no idea whether it was complete or not. Honestly, I did not care. I chucked the most basic rule of puzzle collecting, "Do not buy it if it is not complete," right out the window. In my heart, I knew it was complete.

I have never understood why anyone needs to take drugs to get high when all they need to do is collect. I was floating ten feet above the ground. The euphoria lasted for hours, another advantage that a collecting fix has over a drug fix.

With my advertising puzzle safely at the front counter, I did some other shopping at the mall. I found a second great jigsaw puzzle, a Vitaplay juvenile mystery puzzle of which I was unaware. It did not hold the same sense of discovery and excitement as the advertising puzzle, but it certainly increased the mellow feeling I was experiencing.

What do you think was the first thing that I did when I returned to the hotel where I was staying? You only get one guess. No, I have good kidneys; it was not that. I sat down and put my advertising jigsaw puzzle together. Missed the cocktail hour; did not care.

Putting puzzles together serves as a form of relaxation for me only when I find that they are complete. If they are missing one or two pieces, all I get is frustrated. In most cases, I am never certain until the last few pieces.

In fact, I hate it when a puzzle is missing one piece. Better it should be missing fifty pieces. When just one piece is missing, I spend hours searching around the area where I put the puzzle together and inspecting and re-inspecting the packaging, convinced that I lost the piece. Talk about sleepless nights.

My advertising jigsaw puzzle turned out to be complete. The surface was in great shape. I ate dinner in the midst of another collecting high.

What is the point? One of the joys of collecting is sharing the war stories. I wrote this column as much for me as I did for you. It is a reminder. When I no longer lose my cool over collectibles, it is time to hang up my computer. Hopefully, that will happen only when they are ready to plant me six feet under.

How Funny a Business Is This?

I find the antiques and collectibles business funny. Everywhere I turn I can find something about which to laugh.

Alas, most collectors, dealers, and others in the business disagree. Their approach is serious, VERY SERIOUS. When someone makes a humorous comment causing laughter or even a mild chuckle, they take immediate offense. They view laughing about the business as a personal attack, equivocal to a disparaging remark made about their child, spouse, or favorite relative.

Laughing is easier to accept when times are good as opposed to when they are bad. The current economic difficulties in the trade have created an atmosphere of uncertainty. Times are not bad, but they are not good either. Seriousness prevails where laughter should reign.

Does the level of seriousness differ regionally? Are collectors and dealers on the West Coast far more likely to laugh than collectors and dealers in New England?

I started thinking about this topic when I received an e-mail press release from Hallmark providing information on their ranking of the funniest cities and states in the United States. Simmons Market Research Bureau and Shoebox, a Hallmark division that sells humorous cards, decided "to measure regional differences in America's Laugh quotient."

Before reading further, make a list of what cities and states you think would rank one through five in each of these two categories. I did and missed the mark entirely. I am willing to bet the same happened to you.

Here are the results reported by Hallmark. The top five funniest states were: (1) Rhode Island; (2) Massachusetts; (3) Minnesota; (4) Colorado; and (5) Wisconsin. The top five funniest cities were: (1) Mankato, MN; (2) Helena, Mont.; (3) tie between Cheyenne, WY and Scottsbluff, NB; (4) tie between Providence, RI and New Bedford, MA, and (5) Milwaukee, WI. Well, how did you do?

Before going further, I think it only fair to note how Pennsylvania, my fair state, fared in the poll. It ranked 25th. In the list of 205 metropolitan areas, Harrisburg-Lancaster finished 27th, Philadelphia 38th, Wilkes Barre-Scranton 131st, Erie 152nd, Johnstown-Altoona 173rd, and Pittsburgh 185th. The Lehigh Valley area (Allentown, Bethlehem, and Easton) failed to make the list. I was surprised by this since the area is home to the Pennsylvania Germans, a group notorious for its ability to laugh at itself. I suspect the region's exclusion is based upon the fact that Hallmark's Shoebox division has little interest in preparing cards driven by local humor.

Back to the point of this article—does humor differ regionally between individuals involved in antiques and collectibles? The answer is a decided yes.

Clearly, New England is the most serious and least humorous section of the country in respect to antiques and collectibles. This staid, conservative region has trouble admitting the twentieth century exists, let alone the twenty-first. Individuals still dress up to go to antiques shows that are loaded with eighteenth- and nineteenth-century antiques and folk art. New Englanders take everything so seriously. Given this, one has to wonder if any of the Simmons Market Research Bureau researchers visited New England. If they had, I seriously doubt that Rhode Island and Massachusetts would have achieved the first and second ranking.

Be honest with yourself. The antiques and collectibles business is loaded with humor. First, look at the participants. While I am continually touting the principle that people who collect are normal and those who do not are sick, I am aware that the trade is comprised of far more unique (I am loathe to use crazy, obsessed, possessed, and other derogatory terms) individuals than found in other general populations. How normal is it for a person to spend hours a week on the hunt, whether on the Internet or in the field, for an object to add to an already esoteric collection numbering in the hundreds of pieces?

Second, look at what we collect, how we collect it, and how we store and display it. Connie, my second wife, and I once visited a collector of collector edition whiskey bottles who had purchased a house in which to display his collection. He painted all the windows black so no sunlight could enter and fade the color. He only turned on the lights in each room for no more than ten minutes at a time. The tour of his collection took several hours. The collector owned a bar that was located nearby. After the tour, we went to his bar. The collector offered us a drink. Connie thought she would be safe ordering a screwdriver. Her eyes glistened as he poured the vodka into the glass. He did not see the look of horror on her face when he poured in carbonated orange soda rather than orange juice. Having just spent two hours in the near dark, Connie cast caution to the wind, chugged the first drink, and immediately asked for a second. Everyone deals with their own nightmares separately.

If you do not see anything funny in this story, you have a problem. It should not only have brought a smile to your face, it should have made you laugh.

How many jokes featuring antiques collectors or dealers do you know? I know less than half a dozen. Comedians obviously do not think we are funny. I beg to disagree. I find something to laugh about every day in the trade, if nothing more than the ridiculous price somebody paid for something or the reserve set by an eBay seller. Trust me, if you only used eBay reserves, you could laugh yourself to death.

In 1985 Frank Hill and I authored *The Joy of Collecting with Craven Moore* (Wallace-Homestead, 1985), a cartoon book featuring seventy-two single panel cartoons involving two couples, Craven and Anita Moore and Howie and Constance Lee Bys. It was supposed to be the first of three cartoon books, the others to have been titled *More Joys of Collecting with Craven Moore* and *The Revenge of the Collector's Wife*. The second and third books were never published. The first book did not sell well enough to justify them.

Over the years, several other antiques and collectibles focused cartoon panels and strips have appeared in trade publications. Their life span ranged from a few months to a few years. Most were funny, little wonder they did not survive.

Always one to go out on a limb, here are my humor rankings by region for the antiques and collectibles trade: (1) West Coast, (2) Mid-West, (3) Middle Atlantic Region, (4) Plains States, (5) Southwest, (6) South, and (7) New England.

How Come We Are Never the Good Guys?

Whenever antiques or antiquities are involved, whether it is television, the movies, or comic books, the antiques dealer is always the bad guy. Face it. The accepted public perception of antiques dealers, just like used car salespersons, is that they are crooks.

It is not true. While the antiques and collectibles barrel contains a few rotten apples, and which barrel does not, the vast majority, 95 percent plus, of antiques and collectibles dealers are honest, hard-working and ethical. It is unrealistic to claim they never make mistakes. Everyone does. The key is how the mistake is remedied.

On Wednesday, June 13, 2001, the *Baltimore Sun*'s "Today's TV" section was headlined "*PrimeTime* focuses on antiques dealers." The story read: "In a three-month investigation into the antiques business, *PrimeTime Thursday*…puts a new spin on the age-old adage: Hidden cameras reveal that the best advice may be 'Let the Seller Beware.' The

ABC investigation reveals that some dealers may cut sellers out of prime profits, offering a pittance for valuable antiques, then turning them around and selling them for top dollar." I am certain identical or similar summaries of the program appeared in other daily newspapers.

Some is the problematic word. If the accepted interpretation of some is perhaps one in a hundred, I would not have a problem. Unfortunately, it is much higher. Few would have been a far better word to use. Given the fact that the program focused on four dealers, three of whose dealings were questionable and one of whose were honorable, the conclusion that could easily be reached is that, in this instance, some means seventy-five percent or higher.

For those who did not see the *PrimeTime Thursday* that aired on June 14, 2001 the program focused on individuals selling several objects to antiques dealers located in New York City and Hudson, New York, allowing time for the dealers to price and offer them for resale, and then having a second group of individuals buy them back. It was a setup from the start, especially in the selection of dealers chosen to represent the trade.

The first dealer paid $25 for a Cartier silver box. He priced it at $800 and eventually sold it for $650. During the selling process, he said he had just paid $550 for the piece.

The second dealer, a coin/jewelry dealer who advertises that he buys estates or individual pieces, bought a Tiffany silver tray for $45 and sold it to the *PrimeTime* undercover buyer for $695. Further, the dealer wrote a fictitious appraisal for $2,500. *PrimeTime* never commented on the appraisal scam, a story of equal if not greater importance.

The third dealer paid $75 for three American historical view English Staffordshire plates. He sold them for $890. He was taped telling the person from whom he bought them that he would "probably make $20 on the deal." When confronted following the sale, the dealer was arrogant. His attitude was simple. It is "just business."

PrimeTime noted that they paid $2,235 to buy back the antiques they sold for $145. The profit margin was times fifteen. "For shame," said Helaine Fendleman, author of several books on antiques and a guest expert on the show, "How can they live with themselves?" I assume she was referring to the antiques dealers and not the producers of the segment who skewed the truth. Robert Jackman, a member of the

Appraisers Association of America along with Fendleman, also appeared as a guest expert.

ABC's June 14th *PrimeTime Thursday* enhanced the public perception of the crooked antiques and collectibles dealer. Adding insult to injury, early that same morning ABC's *Good Morning America* broadcast portions of the *PrimeTime* piece as a tease for the evening show. Dena George, a staff researcher, saw the show and told me about it.

Further, it is highly likely that *PrimeTime* will repeat the program. Rip-off stories attract audiences.

The trade will never fully negate this adverse publicity. The affects will linger for years. Because the antiques and collectibles trade lacks a professional trade organization, there has been virtually no damage control. No spokesperson appeared to counter the claims made in the program.

The facts are not in dispute. Their objectivity is. Could *PrimeTime Thursday* have found antiques dealers whose actions would have mimicked the New York dealers elsewhere in the country? The answer is yes. Could they have found them as easily? The answer is no.

I am convinced that 95 percent or more of the antiques and collectibles dealers would act differently if approached by an individual wishing to sell something. Recognizing they are the knowledgeable party in the transaction, the dealer would do his or her best to level the playing field. Although "caveat emptor" (let the buyer beware) applies to purchases and sales within the antiques trade, dealers know that they have to level the playing field and pay a fair price if they hope to (1) stay in business and (2) gain a reputation that brings other sellers to them.

What is a fair purchase price? I nearly choked when I heard that "experts say fair value is half." Not this expert. Dealers, especially those selling objects valued below $250, need to triple their money in order to turn a profit. In the case of commonly found objects, a purchase price of twenty cents on the retail dollar may be extremely fair. The dealer will probably have a common object in inventory for months, even years, before selling it.

PrimeTime stated that pricing in the trade is subjective. There was nothing subjective about the fifty cents on the dollar assertion. It was made as a statement of fact.

Never one to duck an issue, I offer the following guidelines for determining a fair purchase price for an antique or collectible. The following are my suggestions, using a percentage of field/book value, to determine a fair purchase price: (a) 10 to 20 percent if the value is less than one hundred dollars; (b) 25 to 30 percent if the value is between $100 and $1,000; (c) 40 to 50 percent if the value is between $1,000 and $10,000; and, (d) 60 percent on objects above $10,000. These percentages are higher than those set forth in several court cases. When a seller beats my percentages, he should consider himself ahead of the game. If he wants field/book retail, let him go into business and incur the overhead and other expenses involved with receiving field/book value.

PrimeTime devoted more than 90 percent of their programming time to setting the stage and documenting the misdeeds of the three antiques dealers. Less than 10 percent was devoted to solutions. The solutions proposed are worth examining.

Solution One was to do research. Find out what your piece is worth—in this case, the retail (book/field) value of the piece. The sellers knew the value of the pieces they were selling. Knowing this, there is no way they should have accepted the prices the dealers offered. Instead, they played dumb. They wore an invisible sign that read "Please take advantage of me."

Solution Two was to get an independent appraisal. Given the standard per hour appraisal fee of a professional appraiser, a suggestion to consult auction catalogs and general/specific price guides and showing how to do so effectively would have been far better advice.

Solution Three was to shop around and talk with several potential buyers. I kept waiting for the two consultants to object strenuously. Instead, there was only silence. Asking "How much will you offer?" is equivalent to asking for a free appraisal. It is the responsibility of the seller to set the price. The buyer's obligation is to say yes, no, or counteroffer. When the buyer is the more knowledgeable of the two, he must level the playing field.

Solution Four was to sell on consignment or at auction. Although unsaid, the implication was that this would result in a price equivalent to field/book value. Nothing could be further from the truth. Dealers dominate auction buying. By the time the seller pays the auction commission, his return will typically duplicate the percentages I gave earlier.

It makes no difference that the *PrimeTime* presentation was unfair and unbalanced. The public believes what it sees on television.

The key is not to allow this misrepresentation to go unchallenged. I have done my part. Now it is time for you to act.

CHAPTER 15

The Future

There was an antiques and collectibles industry long before I arrived on the scene. It will continue long after I die. Hopefully, it will last for as long as the human race exists.

Unfortunately, no Antiques and Collectibles Hall of Fame exists. The industry has a bad habit of ignoring its past. If you asked twenty-five collectors to name the leading antiques and collectibles auctioneers, collectors, and dealers from the first six decades of the twentieth century, I doubt if twenty of them could name even one individual. The past may be prologue, but not in this business.

Change is an inevitable part of life. There is no reason for the antiques and collectibles business to be different. If you made it this far, you know I am one of the strongest proponents of change in the business. I relish change. I see change as only good, never evil.

I cannot wait for the future. As I noted in the introduction, I have lived through two major revolutions in the antiques and collectibles industry. I hope to experience one more. Two would be great.

I am sixty-three, an age when most people think about retiring. Not me. I currently am working on Pop Nation, *a new television show on Discovery that will premier in September 2005. The show will focus primarily on objects made after 1960. Talk about the future. Here is a show that understands what the future is all about.*

I plan on writing "Rinker on Collectibles" for another ten to fifteen years. I became concerned a few months ago that I had said my piece and it was time to walk away. Dumb me. I have plenty left to say.

Let the future come. I am ready.

Life Will Never Be the Same

It is noon on Wednesday, September 12, 2001. Like many individuals around the world, I have been glued to the television set since approximately 9:30 a.m. on Tuesday, September 11, the time when I first heard that an airplane struck one of the towers of the World Trade Center in New York. As a result of this and the tragedies that followed, September 11, 2001, has become a defining moment in world history.

Each generation seems to have a defining moment—where were you when you heard: Lindbergh landed in Paris, the stock market crashed, Pearl Harbor was bombed, John Fitzgerald Kennedy was shot, or the space shuttle *Challenger* blew up. Now the question that will be asked again and again over the next fifty years is: "Where were you when you heard about the airline hijackings and the subsequent destruction of the World Trade Center towers in New York?" How and if you are able to answer will define when you were born and the generation to which you belong.

America supposedly lost its innocence in World War I. Yet, the Lindbergh date is one associated with hope and optimism. Tragedy dominates the balance of the dates. Perhaps America really lost its innocence during World War II.

The real tragedy is that every time America and the world appear to be steering an optimistic course, a tragedy occurs. During the Kennedy administration, I represented Lehigh University as a participant in American University's Washington Semester program. Donna E. Shalala, Secretary of Health and Human Services during the Clinton presidency, was a member of my group. At the time, my political views leaned strongly to the far right. Donna's political beliefs were in marked contrast to mine. Yet, I vividly remember the confidence and faith we shared in the American governmental system. Having escaped the horrendous memories of World War II and not yet disillusioned by Vietnam, we were optimistic and eager to participate. John Fitzgerald Kennedy's death ended the innocence of our generation.

The space race and man's landing on the moon renewed some of that optimism in the generation that followed. Vietnam tempered it. The destruction of *Challenger* ended it.

The economic boom of the 1990s coupled with a feeling that the world was at peace, not forgetting regional conflicts throughout the world, once again fueled an era of innocence among America's teens and twenty-somethings. The tragedies of September 11, 2001, shattered that innocence. America was vulnerable.

The events of September 11, 2001, were not random acts of terror. They were organized. Life will never be the same.

I travel extensively, primarily by plane. I doubt if I will ever be able to step on a plane again without thinking about the events of September 11.

If a small group of terrorists can create this level of havoc, what is to prevent them from smuggling a nuclear-powered device or crippling virus into the United States? Years, perhaps decades, will pass before Americans and the rest of the world can walk again without looking carefully over their shoulders.

On September 10, I taught a seminar on twentieth-century collectibles for the thirty-five participants in the Auction Marketing Institute's GPPA 201, a course designed to immerse participants in the basic skills and tools they need to appraise appreciating personal property. One of the questions that I raised was: When did the twentieth century begin?

While the twentieth century may have begun from an astronomical point of view in 1900 or 1901, it did not begin until 1920 from a collecting prospective. America in 1905 was very much like America in 1895. In order for one period to end and another to begin, there has to be a significant change in lifestyle. Largely due to World War I, America's lifestyle underwent a significant change in the early 1920s. The Roaring Twenties ushered in a new millennium.

The twentieth century did not end in 1999 or 2000. America in 2001 was very much like America in 1999, at least until September 11, 2001.

Normally technological and/or social advances trigger major lifestyle changes. This certainly proved the case following World War I and World War II. The Civil Rights movement and the computer are two factors responsible for the changes America has experienced during the last three decades.

As the millennium hype ended in early 2000, I could not help wondering what advance would trigger the next major lifestyle change.

It never occurred to me that it might be a tragic event. Like so many others, I was lulled into believing that the world had entered an era of peace that would last during my lifetime. America was the world's peacemaker. While not all its efforts were successful, it was able to keep the world on a relatively even keel. Further, America's economic and military might would certainly keep it immune from attack. No nation would dare. Alas, a small group of individuals demonstrated they had the ability to do what no nation would.

As I write this column, uncertainty prevails. Some media commentators and economic pundits are predicting a collapse of the American economy that conceivably could lead to a worldwide depression. There is talk of war, albeit President Bush has indicated he does not plan to ask Congress for a formal declaration of war at this time.

I am an optimist. Deep inside I want to believe that this recent tragedy will bring out the best in America, and in six months to a year America and the world will be able to put it aside and return to status quo anti-tragedy. I suspect it will not.

In previous "Rinker on Collectibles" columns, I argued that we are now participants in an international antiques and collectibles market. When I checked my e-mail this morning, there were two messages from outside the United States. Alan Carter of *Carter's* in Australia wrote: "God bless America, Harry. Every true Australian person is with you and will give whatever help is needed." Tony Crane from England and from whom I just bought a jigsaw puzzle noted: "I just want to say how sorry I am about today's events in the U.S. Words cannot be found to describe the impact on those affected by what has happened." I am certain these will not be the only messages from my worldwide contacts.

Americans need to remember that the terrorist attacks of September 11, 2001, were not solely an American event. They also were attacks on the world as a whole. No one in a skyscraper, whether in Chicago, London, Sydney, or Tokyo, will ever feel safe again. It is not just life in America that changed, but life worldwide.

As this column neared its end, I questioned whether I was unduly negative in my selection of "where were you when you heard" examples. Were there positive examples from the post-1945 period that I could have used? The fall of the Berlin wall came immediately to mind.

Quickly balancing this positive event were the death of Martin Luther King, the death of John Lennon, and the resignation of Richard Nixon. Alas, tragedy dominates.

As happens with many of my columns, the idea that triggered the column has become secondary or lost entirely. Dana Morykan's observation that eBay temporarily discontinued its listings of New York World Trade Center memorabilia was the impetus. I asked Dana to research developments over the last twenty-four hours to see if events similar to a "celebrity bounce" had occurred as a result of the September 11, 2001, tragedies. As you probably guessed, it did.

What Triggers the Market in the Twenty-first Century?

It would be an ideal world if the value of every antique and collectible increased linearly—as time progressed, value rose. Most collectors and dealers probably would be happy if the value of objects kept pace with inflation. Alas, it is not an ideal world.

The twenty-first-century market is trendy. Value for a specific collectible or object within a collectible category can rise or fall spectacularly in months, sometimes in weeks. A category that was running hot can be in the cooling stage by the time the news appears in trade publications. In this instance, "hot" means a rapid increase in value for all levels of objects within a collecting category.

Realistically, most collectibles prices are stable, i.e., they are the same today as they were three months ago and are likely to still be the same three months from now. Up and down price movement occurs within a narrow range—plus or minus 5 to 10 percent.

Prices advance when something triggers interest in an object or collecting category. Although most collectors and casual buyers would deny it, they can and are led by events and/or the media. The average American collector is a follower. He responds to market stimuli. There are exceptions, but they are in the distinct minority.

In order for a market to run hot, it has to be triggered. Something has to happen to generate collector and/or public interest in a specific object or collecting category. In the mid-twentieth century, these triggers were largely internal to the trade—a new price guide or reference book, articles in several major trade periodicals, a spectacular private owner/themed catalog auction, or a museum exhibit. In some cases, a trend developed at regional flea markets, antiques malls, and/or antiques shows and then quickly spread throughout the country.

Does the antiques and collectibles trade have the ability to trigger a market run—i.e., collecting craze where prices increase dramatically over a short period of time—internally in the twenty-first century? This is a critical question. In the 1970s and early 1980s, most market runs were triggered internally. Since the early 1990s, market runs have largely been triggered by outside sources. The dominance of outside rather than inside market triggers is an indication that the trade has lost the ability to control its own destiny. It has become reactive rather than active.

In the twenty-first century, outside sources—e.g., the media, movie moguls, style leaders such as Martha Stewart, and eBay—are the triggers that jumpstart a stable collecting category or create a new collecting category. The result is a market that is time-focused and easily manipulated.

The media is the most important antiques and collectibles market trigger in the early twenty-first century. In the 1990s television and newspapers were the key media triggers. Style magazines have assumed that role in the first decade of the twenty-first century. Television, thanks to antiques and collectibles shows on PBS, HGTV, and other cable channels, still plays a role, albeit a secondary one. It no longer triggers markets. Television's primary role is keeping the general public's interest in antiques and collectibles at a high level. It succeeds admirably.

In the 1990s a single story in a prestigious newspaper such as *The New York Times* or *Wall Street Journal* had the potential to trigger a market, especially if the story was distributed nationally by one of the wire services. The continued appearance of the story over a several-week period spread interest. The ability of these stories to serve as triggers was aided by the fact that the general public was not subjected to a daily dose of antiques and collectibles stories.

Antiques and collectibles junkies have no trouble getting a daily fix today. All they have to do is turn on television. However, there is a major difference in approach between the newspaper stories and the television shows. While the newspaper stories focus on a single object or collecting category, the typical antiques and collectibles television show touches on a dozen or more object groups. Further, the objects differ from week to week. There is no reinforcement period.

This explains why style magazines have the greatest ability to trigger a collecting trend. Style magazines often continue a theme's focus through several issues. An object group featured in an earlier issue appears regularly in room settings in subsequent issues. This is especially true in style magazines associated with specific individuals rather than decorating styles.

Decorating with antiques and collectibles has become America's favorite pastime. Today's style magazines are past-, not contemporary-focused. When contemporary pieces appear, they are either blended with older objects or feature forms, shapes, and patterns associated with the past. Since September 11, 2001, America has become nostalgia driven.

By the 1990s, movies replaced television shows as the dominant licensing vehicle. Alas, greed on the part of the movie moguls and manufacturers created product markets that were easily manipulated by toy scalpers or bloated with an oversupply of product. The good times were a memory by the start of the twenty-first century.

Adult collectors finally wised up. The subdued adult collector interest in *Lord of the Rings: The Fellowship of the Ring* and *Harry Potter and the Sorcerer's Stone* licensed product was a trend that continued unabated in the spring of 2002 when *Spider-Man* and *Star Wars: Episode II—The Attack of the Clones* licensed products hit the toy shelves. Even Dreamworks and Disney feature-length cartoons failed to generate a buying frenzy for their licensed products.

It is time for an important aside. This column relates to the American antiques and collectibles market. An entirely different picture emerges when examining the worldwide market, especially Japan. Collecting trends remain confined to the national level. Will worldwide collecting trends develop? Yes, they will, but not for several more decades.

Style gurus such as Martha Stewart have replaced television and movie licensing as the second most important outside trigger of antiques and collectibles trends. Although Martha Stewart may be the first name that comes to mind, she is not alone. Cable television, periodicals, and book publishers are personality-focused. Right or wrong, personalities can shape markets based solely on the premise that viewers and readers love them and their advice. The goal is to mimic and imitate, not originate.

Finally, there is eBay. The temptation is to list eBay as an inside rather than outside source. I view it as an outside source for several key reasons: (1) it auctions a wide range of material, not just antiques and collectibles; (2) it is run by individuals who are not antiques and collectibles trade-focused; and (3) it is merely a sales vehicle.

eBay is a place where trends originate and die overnight. It is a constant source for new material. It provides almost instant satisfaction once an individual decides he wants to purchase a specific object.

While imitation may be the sincerest form of flattery, it is an invitation for disaster on eBay. The moment a certain object or collecting category starts selling well, other sellers join the bandwagon. The result is a flooded market resulting in a moderate to rapid decline in prices and/or sell-through rate.

Beware of reports listing the most popular categories on eBay. Most reports are based on the number of items listed and not the number of items sold. In many categories, unsold items far outnumber sold items. Further, the market shifts so rapidly on eBay that by the time information appears in the trade media it is often stale.

As the twenty-first century progresses, the ability to trigger an antiques and collectibles category into running hot is becoming harder and harder, thanks in large part to an increasingly aware and skeptical buying public. Triggers are now obvious rather than hidden.

Identifying a potential trigger is one thing. Determining whether the bullet fired by that trigger has hit the market run bull's-eye is another. It misses far more than the general public, collectors, and dealers realize.

The Antiques / Collectibles Dealer of the Future

In the mid-1990s, I was asked to describe how I envisioned the antiques/collectibles dealer of the twenty-first century. I had visited a technology convention in Los Angeles and saw a demonstration of a virtual reality device. This, I thought to myself, has to have future applications in the antiques and collectibles field. The cellphone, personal computer, and Internet also were in their infancy in the mid-1990s. There was no question in my mind that these devices as well would play a role in the daily life of an antiques/collectibles dealer.

I envisioned my twenty-first-century antiques/collectibles dealer as wearing a wire clamp around the back of his head that had two attachments, a voice mike and a miniature video camera located beside one of his ears. A cord led from the wire clamp to a miniature combination computer/cellphone on the dealer's wrist. The computer housed the dealer's client base and client want list. Access to research information regarding object identification and value was available via a connection to the Internet.

When the dealer found an object for which he had a potential buyer, he would contact his client by phone. Turning on the miniature video camera, the dealer and buyer would examine the object through the use of streaming video. If the potential buyer was dissatisfied with this process, the dealer would transmit an image that allowed the buyer to examine the object three dimensionally through virtual reality. The dealer would converse with the potential buyer during the entire examination process.

Is my vision still futuristic or reality? Actually, it is reality or extremely close to it. The technology is available. The good news is that its cost is rapidly reaching the point of justifiable affordability. I expect to see it in use in the field well before the first decade of the twenty-first century ends.

On September 18 and 19, 2004, I was in Plano, Texas, conducting verbal appraisal clinics on behalf of a newly opened Quick-Drop store. During my visit, I learned about eViewLink.

What is eViewLink, you ask? A recent press release from ESPRE Solutions describes the device as: "A method and system providing wireless personal telepresence facilitating collaboration by two or more persons, each in a different location, on a task at one of the locations and requiring visualization by multiple persons. A portable wireless unit captures/transmits video depicting the technician's first-hand field of view while keeping her hands free to perform the task. The expert employs a management console for visualization of the task being performed by the technician while communicating in real time with the technician. The management console also provides control over video and audio functions, record, playback, freeze frame, and image attributes. Communication between the two persons is accomplished by exchanging digitally compressed video and audio via voice or data network, either public or private. A community server augments the system by supporting three or more participants and enabling communication across public networks."

Do not be confused by the technical jargon. Substitute "potential buyer" for "expert" and "dealer in the field" for "technician." The management console is a computer. A personal computer is fine. A public communication network is any carrier you use for your cellphone.

The eViewLink device is virtually identical to the one I forecast. The dealer can use the device to establish immediate contact or to record up to several hours of information which he then can download on his computer and edit before transmitting it to a potential buyer.

Image quality has been the major drawback in streaming video over the Internet. ESPRE Solutions is a technology company specializing in compression video technology. I saw several examples of video generated by an eViewLink device. It was equal to high definition television when viewed on a personal computer screen or monitor.

What I did not envision was the ability of the potential buyer to take control of the video viewing process. The eViewLink program allows the potential buyer to point the video camera. The camera comes with a zoom lens. Whether the image is as large as the horizon or as small as a postage stamp, quality is maintained.

The eViewLink system is priced between $4,000 and $5,000 depending on the features the customer wants. The price includes all hardware and software required to make the system operational.

I was so engrossed by the eViewLink demonstration that I failed to ask about virtual reality possibilities. If not available now, they most certainly will be in the immediate future.

Obviously, my futuristic vision of the twenty-first-century antiques/collectibles dealer has limits. First, it assumes the technologically oriented twenty-first-century antiques/collectibles dealer will operate without fixed inventory. His emphasis will be on finding and filling client wants. Second, it assumes that the traditional selling forms—auctions, flea markets, malls, shops, and shows—will continue to exist. The technology-oriented dealer's business methodology will be sell-it-before-you-buy-it.

When discussing a final selling price with his remote client, the dealer will factor in the cost of the object, a profit to cover his time and expertise, and shipping and handling costs. Payment will be instantaneous, either through the dealer's own merchant card service or via one of the Internet's established monetary transfer methods, e.g., PayPal.

I have been around the antiques and collectibles trade long enough to remember life before the arrival of the antiques mall. Younger individuals involved in the antiques and collectibles trade will use the arrival of eBay as a landmark event to separate them from their even younger colleagues. I have expressed on numerous occasions a wish to still be around to see the advance that challenges and eventually replaces eBay as king of the hill.

I know it will not be eViewLink. The cost of eViewLink technology and the fact that it relies on an established dealer-client database means that its application will be restricted to dealers serving buyers in the upper and middle portions of the antiques and collectibles market.

Heavy volume eBay power sellers may be able to amortize its cost through the inclusion of a short streaming video describing and touting the listed object. The video has to result in the object selling for several bid jumps more than it would have had the video not been available. This will prove difficult to measure.

The appraisal area is where I see an immediate use for eViewLink technology. Appraisers are receiving more and more requests for walk-through, verbal appraisals rather than formal written appraisals. Walk-through, verbal appraisals are helpful to a wide variety of individuals: (1) executors who simply want to know if there is anything valuable in the house; (2) individuals who are downsizing and want to make an informed decision on what to take, give to the family, sell, or throw away; and (3) individuals doing estate planning [today parents not only must distribute the objects equally, they also have to make the cash value equal].

When I do a walk-through, verbal appraisal, I encourage my client to make a videotape or cassette tape of the process. EViewLink technology would allow me to record the process, return to my office, edit and research-enhance the video, and present my client with a DVD or VHS recording of the final result. Assuming an added cost of $100 or more per appraisal, it would take between forty and fifty visits to amortize the cost of the eViewLink technology.

I remember writing an anti-computer article shortly after the arrival of the first main frame computer on the campus of Lehigh University, my alma mater. I always have been a little frightened by technology, and I confess that I am more resistant than adoptive. Yet, I am no fool.

The future of the antiques and collectible field is directly linked with technology. Technology has produced more change in the last fifteen years than the hundred years that preceded it.

Currently, there is a technological divide between the traditionalist and net-generation antiques/collectibles collectors and dealers. As the years pass, this divide will lessen as the traditional collectors and dealers die off.

I have given up fighting technology. I am now wired. Heaven help all of you when virtual reality Harry pops out of your computer screen.

What Collectors Dream About—The Good Dreams

Collectors obsess. It is the nature of the beast. Collecting is such an integral part of their lives that they cannot help themselves. Collecting is always on their minds—awake or asleep.

Collectors dream. It follows logically. The vast majority of the dreams are good. The balance are bad. I plan to deal with the bad dreams in another column.

Before discussing the wide range of topics about which collectors dream, it is important to note that all collectors' dreams are in color. Collectors' dreams cannot be in black and white. Color plays a critical role in the collecting process. Color creates difference in price, identifies variations, and helps in separating period pieces from reproductions (exact copies), copycats (stylistic copies), fantasies (forms, shapes, and patterns that did not exist historically), and fakes.

Collectors dream in realistic terms. Collectors' dreams include places, people, and objects with which the collectors are familiar. There are no fictional paradises in collectors' dreams. Everything is immediately identifiable.

Collectors dream in the present and future. Their dreams are focused on immediate opportunities and long-term possibilities. When collectors do dream about the past, the dream is likely to be a bad one, e.g., a piece they should have bought but did not. Collectors sleep better when their dreams are positive and optimistic. Better to awake with a smile on one's face than a headache over past lost opportunities.

The vast majority of collectors' dreams involve one or more objects that they wish they owned but do not. True collectors never reach the point where they are totally satisfied with what they have. There always are pieces that have eluded them, no matter how diligent they have been in their hunt.

I quite clearly remember the day when Ken and Daria Dolan asked me during my appearance on their *Smart Money* television show, "If you could have any object you wanted, what would it be?" I did not have to think about my answer. I had dreamed about it often enough. I wanted to own a ten-piece Hopalong Cassidy bedroom suite. I had never seen one except in a newspaper advertisement. My dream came true when I was contacted a few weeks later by a viewer in Alabama who had seen the show and told me he had the bedroom suite of my dreams for sale.

Collectors dream about the objects that they need to make their collection complete. They know what they are because they have seen the objects pictured in manufacturers' catalogs, reference books, or other collectors' collections. Collectors want their collections to be as complete as possible. Few collectors own one example of every object in their collecting category.

Collectors know that dreams can become reality. They know this because they have had numerous experiences finding the objects about which they dream during the hunt. Almost all the collectors I know, albeit they are often reluctant to admit it, have had more than one just-as-in-my-dreams moment. The initial moment is magical and mystical. This feeling dissipates quickly. It is replaced by collectors rationalizing that what happened is nothing more than a reward for the commitment they made to their craft and collection.

Collectors understand that if they persist, everything they seek will come to them eventually. Failure is not an option. This position is reinforced by their dreams.

Dreams often involve the hunt. Hunt dreams can be divided into two types, those involving (a) the hunt process and (b) the rewards of the hunt. Surprisingly, most collectors' hunting dreams involve only themselves. Their rivals are nowhere to be found. The dreams focus on those unique skills that separate collectors from each other. During the dream process, collectors review existing skills and evaluate untried collecting strategies. Dreams also allow collectors to experience new collecting opportunities. A portion of the sixth sense collectors attribute to their skill set is dream-driven.

No matter how much collectors deny it, luck does play a major role in whether or not collectors are successful in the hunt. Collectors prefer to think they are responsible for creating their own luck. Yet, when they review their dreams, they will find that luck is a vital component in a success hunt. A sudden turn of the head in an antiques mall or show booth that results in a find that had been missed when passing by, a random eBay search revealing a long sought-after piece closing in minutes, or a causal conversation that leads to a "I have one of those I would be glad to sell you" response are just a few examples that occur regularly in collectors' dreams.

Dreams involve more than just finding long-desired objects. There is more to the story. A key element is that the objects have to be a bargain. While free would be nice, collectors understand that they have to purchase their treasures. Few dream about walking along a back alley and finding an object destined to become the most prized piece in their collection discarded in a garbage can. Finding the same object highly underpriced at a garage sale, flea market, mall, shop, or show is a dream staple.

In collectors' dreams objects are always in mint condition and in their period box. Condition problems exist only in the real world. Collectors' dreams star objects just off the assembly line. Everything dreamed about is ready for the display shelf.

In their dreams, collectors are king of the hill. Their collections are without peer. Their collections extend throughout their home and, in many instances, are housed in a separate building, often equivalent to a classical-designed museum.

Collectors dream their collections are carefully organized and displayed. Pieces are housed in the finest display cabinets, set on pedestals, or hung on the wall. Displays are spacious, allowing each object or object group to be easily viewed and accessible. Collectors always dream about holding their favorite pieces.

There are no unidentified objects in collectors' dreams. There is a reference library that contains all known reference books as well as a wealth of peripheral material ranging from manufacturers' catalogs to advertising literature. Collectors are linked to the information of cyberspace through a computer. A fully cataloged collection is the one element that is missing in these dreams. Collectors do not want to know what they spent.

There are gaps in the collection. Collectors do not like to admit that the hunt has ended. However, these gaps are minor. The collection contains the top pieces—the ultimate (masterpiece) units, i.e., the top five to ten items in the category; and most upper echelon pieces, i.e., the second level consisting of the top one hundred to one hundred and fifty pieces.

Collection dreams are the one type of dream where other individuals enter the dream. Collectors love to showcase their collections. While some dreams involve friends, most collectors' dreams include their biggest rivals. In the good dreams, the rivals are astonished at the depth of the collection and offer one complementary remark after another. The entire dream reinforces collectors' beliefs that they are the king of the hill.

As you might suspect, collectors' dreams do not include their spouses or children. Collectors are a secretive group when it comes to their immediate family. In their good dreams, collectors never have to answer critical questions regarding how much they are spending, why they need this, or where they are going to put this one.

Although claiming never to have to justify their actions, collectors know that deep down inside they need this. Their good dreams accomplish this goal. Good dreams provide the justification that what they have done, are doing, and are about to do is right, part of the natural order of things. Collectors wake up refreshed and ready to go forward.

There also is a devil inside of all collectors. Collectors are competitive, greedy, and covetous. It is these elements and more that turn collectors' dreams into nightmares. Or, do they?

What Collectors Dream About—The Bad Dreams

There is a devil inside of all collectors. Most collectors do a good job of keeping it under control. They hide it so well that it often goes unnoticed. Unnoticed, that is, until they fall asleep.

Collectors dream. Not all their dreams are pleasant ones. Collectors have nightmares just like everyone else. Anxiety, competitiveness, greed, and coveting are just a few of the hidden devils that cause collectors' bad dreams.

Collectors relish telling tall stories involving their finding a long-sought-after treasure at an auction, flea market, shop, or show. Two elements can enhance the stories even further—obtaining the object at a bargain price, and snatching it out from under the eyes and hands of one of their rivals.

Of course, none of this can happen if collectors do not get to the auction, flea market, shop, or show on time. Dreams rarely are momentary. They tend to cover an extended period of time. Most collectors' nightmares begin with the collector leaving home.

Trouble starts immediately. The car has a flat tire or is stuck in traffic. In their nightmares, collectors always are in a rush. Time is of the essence. There is no margin for error. Delay causes frustration and anxiety.

They begin to lament the bargains they know they are missing. Experience has shown collectors that the early birds get the bargains, not the worms, in collecting. Bargains mysteriously vanish after the first hour. This is a myth but is widely believed within the collecting community to be a truism. In order to win, collectors need to be present when the auction begins and/or the doors open. Anything that prevents that puts collectors at a distinct disadvantage. It is almost better not to arrive at all than to arrive late.

During the imagined delay, collectors' nightmares flash forward to the event they are missing. They see the objects of their dreams on the preview table at the auction or in booths at the flea market, mall, shop, or show. In their innermost minds, collectors know the objects have to be there. They see them but cannot touch them. It is enough to drive collectors mad.

When they finally do arrive at the auction, flea market, mall, or show, the first thing they see is their principal rivals. What are they holding? All the objects the collectors would have purchased had they arrived on time.

Their rivals cannot help gloating. They wander over and begin a conversation. First, they express their surprise at the late arrival of the collectors. Did the collectors not know what time the event started? They arrived last evening to make certain they were present the moment things began. The rivals express sadness at the events that delayed the collectors.

Meanwhile, the collectors are doing everything they can to keep their tempers in check and to avoid looking at the objects their rivals have just purchased, the very objects they would have purchased had they been there first. Of course, their rivals cannot wait to show the collectors the objects they found and explain their incredible good luck in finding them at greatly reduced prices. The moment is agonizing and torturous for the collectors.

As the collectors and their rivals continue attending the event, the nightmares continue. If an auction dream, the collectors always are the under bidder. If a flea market, mall, shop, or show dream, the collectors continually see their rivals a booth or two ahead finding and buying yet another object they would kill to have in their collection.

Hunt nightmares end with collectors returning home with nothing to show for their efforts. They wasted their time. The sense of frustration is overwhelming.

Collectors share their collections with each other. In reality, this usually is a very pleasant experience, a chance to see objects never seen before and to broaden their research knowledge. While there certainly are some grin-and-bear-it moments, the overall experience is positive.

In collectors' nightmares, visits to view other collectors' collections only reveal how puny and pitiful their own collections are. Their rivals' collections are two, three, four, and even more times larger than their own. The fact that the rivals' collections contain duplicates and triplicates of objects they still need depresses them further.

The availability of unlimited display space is probably the cruelest blow of all. Collectors always are short on display space. There is never enough room to display their collections adequately. Far too many things are in storage. Most collectors would spend their money buying another object before spending it on display cases. In their nightmares, collectors' rivals have enough money to do both. In fact, their funds appear to be unlimited. So also are their sources of supply. Nothing eludes their rivals. The thought of "If only I ..." plays over and over in the collectors' heads.

Occasionally, this nightmare reverses itself. The collectors are showing off their collections to their rivals. The visitors notice a duplicate of a hard-to-find object they do not have. They indicate a desire to buy it. The collectors emit a devilish chuckle that grows into a hellish laugh. "Never," they say. "I will never sell."

In the previous version of this dream, collectors forced themselves to keep their emotions inside. To show emotion was to admit vulnerability. In the reverse, they are the devil personified. They are conquerors, masters of kingdoms fit only for themselves.

Collectors do not want to think about loss. In the idyllic world, nothing ever gets misplaced, broken, or lost. It most certainly does in collectors' nightmares.

The fire nightmare is the worst. Collectors return home to discover their homes are on fire. When the nightmare includes a fully engulfed home, all the collectors can do is sit and cry. Painful though this scenario is, it is far better than the one involving a fire that has just started.

First, there is no way to put the fire out without damaging some or all of the objects. This realization occurs very quickly to the collectors. Now the dilemmas begin. What objects are the collectors going to save? Do they save the most valuable objects in their collections? Do they save the objects that mean the most to them? How much can they save in the time available? The answers to these questions differ each time the collectors dream this nightmare.

The theft nightmare is a close second to the fire nightmare. Collectors return home to discover that their collection has been vandalized. Their prized pieces have vanished. What are they going to do? They can call the police, but they know that vandalized collections do not rate high on the "let's solve this crime" list. The collectors quickly realize that they have no actual record to document what has been stolen. They were too busy acquiring to keep records. The cruelest blow of all is a growing recognition that what they collected is mass-produced. There is no way to tell their piece from any other piece in the marketplace. Forget insurance coverage. Most collectors do not want to spend the money.

Last, but certainly not least, are collectors' spouses. While there are plenty of examples of husbands and wives who collect, the simple truth is that rarely do they collect the same thing. It is far more common for collectors to be the only spouse in the relationship who collects.

The worst spousal nightmare involves divorce. Collections are community property. Angry spouses get their revenge by forcing collectors to sell off part or all of their collections. Pent up rage and resentment over all the money collectors spent on building their collections rather than on their spouses and families finally comes to the fore. Each piece collectors lose to divorce devastates them further. It is a no-win situation.

Collectors dream of dealing with angry spouses. Spouses have been known to hide items or even sell them behind collectors' backs. Spouses extract their revenge by simply saying nothing. Collectors suspect what has happen but are never in a position to confirm it.

I am a collector, and I dream. Most of my dreams involve collecting. Good, bad, or indifferent, I do not care. I love to collect. It is part of me. It is only right that I do it on a twenty-four-hour-a-day basis.

Old Collectors Never Die ...

Every collector enjoys sharing his collection with other collectors. I am no exception. Inevitably, any visit includes a question that would best be left unasked: "What's going to happen to all your stuff when you die?"

No true collector or accumulator ever thinks of dying. It is something that happens to other people, not to them. Collecting goes on forever and so do they. The bumper sticker on my car reads "Born To Collect," not "Dying To Sell."

Most collectors fall in love with their collection. Their collection is an extension of their family. It assumes a personality. It is alive; it grows. Selling one's collection is equivalent to selling one's children (something I know to be socially unacceptable, but contemplated once or twice during the raising of mine). The end result is that most collectors do not sell their collections during their lifetimes.

Collections tend to be assembled by an individual. They rarely are family affairs. Most widows and children who inherit collections could care less. Their interest in maintaining the collection is minimal or nonexistent. In fact, the collection often represents the trips to Hawaii or the new car that the family did not buy because the collector could not pass up the opportunity to add the one piece he truly needed to make his collection great. Unfortunately, this "one" piece has a bad habit of multiplying.

When I visit a fellow collector, I often see an object or two that I would like to add to my collection. I make it a firm practice to tell the collector that if he should ever wish to sell that object, I might be a willing buyer and would he please call me. If you do not ask, how will the collector know you have an interest? I also make it a practice to make my remarks within hearing of the spouse. It may seem bloodthirsty, but that collector dies, I want his spouse to remember that nice man offered to buy some or all of the collection.

Individuals who inherit collections usually face two problems: (a) they are overwhelmed by the collection and (b) they want to sell it as quickly as possible. Haste makes waste. Collectibles are not liquid. In order to achieve a maximum return on investment, a firm selling plan needs to be developed.

If the person inheriting the collection does not have the expertise to evaluate and sell the collection properly, he should seek outside help. First, obtain an appraisal of the collection. A good appraiser not only provides values, but also can develop a sales plan indicating where to obtain the values that he has assigned. Make certain that the appraiser has high ethical standards. When you pay a professional for an appraisal, ethics dictate that the appraiser be prohibited from buying any object that he has appraised or directing the sale of the appraised objects to his place of business. Since there are no licensing standards for appraisers, many do not practice these strict ethical considerations. You are well advised to find someone who does.

Second, move slowly. You do not have to take the first course of action that presents itself. There are many options, including auction, consignment, private sale, or donation. It is your choice. Take time to make a wise one and one that fits your needs.

Why don't most collectors dispose of their collections during their lifetime or leave behind adequate records and a sales plan for the person inheriting the collection? The answer rests in how many collectors view their collections. Rarely do they see the collection as an investment. The value of the collection is measured by the joy involved in the collecting and not in potential for financial gain. They never intend to recover the money they have invested. It is an alien concept to the true collector.

Personally, I plan to amend the adage of "live long enough to be a problem to your children" to "live long enough to leave a big problem for your children." If all goes well this is what I will do. My collection is growing at such an alarming rate that I simply do not have the time to adequately catalog it. I hope to do it someday, but ...

My collection is my children's legacy. But, if they are going to get rich from it, they are going to have to work for their money. Unless

they research the objects and their values plus develop a multiplic
sale approaches, they will never receive the best value possible. I v
them to gain their inheritance the old-fashioned way—earn it.

Most collectors have a sadistic streak in them somewhere; I a
no exception. Sometimes I am not certain that I want another collect
to own my things. They are mine and ought to remain mine. King Tu
showed one solution to the problem. He was buried with his collection.
What a way to go! I thought about this, but I simply do not have the
money to build a pyramid.

I do have one recurring dream. My heirs have invited all my rival
Historical Staffordshire collectors to my funeral. High above my grave
is suspended a trapdoor-bottomed box that holds my entire collection.
At a given signal the door opens and my collection falls to Earth. Any
pieces the collectors catch they can keep. The rest are broken,
destroyed forever. As I said, it's only a dream—a nightmare to my
rivals, but I always wake up smiling.

Well, it is time to give my answer to the question I posed earlier:
"What's going to happen to your stuff when you die?" I thought and
thought. Then I realized how simple the answer really is. After I die, it
is not going to be my problem. Who cares? I am just going to keep on
collecting.